YVONE LENARD

LOVE IN
PROVENCE

ROMANTIC ADVENTURES
IN THE SOUTH OF FRANCE

ELYSIAN EDITIONS
PRINCETON BOOK COMPANY, PUBLISHERS

Published by Elysian Editions,™
an imprint of Princeton Book Company, Publishers
614 Route 130, Hightstown, New Jersey 08520
Phone: 609-426-0602 • Fax: 609-426-1344

Library of Congress Cataloging-in-Publication Data

Lenard, Yvone.
   Love in Provence : romantic adventures in the south of France /
Yvone Lenard.
        p.   cm.
   ISBN 0-87127-240-7
      1. Lenard, Yvone—Journeys—France—Provence.
   2. Provence (France)—Description and travel. 3. Provence
   (France)—Social life and customs. 4. Cookery, French—
   Provençal style. I. Title.

   DC611.P958 L43 2001
   944'.9—dc21

                                                        2001018556

Designed by Elizabeth Helmetsie
Composition by Doric Lay Publishers

Printed in the United States of America
10   9   8   7   6   5   4   3   2   1

LOVE IN
PROVENCE

Contents

About
Love in Provence

I first went to Provence in the company of fifty
attractive American college students who brought to
France high hopes for an exciting adventure and the enthusiastic desire to find love there. While officially their studies represented my essential source of concern, I could not
be blind to the fact that, to quote Provence writer Alphonse
Daudet, "They were all of twenty-years old and dying to
make good use of those." So love, in turn, smiled upon
them. Many found romance—perhaps affairs of the short-
lived variety, happily repeated in quick succession, or else
long-term attachments, even, for a few, marriage. Being with
them is probably why my own thoughts turned to love.
However, happily married and wishing for nothing more, I
became a spectator, a gatherer of images and stories of love.

Another sort of love, affection, grew between the students and me. I am grateful that this affection endures to this day, and I cherish Christmas cards and newsletters that tell of their growing families, personal and professional success. All fondly remember that year they spent in Provence.

None of the students—or anyone else—could recognize himself or herself in this book, however, for I have not only invented names but created entirely different characters. Any resemblance, therefore, could only be coincidental.

About the *Experience Romance* Sections

In the course of the time I spent in Provence, then and since, I discovered many places and the possibility of adventures lovers would enjoy. It might be sunbathing—in any attire—on little-known beaches, wading knee-deep in lavender fields, antiquing in Petrarch's footsteps, climbing the Mont Sainte-Victoire for a night under the stars, stirring up the flocks of flamingoes of Camargue or even going on a pilgrimage to the haunts of Mary Magdalen, that biblical woman who, saint or sinner (and who cares about that, anyway?), certainly *did* know how to love.

Then, there were hotels and restaurants, so exquisite and romantic that they seemed to call for lovers' visits. So, the few lines of *Experience Romance* are meant to share ideas, tips and addresses that will contribute, I hope, to your happiness in Provence.

These notes are not, of course, meant to replace a guidebook. There are several excellent ones. My favorite is the *Red Michelin Guide* for hotels and restaurants. I find it easy to use, complete, objective and inclusive of prices. A new, updated edition is published each year in March.

For sightseeing, I like best the *Green Michelin Guide.* It comes in separate slim volumes for each region and is published in English as well as French. You'll find there a wealth of information on history, the land, food, cities, monuments, recommended tours and more.

Also, in each city, even in many villages, you'll find an *Office du Tourisme* (the phone is listed in the *Red Michelin Guide*) where lists of available housing (hotels, rentals, even campgrounds) are kept. They'll know where you can rent bikes or ride horses, join in group hikes or guided city tours, hand you calendars of local events, sell you regional wine and try to answer all your questions.

About the *Dinner à deux* Sections

You'll find there ten dinners meant for those who prefer not to spend hours in the kitchen. They are simple, easy to prepare, suitable for various seasons and occasions from everyday to festive. They are also light on calories.

I recommend that you do not fear the French ritual of *flamber.* It adds subtle flavor, easy glamour and practically no calories, since the alcohol is burned off. And should you feel very strongly about cholesterol, cut down on that by omitting cream and butter altogether. (Olive oil is cholesterol-free.)

But no matter how dedicated dieters you may be, I can think of no reason why you should not complement your *Dinner à deux* with two glasses of a good wine, the first to enjoy while you prepare the food, the second to sip throughout the meal. As you know well, wine is not only good for your health, it also does wonders for your mood.

Bon appétit, and I wish you love in Provence as well as anywhere else.

Yvone

Sex and
the Ambassadors

*S*eptember 1, 5:30 A.M.: In this early, drizzly dawn, a charter plane is going to land at Charles de Gaulle Airport near Paris. It carries 50 American students arriving to spend their junior year in France at the University of Aix-en-Provence.

"What do you suppose they're thinking about right now?" I ask my husband, standing next to me.

"Sex, mostly, I'd guess," replies Wayne.

I can only sigh in exasperation. Just like him, callous, insensitive at a moment like this! But I know better. "Sex is *not* one of their concerns. I've read their statements of purpose, you see, and *that* wasn't mentioned once. What they *really* want is to serve here in France, as *ambassadors of culture.*"

I am the Resident Director of this International Program of a large university system, appointed for the year because, as a professor of French, I'll presumably be able to guide students in both their studies and their adaptation to a new way of life. To prepare for this assignment, a training week gathered all 12 Resident Directors assigned to the various countries where students can qualify to spend the year.

France is decidedly the plum because the Program rents a large villa in Aix, which serves both as offices and as the Director's residence.

Colleagues are a little jealous, since most of them will have to be satisfied with small apartments that they'll even have to find themselves! I am the only woman in the group, and my husband will join me whenever his own work allows. An easy situation for us, but I can see possible financial hardship for those with large families, whose wives will, on top of it, have to leave their jobs at home to accompany them. In their naiveté, some hope to complete research on doctoral dissertations or on scholarly articles. None of us has any idea of what the job really entails.

At the Chancellor's office, the General Director is cordial and competent. He informs us that we are not going there *in loco parentis*, since all students, aged at least 18, are *adults* in the eyes of the law. Their housing needs will be seen to by the assistant, a resident of the country, who remains on the job permanently. Meals are available at student cafeterias. Therefore, our main concern will be of an academic nature. This is explained in detail, and we all feel on firm ground because, so far, we see nothing we can't handle with ease. We'll also have to deal with the budget, a more complicated matter, but most of us have served as chairs of departments and become familiar with, at least, *that* type of budget. It is all very formal and professional. Students are referred to as FTEs, Full Time Enrollees, and remain, so far, totally faceless.

We are handed a thick resident director handbook, which I surreptitiously leaf through while other staff members address us. Budget is dealt with at length. Equivalencies between the French courses and those offered on our campuses seem reduced to simple equations. No problem I can see here. Another section deals with the process of acculturation our students will necessarily undergo, but written by a professor of psychology, its unforgiving academic style discourages me, so for the moment, I give up reading its arcane columns of statistics.

The purpose of the Junior Year Abroad, we are told, is to expose students to a different culture, offer opportunity for mastery of a foreign language, broaden their horizons and introduce them to another system of higher education. All have studied French for at least two years, and demonstrated, in their applications and a series of interviews, both seriousness of purpose and maturity of mind. Only at lunch will the General Director allow himself a chuckle as he refers to what he calls the "Inn of the Lost Pajamas," the motel where students are gathered to spend the night before departure. "Why not just have them meet at the plane?" asks the New Zealand director, a professor of agronomy, whose charges will be studying methods of sheep farming. "Because half the group would be late and miss the plane," answers the General—as we affectionately call him by now—frankly laughing this time. Behind the mask of FTEs begin to emerge real young people who'll forget their pj's in a motel and miss a plane.

So now the day has arrived. Emotion, on that early morning, tightens my throat as I stand there, near the arrival gate, in my festive red blazer. Emotion caused not by concern over the difficulties the job might present—I don't even know enough yet to suspect there might be some. Instead, I think of those kids and the months of worry, hope, anticipation and preparation that preceded this moment. Many must have worked extra jobs, too, in order to bridge any gap remaining after scholarships and parental help. Now that they're about to set foot on that land they've studied so much, and about which they know so little, I wonder what their feelings can be. Are they happy? Excited? Apprehensive, as many of them are leaving home for the first time? What is foremost in their thoughts?

I must have voiced that last question aloud, because Wayne replies:

"Sex, mostly, I'd guess."

This could annoy me, except that I know better.

All the successful candidates' application files have been made available to me, so I could familiarize myself with information I'll need for advising: home campus (there are more than 20 in this system) area of specialization, degree requirements to be fulfilled, scores on language achievement tests, and so forth. Each file includes a statement of purpose in the form of an essay, in which the applicant must state both purpose in spending the year abroad and personal goals he or she is determined to meet.

True, these essays, written in an attempt at formal language and probably rewritten by parents and teachers, reveal little of a personal nature. Predictably, most express a desire to perfect their knowledge of the French language, literature and culture. They feel, at the same time, that they should make it a personal duty to introduce the French to the finer aspects of American life. Or, as several put it, "to serve as *ambassadors of culture.*"

Photos are attached to each file, and this is when I forget all about FTEs. Instead, I spend hours learning to connect names with faces, so I can recognize and greet them as they file out. And now, the moment is at hand. Just time to sneer at my husband.

"I'm happy to tell you they have higher goals than you seem to think." Unfazed, Wayne winks and whistles the theme song of the Folies-Bergère show:

Paris, c'est une blonde. . . .

And suddenly, they are here, many more than 50 it seems, in a flurry of jeans, windbreakers, brightly colored hand luggage, one pair of skis in a carton, curly heads, one spiky red beard, petite Asian twins, a great deal of flying long, blonde and dark hair. I recognize Carola, with a perfectly straight golden mane to her shoulders; Maria, a stunning Latina; Phil, with a handsome, serious face and glasses; Dana, scowling, with heavily charcoaled eyes; Jennifer, short bob and determined expression; Rob in a backwards baseball cap.

Parker, who brought the skis, is the one who'd written the Chancellor's office to inquire about rumors she'd heard of the University at Aix being "a party school." She needed to know, for she might reconsider and withdraw her application. A copy of both her letter and the answer were clipped to the file. Instead of addressing her concern, someone had written, over the General Director's signature, an irrelevant note listing the various fields of study available to American students in Aix. Encouraged, apparently by the variety of options, she has not reconsidered, and here she is, lively, pert and not at all bookish-looking, with fingernails painted blue.

There is a married couple, both solid and cordial. She, Ginny, intends to become a park ranger, but her grandparents emigrated from France, and she wishes to learn more about their homeland and her heritage. Sam, her husband, is a playground director on sabbatical, coming along as a dependent. Two others, Larry and Mona, though single, look like a couple to me: from the same campus, luggage tagged with both names, he with a prematurely weathered face—a cowboy type—she small and dark with a Madonna profile, standing very close.

No one could miss Faustino, black, tall and willowy, who makes a point of introducing himself with exquisite courtesy and informs me that he'll be looking for spiritual enlightenment in France.

Two students, I know, will be older, engineers completing a master's degree, who need to learn French in order to accept positions in West African countries where that language is required. Burt and Stan, both geologists specializing in petroleum prospecting come out together, carrying professional-looking cases, a little abashed, perhaps, to find themselves mixed in with such a young crowd. . . . As for Kevin, I totally fail to recognize him because his hair, shoulder-length on the photo, has now been shaved clean to his skull. They all crowd around Liz, my assistant, and me, while more pour out of the narrow exit: Rosalind, plump and pink like a cherub, who hugs me effusively. "I'm so glad you don't look *at all* like a professor!" she squeals in a high-decibel voice. Madison, slender, with a white-blonde braid swinging down her back, is—how could I overlook that entry in her application under "sports?"—a black belt judoka, winner of championships at college meets. A few I cannot identify from their photographs, and all year I will have trouble at times remembering their names. Constance, however, who comes out running in a very low-cut sweater, will not be one of those.

And now, it looks like everyone is here, but Liz, who keeps tally against her list, finds one still missing. So we all wait, eyes fixed on the gate.

Finally, after what seems like minutes, Sarah, the last one, appears, long pale hair, round face and green eyes streaming with tears, walking so reluctantly that it seems she might go into reverse at any step. She makes straight for me:

"I want to go home. Let us sit down and talk. Then, you'll put me on the next plane home."

Now this is a new one, and the first of many eventualities not considered in my Resident Director handbook. Sure, I am anxious to satisfy all requests, but still . . .

"Look, Sarah, I cannot sit and talk *right now*. The whole group must be looked after and get situated. Of course, we'll discuss matters as soon as possible and find a solution to your problem. If your reasons for wanting to return are valid, we'll find you a student charter, reserve a seat, etcetera, but it will take a few days, at least. In the meantime, you *must* stay with us. Please, dry your tears, we're going to visit Paris, I'm sure you can enjoy it."

But this only opens the floodgates wider.

While we wait for luggage to appear on the carousels, Liz runs outside to check on the chartered bus, the *autocar*, which is going to take us first to a student dorm in the Latin Quarter, remain with us to see Paris for two days, and finally bring us to Provence. She returns, beaming:

"It's here, ready and waiting. A light blue and silver Mercedes bus, its bar stocked with soft drinks. And wait 'til you see the driver! His name is Jean-Luc. A young Alain Delon, dark and terribly handsome," she tells me. "The girls will go crazy."

Luggage is retrieved and stowed in the cargo compartment underneath. At that point, Wayne says goodbye. He is working on an assignment on the other side of Paris and has shown up this morning only to lend a hand as needed—not to mention annoying me with his dumb remark. He leaves, waving to the students and whistling again:

> *Paris, c'est une blonde,*
> *Paris, reine du monde.* . . .

He'll meet us in Aix-en-Provence, at the end of the week.

Now, Jean-Luc, the driver, is standing by the open door, black silk shirt unbuttoned on a smooth tanned chest with gold chain and medal, one dark curl falling onto his forehead, single dimple in the right cheek.

Several girls scramble and fight—with admirable presence of mind, I'd say—for the seat directly behind and to the left of the driver's. Jean-Luc couldn't miss the commotion, but only puts on a pained expression and reins in the dimple. Jennifer ruthlessly elbows all others aside and settles triumphantly on that most desirable of seats, indifferent to the volley of dark looks.

The sky is so overcast, and the horizon so closed in, that the Eiffel Tower isn't even visible when the bus follows the *périphérique*. Tall buildings loom on both sides, topped by neon signs of mostly Japanese companies: Sony, Mitsubishi, Daewoo, their neon fading in the dull early light. The group is silent, tired from 12 hours on the plane, and before that, probably not much sleep at the "Inn of the Lost Pajamas." I take the microphone hanging from the side of my seat.

"Welcome, all of you! You have arrived in Paris, this is Sunday morning, and the time is now 7:00 A.M., if you wish to set your watches." A few wrists are raised, watches adjusted, but most seem to be slumbering, except Jennifer, who is leaning forward, trying to converse with Jean-Luc, who stares straight ahead, speaking out of the corner of his mouth. I continue: "We'll be staying in a very modern student dorm in the Latin Quarter, where French students are in residence . . ." A hand goes up. "Is the dorm co-ed?"

I don't know. Is it? So it is Liz who answers, "Dorms are co-ed in France." Now, that wakes up the slumberers and a cheer goes up, "Hey, you guys, like, French girls!" shouts Rob with the baseball cap.

The first problem arises upon arrival at the dorm where we will spend the first two nights while visiting the highlights of the capital.

They rush into their rooms and rush out in consternation.

"What? No hangers in the closets?"

All have been instructed, as part of a long list of packing recommendations, to bring wire coat hangers, as these are not provided in French dorms. It seems that many forgot, and now they can only wail helplessly. The girls, that is. The guys couldn't care less, throwing clothes around and seeing where the hell they'll land is their idea of unpacking.

But attention is soon diverted by a more serious crisis, and a great cry is heard:

"What is that *thing* across my bed?"

That *thing* is a *traversin*, a bolster, a long, round, log-shaped pillow seemingly stuffed with sawdust, that you wrap in the *top* part of the *bottom* sheet (got that?) and where, on French beds, you rest your head.

"I want a *regular* pillow! I couldn't sleep on *that!*"

All of us appointees to the job of Resident Director have been advised, as an aside, not to dismiss lightly students' problems and requests, but to make every effort to satisfy them if they appear in the least legitimate. "Remember, ours is a lawsuit-happy country, and letters to Congressmen will not give *your* side of the story," said an assistant to the General. Anyway, *I* am anxious to keep my flock as happy as possible. So I reassure them:

"Don't worry. We'll get you *regular* pillows for tonight."

But Liz whispers to me:

"Don't be silly. Where are you going to find 50 pillows, on a Sunday morning yet? Let me handle this."

She gathers the group, loudest protesters crowding in front:

"*Of course,* we are going to get pillows for those who feel they *must* have them! And while we're on the subject . . ." she lowers her voice to conspiratorial tones, "I am not sure I should mention this, and I hope you won't be *shocked.* But we're all adults here, after all, aren't we? You might have heard of the reputation the French enjoy as great lovers? Oh, you *have?* Then you won't be too surprised to learn it was acquired on *traversins* just like these. That's right. The French wouldn't use anything else." She pauses to survey the effect of that valuable information. "I only bring this up because it is a cultural fact you might find interesting. . . . Now, where was I? Oh yes, how many of you *must* have an American-style pillow while in Paris?"

One young man elbows another in the ribs, a few snickers are heard, but not a single hand goes up. The deft way in which Liz has defused the situation fills me with admiration.

As I am walking down the hall, two of the guys catch up with me. "What is it they do with those contraptions?" they want to know.

Now, we have just arrived, and I am supposed to stand

there, describing Kama Sutra–like, erotic positions involving a *traversin* that I would have to invent? I cannot recall a single paragraph in my handbook on the subject, but I can imagine a letter written home tonight:

> *Dear Folks,*
>
> *France is sure a weird place. Our director is some crazy type who couldn't wait to tell us what they do in bed here! But don't worry, Mom, I didn't even listen. . . .*

So I answer:

"That's what you're here for, to learn for yourselves about the culture. I am sure you'll find out."

But they insist, "What if we *don't* find out?"

"Then," I declare, "if you still don't know, I'll tell you on the last day of the Program. Remember to ask me." They groan in disappointment, but I suspect they look forward to finding out on their own.

Dorms do not serve breakfast on Sundays, so as soon as everybody has freshened up, we herd our group into a large café just across the street, a typical Left Bank establishment with marble tabletops, baskets of croissants and no-nonsense waiters in long white aprons.

"What would you like for breakfast?" I ask naively, forgetting the choice is nothing like what you find in American coffee shops.

But Steve—his brother participated in the Program a few years earlier, so he comes here prepared—asks for a *pastis.* "*Serré,* strong," he specifies. *Pastis* for breakfast? I pointedly ignore the waiter's questioning eyebrows raised in my direction. Let Steve have what he wants, for God's sake, he is old enough to drink, under French law! Two girls want salads. It seems they've been dieting for months—in order, I presume, to present sylph-like figures to admiring French male eyes. Salad is all they can have for breakfast. This time, the waiter's eyebrows shoot up to his hairline.

"Surely, you must have *some* kind of a salad," I say coldly, siding with my charges. After reflection, he brings out the lunch menu, which does list one: *salade niçoise.*

"Okay, like, then that's what we'll have."

It takes a while, but the *niçoises* finally arrive, artfully arranged on vast platters, complete with hardboiled eggs, potatoes, green beans, tuna, tomatoes, onions, olives and (Ugh! Yeccch!) anchovies. "But it was just, like, an appetizer salad we wanted, with lettuce, you know, non-fat dressing on the side, maybe a piece of tomato, but nothing like that stuff . . ." moan the dieters. In vain. French cafés have heard of no such dish.

Meanwhile, however, most, eager to dive into the French experience, do ask for the classic French breakfast fare of café and croissants. "Café au lait?" I suggest helpfully, because I know how much stronger French coffee is than the American version. But someone mentions that Jean-Paul Sartre—the revered existentialist, whose works are still read in American universities by students unaware that existentialism is nothing but, in Sartre's own words, "an enclave in Marxism"—Jean-Paul, it seems, always drank *his* coffee black at the Deux-Magots. Another voice weighs in with the opinion that Camus' *The Stranger*—which they've all read, too—was surely fueled with *café noir*. So café noir it will be all around.

"Watch what happens next," cautions Liz, who's been through it all before.

Sure enough, the first sip brings out sputters and gags.

"Too strong! Ugh! What do they put in that? I want *regular* coffee, not this black mud!" I explain that this is, in fact, *regular* coffee here, and pass pitchers of *hot* milk—yes, *hot* milk. Sorry, but it is the only kind readily available for café au lait—to dilute the offending brew. This reduces gasps to grumbling.

Sarah, sitting alone, is munching candy bars, swimming green eyes and wet round cheeks. I walk over to her table.

"It was at the airport, I wanted to talk to you," she sobs, "but you wouldn't listen to me and help me return home. . . . I feel too terrible now to. . . ." She gets up and runs out in the direction of the dorm.

Well, I am getting depressed, too, by such bottomless despair. Oppressed, also, by that crowd of unruly, dissatisfied kids. So that's the way it is going to be? Only on our first day, I think, not even 9 A.M. and nothing but problems, petty, selfish grousing. Can I take a full year of *that*? How did directors in previous years survive it? My respect for those unknown colleagues grows.

Better pick up a paper and scan headlines. This way, if I don't look up, I won't see what's wrong, and I *do* need a break. After a few minutes, though, I steal a glance.

Everybody is wolfing down croissants, cups and baskets held aloft for refills. Steve's *pastis* has been abandoned, untouched, as, in the company of Rob, still with his baseball cap backwards, he has moved over to the window, the better to watch the passing pedestrians. He leans over to my table, eyes shining:

"See that redheaded woman over there? With the white boots and miniskirt? Is that a *prostitute*?"

Such expectation gleams in the young man's eyes, I could not disappoint him. So I fervently hope that the probably perfectly respectable Parisian lady, who is walking down the Boulevard Raspail on this Sunday morning, in her tightly belted mini–trench coat, will forgive me if I answer, "Oh yes, definitely," and send two ecstatic young Americans scrambling for their cameras.

I don't even smile, but for some reason I couldn't explain, this brings me out of my funk. Wayne's idiotic remark might have contained some grain of truth, and the excitement Steve and Rob project, clicking away through the glass, unaccountably brings a glimmer of cheer to my outlook.

It rains during the first part of our tour of the city, but then, as we turn onto the Place de la Concorde, the sun suddenly breaks through. A Paris sky of pewter and mother-of-pearl opens to reveal patches of intense blue. The wet pavement glistens, the Obelisk rises, dazzling white; gilded bronze lampposts shimmer; fountains gush great arcs of rainbows and diamonds as a cheer, mixed with gasps goes up in the bus. Carola, with the straight blonde hair, reaches over and touches my hand.

"I've dreamed of this moment for so long! Now it's here, and better than in my dreams! Thank you for bringing us here."

The Paris tour has been arranged at my own suggestion. In previous years, students only transferred from the airport to the Gare de Lyon, the railway station, to board a train that took them directly to Aix. But after I had, on my own initiative, inquired about a bus, meals and dorm costs, and found them no more expensive than 50 train tickets, the General Director agreed to give it a try. Students have been informed of this change in the usual arrival plans, and told that it was due to a wish of the Resident Director to offer them a chance to see some of Paris right away. So a few of the cheers are meant for me: "Hey, Madame Lenard! Right on!" Now I know what they will call me, I have acquired my name for the year: not professor, not director, just Madame Lenard, which will soon be shortened into Madame L.

How is that to help steady a still rather shaky director?

For the rest of the day, I am privileged to see Paris through all those 20-year-old eyes filled with wonder. The old tourist sights become new and magical. I had forgotten how majestic the Arch of Triumph really is, raised at the top of the Champs-Élysées as on a pedestal. Even trite old Eiffel Tower, reflected in those eyes, becomes, to its own surprise, young again. But, unfortunately, satisfaction is not 100 percent unanimous.

"What do we do tomorrow?" pouts Dana.

"We'll see more of Paris," I tell her.

"Paris, Paris! Isn't there anything else to see, *here*? How about nightclubs? Have you heard of the Crazy Horse Saloon, where they have total nudity? That's where I want to go."

In addition to her thickly charcoaled eyes, I notice, when her fur coat falls open (A fur coat? On September 1st?), that she's wearing underneath only what looks like a black bra and panties. A training outfit, I'd like to think, but these don't come with see-through lace inserts and a little bow at the cleavage. Strange girl. . . . Should I say something about proper clothing? But then, we don't have a dress code. In addition, she's over 18—an adult in the eyes of the law, and in her own, I guess, even more—so I shouldn't start giving orders I have no means of enforcing or lecture and sound like a martinet.

She is sitting alone, a little apart, as if both she and the others feel she doesn't quite belong to the group. Could a feeling of not belonging lie at the root of the problem? I attempt to converse, asking friendly questions about herself, her studies, her family. But she only shrugs and looks away.

"Don't give me that understanding shit."

And then, I cannot miss in the rearview mirror, Sarah's green eyes still streaming with tears. Would my company be more welcome here than with Dana?

"Sarah, tell me why you applied to the Program, since you were, from the start, so anxious to return home?"

She blows her nose, sniffles, sobs a little and finally answers:

"I didn't want to come. But my parents insisted so much, I felt I had to."

"Why should your parents insist, if that wasn't what *you* wanted?"

"Oh, it was pure self-sacrifice on their part. . . . But my place is there, back home." Sobs interrupt her, her hankie is soaked, so I hand her mine. "I knew it, but then, Jesus told me, too."

Now if Jesus felt the need to get involved, matters must be serious.

"*When* did Jesus tell you?"

"When he appeared to me on the plane. Before, I thought so, but after that, I was *sure*. My place is at home."

I shouldn't allow myself such levity, but I can't help thinking that appearing on the plane rather than on the ground shortened the trip by about 30,000 feet for Jesus.

"But why is it so important for you to be home?"

"Because of my poor parents, don't you understand? I have no right to deprive them of my presence, when they don't have much longer to live. . . ." I visualize an octogenarian father. But her *mother*? How *old* could her mother be? Sarah adds:

"They're both in their late forties, so you see . . ."

I see. Something is wrong here. Something else is hiding behind that oversized filial devotion. And why should her parents insist on sending her away? Did they have some reason, other than self-sacrifice, to want her here?

"May I leave tonight?"

Until I understand the situation a little better, I'll try to keep Sarah with the group. I know that I cannot retain anybody in the Program who does not want to stay, but I also know I don't have to release anyone until the final destination has been reached. Once in Aix, I'll try to contact her parents.

"Sarah, you'll have to wait until we arrive in Aix, otherwise, you'll never know what the trip was all about. Then, if you still feel the same way, you can sign yourself out of the Program, and we'll help you make return arrangements. But give yourself a chance! You've come this far, go all the way. And please stop crying, for heaven's sake! That's not what your dear parents would want from you." And, as tears flow only harder, I feel like a heartless jailer.

As I return to my seat, I regret that for the past hour, I have neglected all the others. But they are engrossed in the sights, the men, especially, in the micro-minis that are all the rage this year.

Dinner in the dorm cafeteria goes smoothly, after everyone has accepted the fact that what looks like skinny chicken with funny legs is, in fact, rabbit. All are gratified to find that Diet Coke, called *Coca Light* here, is plentiful and that very golden fries are piled high next to decent looking pizza and well-sauced spaghetti.

Andouillettes, shaped like large, bumpy, vaguely obscene sausage, sizzle on a grill, and French students are lining up for them (or rather, crowding up, since the concept of lining up is foreign to French ways). Steve, Rob and a couple of other sophisticates join them. Phil follows, after brief reflection.

A moment later, they are staring disgustedly at the barely touched *andouillettes*.

"That's not *regular* sausage," they complain in my direction. "It tastes awful, and it stinks, too! What the hell are those made of?" An attempt to slather the *andouillettes* with mustard only brings tears to their eyes. "*Moutarde forte de Dijon*" isn't *regular* mustard, either.

A group of French girls, at a facing table, is watching the scene. They lean over, point to the *andouillettes* in the guys' plates and make faces. "Yes, awful," grimace back the Americans. The ice is broken. The girls move over to the guys' table, where room is eagerly made for them, but not until the boy-meets-girl ritual of *la bise* has taken place. *La bise* consists of two kisses, one on each cheek. Four girls kissing five boys twice, that makes for a lot of kisses, but that's the way young people in France meet their friends. Our men don't object and a tentative conversation follows, the girls saying things the boys don't get. Phil brings out his pocket dictionary, leafs through it, shrugs in frustration. He comes over to me.

"What is *une bitte*, in English? They keep saying that about the andouillettes, but I can't find the word."

Now, put yourself in my place: This is my first day on this highly responsible job. Am I going to inaugurate these noble functions by telling them what *une bitte* is? No way. They'll have to find out for themselves. I can visualize how the scene would read in a letter home:

> *Dear Folks,*
>
> *Well, Paris is okay, though, like, nothing is regular here and French food can taste pretty gross. The kids are cool, but we have this weird director who teaches us words like Mom used to wash out my mouth for when I was a kid. . . .*

"Translation is not a good way to internalize a language," I declare, sounding as professorial as I know how. "You must learn *directly*, so ask your friends, instead, to explain terms you fail to understand." No need to refer to my handbook; I am certain I would not find there a single line referring to objectionable French slang.

The girls are still giggling. One of them, with incredibly slim hips molded into black jeans and dark bangs down to her eyes, runs to the food counter and brings back two tangerines that she arranges on the plate's edge, on either side of the *andouillette*. She points:

"Tu vois? Une bitte, c'est comme ça."

The guys howl and guffaw so that several other members of the group, boys and girls, leave their tables to see what the excitement is all about. More *bises* all around, and everyone learns, right there and then, what *une bitte* is. Now, I think, still taking refuge in my professor's persona, is that advanced education or what? Isn't this the perfect application of the direct method, following the soundest principles of language skills acquisition?

The language lesson continues with one of my flock asking in hesitant French why that stuff stinks so. A clear French voice replies:

"C'est parce qu'y a de la merde!" (That's because there's shit.)

Andouillettes are made with pork intestine and considered a delicacy in France, although they look like...well, you know, and smell . . . let us say it has to be an acquired taste. Steve, Rob, Phil and a few others are soon marching out of the dining room, Rob chanting, *"Y a de la merde,"* and they inform the crowd at large that they are going to the girls' rooms to *try* and listen to French CDs, then play, in turn, some of their own to give those natives a chance to hear real fusion jazz.

I had thought that all would be eager to make up last night's sleep deficit, but only a few climb upstairs to their rooms. And I mean *climb!* Like seven and eight floors. Signs at the bottom of the stairs indicate that no elevators have been installed in this otherwise modern dorm because exercise will be good for the residents. Others go walking down the Boulevard Raspail in hope of meeting more of those prostitutes like the one they'd spotted earlier. A group that includes Jason with the red beard, Kevin with the shaved head and a few other intrepids wants to find out if they'll be served a beer in some café. I will learn, a little later, that they were, no questions asked. They've even chanced upon an added bonus:

"It was, like, weird, you know. We saw there was a down-stairs room, with lots of people there looking up and laugh-ing, like. So we walked down, too. Can you figure that out? They had like those big, long mirrors angled so they reflect-ed in reverse the feet, the legs—and then *some*—of the peo-ple walking by. I can tell you, with all those miniskirts, and even those that weren't so mini, it was a blast, man."

Dana continues to be unhappy.

"I want to go to the Crazy Horse. Tell Jean-Luc to drive me over."

I am going to point out that, no, Jean-Luc isn't about to take her nightclub-hopping in a 60-passenger bus and that, in any case, his workday is over. But before I can utter a word, one of the girls who lost out to Jennifer earlier cuts in, cattily:

"Ah, Jean-Luc! That's a good one. I wouldn't look for him, if I were you. . . . He went out to dinner someplace with Jennifer."

Unfazed, Dana decides that she'll see for herself what is really going on with that Crazy Horse. I gather she believes there will actually be a horse, a crazy one yet, associated with all that nudity. Liz tries to explain:

"It's a nightclub like others near the Champs-Élysées. No, there's no horse, crazy or sane. It is just a name taken from some old western, I guess. Yes, they have shows with striptease numbers, some in reverse, I heard, where the girl starts nude and proceeds to get elaborately dressed. Yes, some other numbers, in dim, or striped, or changing lights involve nude dancers. In any case, not a place for an unescorted young lady."

But this only confirms Dana in her desire to go there. She'll simply take a cab. By now, she's changed into a dress cut so low and so short that I gasped when she sat down, while Liz remarked cheerfully that, at least, her navel was well covered. What should I do? I don't think I can formally forbid her to go. Don't forget she's technically an adult, and anyway in Aix I won't be watching her every second.

I needn't have worried. In five minutes she's back, furious:

"What's the matter with those cab drivers? I stopped one, but when I told him I wanted to go to the Crazy Horse Saloon, he made me repeat it, burst out laughing, tapped his temple like I was crazy myself and took off. I'll call my Dad, tell him to write our Congressman. I didn't come here to be treated like I was nothing!"

Why would that cab driver refuse to take her there, I wonder?

"Nobody goes to these clubs before midnight, and it is barely nine! The cabby could see who he was dealing with. I didn't think she'd get a ride, but it was better to let her try than forbid her," explains Liz. How wise! I'll have a lot to learn from her.

Sarah, all alone in a corner, is still crying, but devouring a mound of fries. Kevin, shaved head shining under the lights, ambles over, sits facing her and must be trying to console her, because tears turn to convulsive sobs.

"Lost her groove, like big time," he remarks sadly as he regains his seat.

Next morning, it takes some doing to gather the group for the planned sightseeing tour and there are absences, lots of yawns and bleary eyes. With quiet authority, Jennifer takes her seat closest to the driver's with such a proprietary air that the defeated rivals can only shrug contemptuously. Kevin tries to sit next to Sarah, and for a while it looks like she might feel better, but then tears start rolling again, so he moves away, discouraged.

We see the Sainte-Chapelle bathed in the jeweled light of its tall stained-glass windows. There, Maria, the beautiful Latina, astonishes us because she knows when it was built—the 13th Century—and for what purpose—to house the crown of thorns of Jesus, purchased by the

French king. "When I was in high school, we had that great French teacher who showed us a film on Paris. We enjoyed it so, we must have run it five times! Never thought then that I'd see it all with my own eyes some day."

When, a little later, I point out the Sorbonne buildings, site of the original Paris university, Phil, the serious type with steel-rimmed glasses, raises his hand. He remembers a story he's read in French class.

"Didn't it go like this: Some teacher at the Sorbonne had an affair with a student and her uncle was so mad, he had the guy castrated?" This is, of course, a very stylized version of the great Abélard and Héloïse doomed romance.

My duty is clear: Abélard, I explain, a cleric like all university teachers in the Middle Ages, was allowed to give Héloïse, a young lady, learned for her time, private lessons in theology and philosophy, since there was no question of her attending public lectures. The lessons, however, must have veered from their subject, because pupil and teacher fell in love and Héloïse became pregnant, disgracing her family. So her uncle, high in the clergy hierarchy, had her locked up for life in a convent and, yes, his henchmen *did* emasculate Abélard. For 30 years thereafter, Héloïse kept writing passionate letters to her erstwhile lover. Abélard, on the other hand—he's always struck me as a heartless, insufferable pedant—sent her nervy, moralizing ones, quoting Aristotle about the advantage of keeping one's virtue intact. Could *that* have been what drove her uncle over the brink? Anyway, minus whatever, Abélard's fame grew and crowds flocked to his lectures, out of curiosity, I guess.

I fear, though, that I have failed to convey the full pathos of the tragic romance, for my group shows neither reverence nor a trace of emotion.

"All right, like yeah!" shouts Rob in glee. "Like they cut off that dude's *bitte!*" Well, at least he is using newly acquired vocabulary on his own, who could find fault with that, I think.

On a quick tour of Notre-Dame, my charges crane their necks in awe at the soaring Gothic nave and want to know the meaning of the Last Judgment sculptures on the tympanum. But the punishment of sins bores them, except that of the sin of lust, which puzzles them. They just can't figure out why *that* should be punished.

"That stuff is like nobody's business," pipes up Rosalind in her squealy soprano.

Soon, I take pity on the stifled yawns and suggest they might prefer to have the rest of the day free. That wakes them up instantly, and they scatter like a flock of birds.

Dinner in the cafeteria on that second night is almost festive. French and Americans mingle and language lessons continue. There's the French girl in tight jeans, whose name is Pomme. (Yes, *Apple.* For years, first names were restricted by law to those on an official list kept in French city halls. Now that freedom has been granted, parents give free rein to their imaginations.) Pomme exploits last night's success by explaining to a spellbound audience the difference between *baiser* (to screw) and *embrasser* (which does *not* mean to embrace, but to kiss). She demonstrates the latter by grabbing Phil and kissing him at length on the lips, as he blushes furiously and removes his glasses. *"Ça, c'est em-brasser,"* she declares. *Baiser* is demonstrated with hand gestures that embarrass me but no one else apparently.

"Ah, je vois, avec une bitte," cries out Rob, the earlier wise guy, the one who made light of great medieval romances.

Well, perhaps this is not the way information brochures would describe learning in the International Program, but learning *is* taking place! While everybody eats whatever there is without a single sound of complaint, I compose in my mind the lofty terms in which I'll describe our undergraduates' successful acculturation in my report to the Chancellor's office.

The thought of *undergraduates* brings to mind Burt and Stan, the engineers, who are *graduates*.

"I haven't seen those two since we arrived," I tell Liz. "Have you?"

"Yes, I ran into them at breakfast this morning, and they sat down with me. We had a nice chat. Very interesting fellows, especially Stanislav. Born in Czechoslovakia, he came to the U.S. as an adolescent. He is 34, had been working as an engineer, but returned to college for a master's. He's been offered an excellent job in Gabon, but since he'll need to be fluent in French, he decided to join the Program."

"Did he tell you what prompted his return to school and that drastic change in his life?"

"He confessed he'd been terribly lonely and distraught after his wife was killed in a car accident a few years ago. So this is his way of turning a new leaf, so to speak, getting a jumpstart on a new life."

"You've learned a lot about Stan! What about Burt?"

"Burt said that both he and Stan would be on their own in Paris. They've been here before and have friends to look up. They'll show up tomorrow morning in time for departure. But you see, I talked mostly with Stan. Such an interesting man! Did you notice his eyes? I can't figure out if they're blue or gray."

Is there a faraway look in Liz's own eyes? I know little about her yet, except that former Resident Directors and students have commented on her charm and efficiency. She's been with the Program for five years, and the general consensus is that she represents its mainstay. I already like her, her infectious laugh, her resourcefulness and never flagging optimism. Rather tall, blonde, with a full figure and smiling eyes, she is an attractive woman. Her age? Oh, fortyish, I'd say.

I cast a look around. All is well. At a long table, Carola, Faustino and a few others are poring over a large illustrated album of Notre-Dame, while some serious-looking young Frenchmen lean over, pointing, making comments.

Except that Dana is still unhappy.

"Where can I go to meet *real* Frenchmen?"

"Just look around. There are more than a dozen right here who look quite real to me," I suggest, gesturing. But she shrugs contemptuously:

"Kids," she snarls. "Jerks and clowns, like. I mean *real*, like *rich*, you know. My mother said there were, like, lots of dukes, royalty and stuff, who have castles but want to marry American girls so they can come live in the States. When am I going to meet them?"

Remembering that I *must* try to satisfy wishes, I offer:

"You'll have plenty of time to look for them in Aix-en-Provence when we get there." This only makes her stamp her foot irritably. For my part, I cannot help thinking that Dana might be out of place in the Program. Let's see what develops and I'll advise accordingly, but, at this point, some doubt is permitted.

Still, I feel encouraged that by this second day, 48 out of 50 seem to be doing fine. Not a bad percentage. And, to tell the truth, I am beginning to enjoy this group of sweet, unruly, unabashed, serious and raunchy kids.

It will be no hardship to like them all. And that night, in my narrow dorm bed, I fall asleep, feeling already years younger. The company, I guess.

Next morning, our final one in Paris, departure is preceded by a lot of running up and down from one floor to another, doors slamming, and I wouldn't swear that all slept in their own beds, but I know that any question on the subject could be considered an invasion of privacy since I am dealing with *adults*.

Phil, very handsome without his glasses (I hope he hasn't lost them), walks downstairs, looking solemn, arm in arm with Pomme, who kisses him passionately before he climbs aboard.

"*Ça, c'est embrasser,*" chorus voices from the bus. I am gratified to note excellent use of *ça* in its emphatic function, as grammar books would put it. Addresses are exchanged with the French students and promises to meet during the next vacation period.

No more struggles for that privileged seat near the driver. It seems that Jean-Luc has become Jennifer's property, and she sits, smug and satisfied, as close to him as the layout permits. No sooner are we out of the city and on the *Autoroute du Soleil* to Lyon and Marseille than she is whispering in his ear, tickling his neck and ruffling his hair. Terribly embarrassed, Jean-Luc tries in vain to stop her and resorts to looking straight ahead, pretending to be unaware of her attentions.

Liz and I are appalled. Distracting the driver could lead to an accident and cannot be tolerated.

"Do I do something about it, or do you want to handle it?" I whisper to Liz.

"Save your authority," she replies, "you might need it later," and she stands up, taps Jennifer on the shoulder.

"I am afraid I must ask you to let me have this seat. I'll soon have to start giving directions to the driver who is unfamiliar with this area." Jennifer pouts, hesitates and finally rises . . . to sit on the floor, right at Jean-Luc's feet, her face level with his knees. I see him turn dark red.

"Chill out, Jenny," says Carola quietly. "Why do you have to make an ass out of yourself? Come sit by me."

"Hey, Jen," calls out Rob, baseball cap still backwards, "no sniffing his *b*. . . ." Maria has reached over and clamped her hand over his mouth. Everybody laughs. Still Jennifer doesn't budge.

Dumb girl, I think, very angry by now. We could all get killed because of her . . . let's say foolishness, although other words come to mind.

"Jennifer," I say as steadily as I can, "you will get up this instant and take a regular seat. Don't force me to take disciplinary measures." She pretends not to have heard, hoping to make me repeat the injunction, but I just wait. So, after a moment, she makes a face in my general direction, squirms . . . to finally get to her feet and take a seat next to Carola. I am relieved because the immediate problem is solved, and, frankly, I don't know exactly what disciplinary measures I can take. The handbook only mentions signing the student out of the Program after consultation with the General Director, and I am not prepared for such drastic action.

Okay, one down. Now, what's next? But all is calm as we drive through the great royal forest of Fontainebleau. I see Phil squint out of the window.

"Lost your glasses, Phil?"

"No, they're right here in my pocket. Only, I thought I'd try my contacts. Seems they don't bother me here like they did back home." Regular features no longer marred by the steel frames, Phil looks decidedly handsome. Did the bold Pomme have anything to do with this transformation?

Many are disappointed, crossing Burgundy, to discover so few of the famous vineyards. But as Liz explains, *that* kind of real estate is too valuable to be lost to the *autoroute*. The great vintages lie east of our course, closer to Dijon. Instead, we sail through lush pastures where white Charolais cattle graze or crowd around the drinking troughs.

"Hey, look! Just like Disneyland!" Even better than Disneyland, Châteauneuf, an intact medieval castle, stands in profile on the brow of a hill.

When we stop at a rest area for a break and a snack, the kids are entranced to find various services grouped on one side of the *autoroute* with an overpass from the other. They swarm the boutique selling local specialties of cassis—cassis jam, liqueur, candy—and mustards in every imaginable flavor, including cassis mustard, and, of course, acres of Burgundy wines. But where are the soft drinks?

Orange juice is thought prohibitively expensive, but a press, set right in the parking lot, dispenses fresh apple juice. Drop a few of the red and yellow fruit from an overflowing basket into the funnel, watch the attendant turn the crank and *voilà!* A glass of cool, cloudy cidery juice. Cost? About 20 cents. Some cannot get enough, but Dana, who demands *strawberry* juice instead, leaves without drinking anything and will complain for the rest of the morning that she is thirsty. The twins, Keiko and Michiko—I still cannot tell them apart—make it a point to counter what they see as Dana's lack of courtesy by assuring me they've never had such a good time before as since they arrived in France.

Déjeuner has been ordered in Beaune, the loveliest of Burgundy towns, at a friendly restaurant on the market place called Maxime. As we alight, Jason, an art student, announces that he'll forego the meal or else grab a snack somewhere because he *must* see the Roger van der Weyden triptych his class has studied.

"Wait, I'll go with you," calls out Maria, and two others join them.

"You know how to find the triptych?" I ask.

"Sure, at the Hospices, tours every hour. Come on, kids,

next tour is in 10 minutes, I checked, and there's a map of the city in my guidebook." Madison, the judoka, peels from the group and sprints after them, long braid swinging. Liz watches them disappear in the direction of the Hospices, once a medieval hospital but now a celebrated museum.

"Education isn't wasted on kids like those. . . ." she muses. "But then, they all learn something here, whether they want to or not. By the way," she continues, always practical, "that's five less for *déjeuner*. I'll have the restaurant pack lunch boxes for them."

Our tables are already set on the square, decked out in red and white cloths under umbrellas. Faustino, doe-eyed and diffident, approaches me:

"Could I be served a vegetarian meal? Avoidance of meat leads to greater spirituality, don't you think?"

I present the request to a waiter who nods, leaves and soon returns, bellowing "Who's the vegetarian meal for?" That's enough for 30 hands to shoot up, requesting a vegetarian meal, too. If Faustino can have one, why couldn't they? Anyway, they are dieting and this is a perfect opportunity.

I blanch. What about the meal ordered in advance and ready to be served? Once more, Liz saves the situation.

"As part of your cultural experience, a typical Burgundy meal has been prepared for you. I understand how you feel about dieting, so just eat sparingly, only toy with your food if you must. There'll be enough without the meat. But do show the great courtesy of your culture by not refusing food offered to you."

This rekindles the ambassadorial spirit, and all fall voraciously to the appetizer salads, the local *jambon persillé*, chunks of rosy ham in a parsley gelatin, *oeufs en meurette*, another regional dish of poached eggs in a velvety wine sauce. Not a shred is left of the Charolais roast beef or a crumb of the creamy gratin of potatoes. I even observe Faustino accepting forkfuls of beef from a neighbor's plate.

Arrival of the cheese trays is greeted with some suspicion, and a few noses wrinkle at the pungent Époisses, fabled king of Burgundy cheeses. Yet, these, too, are cleaned up in no time. At dessert—wheel-sized plum tarts—the owner appears to ask if everything was satisfactory.

"Alors, tout va bien? Assez mangé? Now I'd like to serve you each a glass of wine from our own reserve, compliments of the house and our welcome to you!" Cheers answer and waiters pour glasses of a fragrant Burgundy red. At that point, Constance calls out angrily from her seat.

"How dare you allow wine drinking? Most of those kids aren't even 21 yet! This is illegal. I wouldn't touch the stuff myself or stay in a place where liquor is served, for that matter. Drinking is immoral and should be outlawed. I'll have to report you."

I sigh. Would it have been too much to hope I'd be spared one of those?

"For one thing, Constance, everybody here is old enough to drink under French law. Second, one glass of wine after a large meal cannot have adverse effects. Third, you don't have to drink any yourself, and fourth, you certainly may leave. Just meet us at the bus."

Constance stomps away angrily, followed by a few catcalls that I sternly hush. "She has the same right to refuse this wine as you have to accept it." They could retort, but the mood is mellow and nobody really cares.

And then, surprise! From my seat, I can see our bus parked on an adjacent street. Jean-Luc, who has finished his own meal, is smoking a cigarette, sitting on a bench. When we stopped at the rest area, I couldn't miss a furious exchange between him and Jennifer. I saw her hang her head, him walk away, and they haven't been speaking since. It looks like the romance is over. But Jean-Luc will not remain lonely for long, because now, Constance runs across the square, turns the corner to the bus . . . and goes to sit on the bench very close to him.

I am distracted from whatever thoughts the sight might suggest when a clear, high voice arises, a voice that should be soaring from some angelic choir, as Rosalind begins to sing, incongruously, a bawdy drinking song! And I mean *bawdy*. Where could she have learned "The Monks of Saint-Bernardin," which leaves nothing to the imagination as to the preferred entertainment of those monks? Surely not in the church where she is a soloist! All the others clap their hands and pick up the easy refrain. This attracts waiters and a few local strollers who stop, hearing the familiar strains. Nobody seems shocked or even surprised, but rather pleased instead that these young foreigners should be so well versed in French drinking songs. So they join in, adding even a few stanzas.

Sarah? She is still moping. As for Dana, she looks away, drumming her fingers on the table. Catching my eye, she mouths: "When are we going to leave?"

We do leave soon after, and would have left even sooner, except that a couple of *monsieurs* (as the students call
them and which I find much more endearing that the correct *messieurs*), older gents with bérets and red faces, have
grabbed the hands of Keiko and Michiko, asking where
they come from, where they're going and couldn't they stay
for a wine-tasting tour of their cellars? When they won't let
go: "Don't worry about those," offers Madison the judoka,
just returned from the Hospices. "I can always throw one
of them and that will cool down the other." But we don't
have to resort to such hardly ambassadorial tactics, as
Keiko and Michiko manage to extricate themselves, bowing politely all the time.

Not surprisingly, most doze throughout the afternoon,
catching up at last on missed sleep. We leave Mâcon,
Tournus, Lyon and the ancient Roman city of Vienne
behind us, no more than exit signs on the *autoroute*. We are
to spend the night in Valence, traditional gateway to
Provence, as a setting sun shows the way.

The brand new youth hostel, featuring balconies as
color blocks of blue and yellow, stands close to the bank
of the Rhône, and the great river flows swiftly by, swirling
eddies high on its banks. After dinner, a group led by Burt
and Stan, the engineers, decides to go dancing on a barge
moored along the other side of the bridge. Its flashing
strobes and strings of colored lights cast impressionist
reflections across the entire river, and we can hear the
music carried over the water with the thump, thump of its
bass drum.

Liz and I are sitting outside, enjoying the calm, cool evening.

"Come dancing with us?" asks Stan. "You should have fun, too, sometimes!" I feel flattered, but Liz laughs, shakes her head and excuses us both:

"Some other time, maybe. Right now, I think we'll stay and look after the others."

"Don't look too close, like, if you get my drift," volunteers Kevin.

Left alone, Liz and I take a walk along the bank, watching a train of barges riding low in the water, carried downstream by the strong current. We pass Faustino, sitting under a tree, deep in his evening meditation.

"I've been doing this job for five years," confides Liz, "and each year is a different experience. Oh, there are predictable moments, like the first cup of French coffee, or the *traversin* business, but group dynamics are not the same twice. You see, I've lived in Aix for many years, my children are grown and have left home, my husband. . . ." She pauses, hesitates. "My husband is busy with his work. He has his . . . his own interests, and I'd be lonely without the Program. These kids exude such vitality, such *joie de vivre*, it's infectious. Even when they're at their worst, grousing, exasperating you, they'll suddenly do something that makes you like them all over again. I correspond with many from the previous years, and I've remained friends with the previous Resident Directors. The office has become the best part of my life. You'll see, we'll have a good year."

After we've said goodnight and retired to our rooms, I stand for a while on my balcony, watching the lights on the river, which outline a dark silhouette by the bank. When he turns and walks toward the entrance, I recognize Stan, who has not gone dancing after all.

Impatience reigns in the bus the next day. Now that a sign has announced "You are in Provence," the kids watch for changes in the landscape. First there are miles of orchards along the road, with espaliered trees and cypress edges as breaks against the *mistral,* the wind that is blowing today, pushing clouds and scouring the sky to clear indigo; then vineyards. "Côtes du Rhône" the students read aloud. The foothills of the Alps appear in the distance. "Is that lavender growing by the roadside?" A little dusty, but yes, these are clumps of scraggly but fragrant wild lavender. A window is lowered—"I can smell it!"—and all the windows go down. Soon the gusts of wind also blow in whiffs of thyme and rosemary that grow in the hills as far as the eye can see.

"Village de Lagarde-Adhémar." Someone reads from a sign and points to a perched village, crowned by its castle and church steeple, cascading from the top of a not too distant rise. "Looks like it's made of Legos!" exclaims Rosalind. "Why should they choose such a site, crowding everything this way?" Phil wants to know. Liz explains that perched villages are common in Provence; that they are ancient, built as protection when pirates' raids from the Mediterranean presented a constant danger.

"How long ago was that?"

"Probably before the 12th century," says Liz, "but you can learn all about them at the university. There is a wonderful course on regional history with field trips every week."

And finally, when a last sign announces *Aix-en-Provence*, excitement knows no bounds. Jason is the first to spot the Mont Sainte-Victoire on the horizon. I have to promise that we'll organize outings so they can climb and paint the mountain made famous by Cézanne.

"That won't be necessary," murmurs Liz. "Right now, they feel a little insecure, but give them a few days and they'll scatter, each will have found his or her own life. Lucky if we even see them all for the compulsory language classes held at the Villa!"

A few hours later, all our ambassadors have been settled, either in shared apartments or in single dorm rooms—the only dorm rooms in the world, comments Jason as he looks out, with a Cézanne in every window: A full view of Mont Sainte-Victoire.

Liz takes me to my *logement de fonction*, as job housing is called in French. I am impressed by the gate, the tree-lined drive that ends at the foot of a broad terrace. The Villa is rather grand, with vast rooms downstairs furnished in Provençal antiques plus a ragtag assortment of plastic chairs. "Our contribution to décor," comments Liz pointing to them. "Otherwise, the Villa is rented furnished."

Mail is piled on the desk in the bedroom that will serve as my office. I skim through, plenty of time to examine it tomorrow. But one letter retains my attention. The address is handwritten, addressed to the Resident Director, with the word "Personal" underlined on a corner. Something tells me I should have a look.

> *Dear Sir or Madam,*
> *I am writing to you because I feel there are certain facts you should be informed of. . . .*

The letter is signed by Sarah's mother. Silently, I pass it to Liz who reads, shakes her head.

"I thought it would be something like that," she says as she hands it to me. I slip it into my desk drawer.

My large bedroom, with a canopied bed and a period chest of drawers, looks down over the drive, just above the front door. Everything is freshly polished, the bed made. Liz has mentioned the very efficient cleaning lady who works at the Villa, promisingly named Madame Bon.

"Get a good night's rest, nothing to do that cannot wait until morning," says Liz. "You'll find groceries in the fridge downstairs if you need anything. In any case, I'll be here at nine in the morning. Good night and *à demain.*"

As I lie down, I make plans to check tomorrow on each of my charges and see how they are faring. We all have the rest of the week to get settled, and I have called for a full meeting on Monday. Wayne will be here in a day or two. Now I can sleep, and I set my alarm clock for 7:00 A.M.

But instead, it is still dark when a ringing shakes me awake. What is this? The doorbell? It continues in fits and starts. I run through the room, lean out the window. Sarah is standing there, pulling insistently on the brass handle.

Okay, she wants to go home. Only *now* I know what's driving her. My hunch was right, it is *not* filial duty.

"Just wait, Sarah, I'll be down in five minutes."

I dress hurriedly, brush my hair and rush down.

"All right, Sarah, now that you're here, let's have a serious talk." She follows me into my office, sits opposite me. My desk drawer is open a few inches and her mother's letter lies in front of me, while Sarah weeps and dabs at her eyes with a soggy wad of Kleenex.

Dear Sir or Madam,

I am writing to you because I feel there are certain facts you should be informed of.

My daughter Sarah has become infatuated with her best friend's father, a man older than her own father. She has built, entirely in her imagination, a thwarted love affair between them, and the poor man is at a loss, having tried every way he knows to make her understand that he cares for her only as one of his children's friends.

But she'll listen to no one, ambushes him, stalks him, pursues him with love notes, phone calls, even anonymous ones to his wife, warning her that she stands in the way of a great love and should simply leave. . . .

Things have reached such a point that we felt the best course of action would be to send her away, and the International Program seemed to offer a solution.

Now, Sarah is extremely good at dissembling, turning the truth into an entirely different story and putting Jesus on her side. She only accepted to apply after she had convinced herself that he would be leaving with her! Now that

*she knows differently, I wonder what her attitude can be
and what she might possibly be telling you.*

*Both my husband and I are terribly concerned about the
child who is in great need of counseling, but refuses help. So,
whatever she is telling you, please make every effort to
keep her there. Time cannot fail to do its work, as will new
friends and surroundings. We see no other course of action
at this time.*

I look Sarah in the eyes:

"Tell me once more, and truthfully, why you want to go
home."

"I said it before: Because I have no right to deprive my
parents of my presence."

"What if I told you they prefer that you stay here?"

"I'd say you're lying, or else they're being brave and lying,
too."

Should I show her the letter? No, it was clearly meant for
my eyes only. Is there any hope she'll get over her despair?

"Suppose I tell you that you cannot leave just now?"

"Then," she says, opening her large bag, "then I'll kill
myself. That's what this knife is for. When I found it in a
drawer at the apartment last night, I knew Jesus was showing me the way." And she pulls out a 10-inch kitchen knife.

Now, threats of suicide are not among eventualities covered in my handbook, but I am sure we do *not* want blood
on our hands. So:

"Sarah, please walk downstairs and wait for me in the
salon. Or look into the kitchen, I think there's some food
in case you want a snack. I'll call you back in a moment."

As her footsteps recede, I dial the General Director's office. With the time zone difference, it is afternoon there. Luckily, the assistants put me right through to him.

"I am so sorry. I had hoped to keep everything running smoothly, but we have a case here for which we need your advice." And I summarize the Sarah story, the terms of her mother's letter and the suicide threat.

The General has seen "cases" before. Still, he is appalled.

"There's no telling what this young lady is capable of, in her unbalanced state of mind. I blame her parents for sending her there; the purpose of the Program is *not* to solve psychiatric problems. When can you get her on her way? No, don't bother waiting for a student charter. Take the first commercial flight available."

A few more calls, and I obtain a booking on a flight home, via Paris, departing this afternoon at five. I leave a message on her parents' machine to meet her at the airport. Then I call in Sarah, who drags in, sobbing and munching on a cookie.

"Good news for you. You are leaving this afternoon and returning home. Just sign here and date this form. Be ready when I come to pick you up at your apartment."

Under my eyes, a sudden transformation: The weeper turns happy, vibrant, enthusiastic.

"Great! I am so happy! You see, somebody back home loves me and *needs* me so much! At last, we'll be together again! I can't wait to see *his* face smiling at me when I get off the plane. . . . Now, do I have some time for shopping?" A pause. "May I use your phone to call him?" I refuse, but I know she'll make the call as soon as she gets out of here. I sigh, a complete failure on my part.

"Don't be ridiculous," exclaims Liz when she arrives later. "Nobody could have done anything else. We get problem cases every year, and best is to let them go. Too bad, she's probably a very nice girl when she is normal. Now, you'll have time for the others. You cannot forget forty-eight . . . or nine well-adjusted kids just because one came who shouldn't have."

As usual, Liz is right. I already feel better as we climb into her car to start the rounds and see how everyone is managing. By the way, what about getting first a few dozen croissants in case some haven't figured out yet how to find breakfast?

Experience Romance
Climb to a High in Aix-en-Provence

To the Top of Mont Sainte-Victoire
It is a tradition among the young and young-at-heart, in Aix-en-Provence, to make the ascension of the Sainte-Victoire on the eve of their birthday, alone, in pairs or with a group of friends. They celebrate with a suitable picnic and spend the night there, contemplating the stars and their own future.

Needless to say, birthday or not, it is also a favorite excursion for lovers: Imagine the romantic setting, on top of the world with all the lights below and the immense, star-studded sky above. The cool night air will even keep champagne at the right temperature.

Our recommendation: A lovely adventure in good weather. While not difficult, the path is rocky and steep in places, so wear suitable shoes. Take a backpack with a picnic, plus something for breakfast, and whatever you'd enjoy drinking. Don't forget a blanket and warm clothes. Bring a flashlight and candles, perhaps, for a magical touch.

There is a shelter at the summit where you can retire if, overwhelmed by the cosmic show, you long for a roof over your head.

For all information:

Office du Tourisme

2, Place du General-de-Gaulle

13100 Aix-en-Provence

Tel: 04-42-16-11-61

Fax: 04-42-16-11-62

www.aixenprovencetourism.com

Play at the Complexe du Val de l'Arc

Just outside Aix, in the valley of the winding river Arc, you'll find this lovely, municipally-run sports complex with a fabulous view of the Sainte-Victoire.

You can play tennis, swim or take a walk in the peace and quiet of the tree-shaded river. I love to feed the ducks and swans and even wade in the cool water.

Hungry? Thirsty? There is a restaurant built on a sort of pyramid, which guarantees an even better view of Sainte-Victoire. Sit on the terrace, sipping an apéritif (probably a kir), and evoke Cézanne as you watch twilight descend over the mountain. Food is simple, but good and inexpensive.

Tired of Hotel Rooms? Stay at the Bastide du Roy René (adjacent to the Complexe du Val de l'Arc)
You will not find a more poetic or romantic apartment-hotel. There are lawns, cypress-lined walks, age-old plane trees and fountains everywhere. View of Sainte-Victoire? Of course!

Built in 1472 as the *bastide* (country home) of Good King René, who reigned over Provence, it was later enlarged as a monastery. When the 18th-century plague epidemics struck, it was turned into a hospital. More or less abandoned since, it has recently been restored with supreme good taste into a charming complex. Most apartments have their own secluded patio with table, chairs and umbrellas. They are simply, but elegantly furnished, with well-equipped kitchens and sleep two to six. Parking is full security, behind electric gates.

Prices are moderate, by the day, week or month. Chemin des Infirmeries, 13100 Aix-en-Provence (Tel: 04-42-37-83-00; Fax: 04-42-27-54-40; www.france-rdv.com/roy; e-mail: bastide.roy.rene@wanadoo.fr).

Simple and Sensuous
An End of Summer Dinner *à deux*

You are both busy all day and come home evenings, look-ing for a quiet, intimate time. You want a simple, but tasty and even sensuous meal that you can prepare together near an open window in summer; a light dinner that serves as a prelude to a romantic evening, the sort that rekindles the feeling of why you wanted to be together in the first place.

Salade de fenouil et oignon rose
Filet de saumon grillé
Pommes de terre à l'estragon
Crème à l'abricot

Fennel (Sweet Anise) and Spanish Onion Salad
I fennel (sweet anise) root or two if small
½ Spanish onion
Vinaigrette

Slice very thinly, by hand or in Cuisinart, the fennel and onion. Add the chopped, soft green leaves from the top of the fennel. Mix and toss with vinaigrette to taste.

Vinaigrette: In a lidded jar, mix 3 generous teaspoons Dijon mustard with ¼ cup white balsamic vinegar and ¼ cup olive oil. Shake well. (If you prefer a milder dressing, use less vinegar.)

Grilled Salmon and Tarragon Potatoes

2 pieces salmon filet (*not* the slices)
4 medium Yukon Gold potatoes
Salt and pepper, dried or fresh tarragon
Butter
Lemon sauce

On a hot, dry grill pan or non-stick pan, grill salmon, skin side first. Turn after 6 to 8 minutes, depending on thickness. If very thick, cover after a few minutes. Continue cooking the other side. Both skin and flesh should become crisp and golden. Salt and pepper flesh side.

While the salmon is grilling, peel potatoes and cook in salted water, enough to cover, until just cooked through (easily pierced with a fork). Do not overcook. Drain. In same pan, add butter and tarragon leaves, chopped if fresh. Shake to melt butter and coat potatoes.

Lemon Sauce: Melt ½ stick butter with the juice of a lemon. Add salt and cracked pepper.

On Your Plate

Arrange salmon and pour sauce over it. Garnish with potatoes and extra lemon. If you wish to eat the salad on the same plate, you'll find fennel and tarragon have complementary flavors.

Apricot Cream

I small can apricot halves, drained (or 3–4 fresh
    apricots)
I ounce apricot brandy
⅓ pint sour cream or crème fraîche

Sugar
Chopped pistachio nuts for garnish

Purée drained apricots in blender (reserving two small pieces for garnish) with I jigger of apricot brandy. Mix with sour cream in a bowl. Add sugar to taste.

Serve in pretty crystal sorbet glasses, garnished with reserved apricot and sprinkled with chopped pistachio nuts.

To Drink
A Pouilly-Fumé, a Loire wine, is perfect for such a dinner.

If too warm for candles, how about just flowers?

Scipio in Love
and the Dancing Police

*T*onight is our big, start-of-the-year party, and the Villa is perfect for such an affair, with its wide terrace surrounded by a stone balustrade, vast entrance hall with dining room on the left and salon on the right. Resident Directors traditionally hold such a party where students can meet faculty and other people they'll be dealing with during the year.

All last week was devoted to advisement. I've met with each student individually, their academic record and the catalog of their home campus in hand. There are more than 20 campuses in our large system. Each, in a spirit of autonomy, lists different requirements for completion of degrees, even in the same area of specialization. At the same time, I consult the French catalog which, to my surprise, does not indicate *where* courses will be held. My attempts at finding out have been stymied when secretaries, asked over the phone, answered that *they* guarded the information and would release it only if and when. . . . But never mind, for the students have already found out, I discover.

Not surprisingly, no course offered here corresponds *exactly*—or even approximately—to what is available on our home campuses, so it is up to me to find rough equivalencies, then adjust units accordingly. This business of *units* that must be assigned to each course worries me because, try as I might, I haven't been able to figure out how the French calculate their *unités-valeur*, as they call them. I can detect no correspondence between *unités-valeur* granted and the number of weekly class hours—which is *our* way of determining *our* units.

Most students are cooperative, they understand the process and readily accept the courses I suggest, or else propose realistic equivalents. Carola, who majors in marketing, will take several courses in International Commerce and Economics of the European Community. For an elective, which we all understand should be fun, Jazz Dance. Jason is ecstatic because he can fill his schedule with courses in History of Art, with Studio Art: Figure Drawing as an elective. Faustino dreamily scans the offerings: dance and music, music and dance. . . . "Is there any way I could be allowed to practice on the organ in the cathedral? I'd record my playing. What a souvenir to bring back!" I promise to look into it, but I don't see, at the moment, whom I could approach. "Yesterday," continues Faustino, "walking by the cathedral, I heard strains of organ, pushed those sculpted doors and found myself surrounded by clouds of incense and music pouring like . . . like the sea rolling. I'd never experienced anything like that!" I rejoice: So the Program is already bearing fruit! He ends up settling for Music Theory, Elements of Musical Composition, History of Ballet and, for an elective, Modern Dance.

Dana's advisement presents the sort of challenge that would drive a saint to sin. Nothing suits her, and after an hour all she has tentatively decided on is a jogging course. But wait:

"Who will drive me to the athletic field?" she wants to know. "I'll take the course only if I'm driven there."

"I suppose you could jog," I suggest.

"You are being defensive," pouts Dana accusingly. "Do you feel insecure? You must have an ego problem."

Well, yes, I do feel insecure. For one thing, I am a novice at psycho jargon, at which she, obviously a veteran of counseling, excels. Then, I am not certain my patience will hold much longer and, finally, all of my appointments for this afternoon are being thrown off.

"Take the catalog, sit in the dining room or in the hall, and mark the courses you *might* be interested in. I'll see you after I've met with the others, who have appointments."

"You are being dismissive now," she snarls. "Your ego is getting in the way of my education." Only nothing will force me into the kind of argument she's looking for and the afternoon continues.

Keith, a heavy-set, silent type, presents me with my next challenge. He has indexed and cross-indexed the catalogs with plastic markers, underlined text in three different color inks. Problem is, the only courses he is interested in are for the *doctorate* program. And Keith is only a junior, not even quite that, since he must make up a few deficiencies to reach that status. His language grades aren't that great, and he refuses to speak French with me. . . . What in the world would he get out of those seminars in which advance reading requirements are enormous? He wouldn't last a minute and nobody'd understand how I could have approved such a program!

"Keith, you indicate here Criticism of the Age of Enlightenment. For that, you must have read the 18th-century philosophers, Voltaire, Rousseau, Diderot, Montesquieu and probably several more. After that, you'd have to theorize on the validity of. . . ." Keith dismisses my concerns with a casual gesture.

"I *know* what the Age of Enlightenment is! Just give me the date when the light bulb was invented, and I can criticize *anything*. I was always good at finding fault."

Does it look like we might be at this all year? Yes, but because all the others are so well prepared and rational when they come to sit across from me, advisement *does* come to an end. Several will take, as an elective, the photo course Wayne has offered to teach, *sans compensation*, since he'll be here between his own professional assignments. The kids look forward to learning how best to make use of their photo artillery, which ranges from Instamatics to multi-lens state-of-the-art Nikons.

All right now. Can we start thinking of the party? Not so fast.

Wayne, who cannot live without music, has gone shopping and bought a stereo. It was supposed to be installed upstairs in our private quarters but, upon request, he agreed that it might as well go downstairs where *everybody* can get an earful. The kids are eager to hook it up now.

Liz is dubious.

"We never had a stereo before because the previous directors felt that music and dancing, which will inevitably follow, might send the kids out of control. Are you sure this will be all right? Can you keep them in check? Remember, this party is a very *staid* affair."

There is more. She cautions me:

"You are the first woman director to be appointed to run this Program. There were murmurs last spring when your name was announced. Some feel America is pushing feminism a bit far and couldn't see how a *woman* would handle those guys, who can get pretty rowdy. People have heard of your books and thought you probably had more experience at a keyboard than at a job like this."

Back home, we've been over that ground long ago, so I only resort to the classic answer.

"Then, it will be up to me to show I can do as good a job as my predecessors." To begin with, I'll see that the kids look presentable and display their best behavior. Privately, I also promise myself that I'll be on my best behavior, too.

So I admonish the men:

"This is a very important event. You'll be making your first impression on the families that might want to host you. So please, no shorts, no sweats, no T-shirts. You must look your best and show the good manners of our country."

For added incentive, I even resort to bribing them:

"You can dance *after* the reception is over and the guests have left. But only after, you understand. It is not that kind of an affair." The girls love the idea: "A party!" they cry. "We'll love getting dressed up! Wow! A chance to wear pretty clothes and really do up our hair."

I have had no chance to see much of the town, busy all day with advisement and making the rounds in the evenings to see how everybody is doing. The girls who brought no hangers went and bought some; the guys creatively strung belts or shoelaces tied end to end across their rooms to fling clothes over, as an alternative to piling them on the floor. Several, mostly the boys for some reason, have been stricken with the flu, the kind that hits you after breathing germ-laden, recirculating air on a long flight. Fortunately, French pharmacists prescribe almost as doctors do and will even give shots if necessary.

Poor Rob is feverish in his dorm room, sitting on his bed, winter parka draped over his shoulders. An open box of medicine sits on his desk.

"Did you take any of those?"

He shakes his head in disgust:

"Those pills, you mean? Man, they're more like machine gun ammo! Huge! You have to break them up to swallow them. And they taste so bad, they, like, make you even sicker. One's more than enough. Here, take a look at them, will you, go ahead! Smell them, too, and taste them, you'll see what I mean."

I certainly can sympathize with Rob. These are suppositories and not likely to be formulated for taste appeal. Suppositories, considered here preferable to ingested products because the medication bypasses most of the digestive track, are a popular form of treatment in France, used to cure a variety of ills, from sleeplessness to toothaches to hives and even undesirable personality traits.

Although I had hoped, in Paris, when the *bitte* matter came up, to limit my conversation to above-the-waist matters, mindful of how my remarks might come across in letters home, I can see now that it won't be possible and regretfully give up the idea. As delicately as possible, I try to explain the proper use of that peculiar ammo. But before I can even finish, Rob is shouting out in the hall:

"Hey, you guys, listen to that! You won't believe it, man. Up your ass, *she says*. Like those pills they gave us, they're supposed to go *up your ass*, she told me." (*Dear Folks, Our director told us today how to take French medication, but Mom shouldn't be reading this . . .*). Heads pop out of neighboring doors, and I have to hesitantly repeat to a bunch of doubting guys just where you place a suppository with Rob doing his best to help, illustrating my speech with appropriate gestures. A lot of unconvinced headshaking follows. . . . Yet, by next afternoon, everyone is feeling better, so it seems that directed to the proper channels, the medication works, or else the bug has run its course.

Liz shrugs, bored, when she hears the story. "Happens every year."

Wayne arrived shortly after the group, bringing with him Truffles, our dog, a yellow mongrel I rescued as a pup last year from a hit-and-run accident on the freeway. We had left her in the care of friends who shipped her to the Paris airport where Wayne picked her up. Truffles, a little too tall for a dachshund, too long for another breed, would not win beauty contests. In fact, the vet tells me she represents the typical end-of-the-line product of indiscriminate breeding, the nondescript yellow dog that, after a nuclear holocaust would emerge, pregnant, out of a hut somewhere in Central Asia, followed by the only survivors, a little brown man and his wife, to start the cycle of life all over again. But she overflows with eagerness, *joie de vivre* and intelligence. After greeting me effusively, she conducts a thorough sniffing tour of the grounds, and finally settles near the entrance door to assume her duty of guarding the house, jumping up every time visitors appear to welcome them with rapturous tail-wagging.

She hasn't been there a day before an enormous dog shows up, apparently out of nowhere. I mean a *monster* of a dog, much larger than any breed I have seen before, closer in size to a young bull than to any canine, with the punched-in face of a boxer, only hirsute, and the body of . . . of a woolly rhinoceros, maybe. He galumphs up to me, rears up, attempting either to put his paws up on my shoulders or else to eat me alive—hard to tell—knocking me down, to sit flat on the gravel. This accomplished, he makes straight for Truffles who stands, quivering with excitement. A lot of joyous barking is followed by friendly tussles, rolling on the ground, chasing all over the unkempt garden, running crazily up and down the drive.

"Dog flirting, like big time," diagnoses Kevin who happens by.

They finally settle down under a scraggly climbing rose, near the door, fur to fur, panting in unison, tongues lolling. The Monster only leaves after dark, when I have dragged in Truffles for the night, but is back the next morning to wake us up. They have remained constant companions ever since. Once in a while, he will open his mouth wide and, touchingly, Truffles will rest her entire head between his jaws in a perfect picture of love and trust. Although the Monster does leap up on them, the students don't mind him; the guys wrestle with him and the girls coo at both dogs. All enjoy seeing him settling down with his little yellow girlfriend.

"Puppy love, like," squeals Rosalind. "I used to be in love like that when I was *young.*"

Invitations have been sent by Liz on my personal card with my impressively long title, which takes almost two lines in print: *Resident Director of the State University International Program in France.* Wow! . . . But Wayne is not impressed. "Long is proof," he says, "that it doesn't mean much. *Real* titles are short, like CEO, boss, chief, czar, duce, Fürher . . . or *man,*" he adds, stepping aside out of my reach, hoping to get a rise out of me. But I ignore the tease, I am way past resenting that man versus woman business. Let guys have their fun, why not? Besides, I have more important things to do.

Most of the professors, whose classes our students shall be attending, will be here with spouses, as well as several deans and academic notables. Liz, who knows everybody in town has, bless her good PR sense, rounded up a number of families who wish to entertain one, or several, American students for dinner, a weekend, a vacation perhaps, and we hope affinities will develop. We are eager to help our kids participate in French life beyond the university.

In order to expand their opportunities outside our city circle, I had the idea of inviting the mayors of several of the neighboring villages. They might open horizons for our young people. Most respond favorably, and the mayor of Villelaure, owner of a wine estate, will bring, in addition to his wife, his son Fabrice "who loves all things American."

Fully aware that my reputation will be on the line tonight, so conscious of the fact indeed, I have even let down the hem of my beige silk suit as far as it will go, *almost* down to the knee. Let's give this affair as much dignity as we are capable of.

A shower this morning has left puddles in the drive, but before noon the sun is shining again. Champagne and hors d'oeuvres will be served on the spacious terrace fronting the house. A long table has been set up along one side to serve as a bar. Later, trays of petits fours will circulate. In the salon, chairs have been lined up along the walls, the carpet rolled away. Phil, assisted by a few others, came this morning to hook up the stereo, bringing an armload of CDs to add to Wayne's. He will be in charge of the music tonight.

"I won't be doing any dancing myself," he confides. "Next vacation period—it's a month from now, right?—I'll be going to Paris. . . . I'm meeting someone there," he adds so mysteriously that I refrain from asking if that person might not, by any chance, be named Pomme.

Now, I repeat once more:

"No music and no dancing until after our guests have left, that's understood? You must act *decorously*. What? All right, I mean, cool it until then. Afterwards, you'll have until . . . oh . . . let's say . . . does eleven sound reasonable to you? No? 'Til when then? No, Jason, certainly not all night. Let's say midnight then and not one minute longer. And promise you'll help put everything back in place before leaving."

Liz has organized every detail and now she arrives, pretty and blonder today in a blue printed chiffon.

"Young Professor Féraud has volunteered to help Wayne behind the bar. Two ladies, friends of mine, will pass the hors d'oeuvres and later, the petits fours."

"Wouldn't it be simpler to ask the students? I'm sure they wouldn't mind passing . . . "

But Liz's laugh interrupts me and she shakes her head:

"I did that the first year. Within half an hour, the trays were empty, and most of the guests hadn't even arrived yet. The kids were even more surprised than I was. They had not *eaten* all that stuff! Barely tasted it, they claimed. So tonight, the dining room is out of bounds to them."

Now, I suddenly remember I must do something about the Monster out front. We wouldn't want him to scare the guests away, or, perish the thought, try to leap on them!

But when I rush outside, I see no sign of our canine lovers. Gone. Nowhere in sight. I panic, call, whistle, call again. No Monster, no Truffles. Where could they have wandered off to? She has a collar with a tag, but I don't know whether or not he does and, anyway, would anybody be brave enough to search for it in that thick fur? I walk up and down the drive, skipping over puddles, look out the gate into the street. In vain.

I meet the first arriving students there. They've been asked to show up a little early as they are, in fact, co-hosts of this affair. Others soon follow in large groups, or else by twos and threes, as friendships have begun to develop. I must admit they look quite ambassadorial tonight. The girls are a whirl of summer dresses, short and long skirts; Carola in a pale blue mini with a cropped jacket, Maria in flowing slacks with a red embroidered top, Rosalind pinker and rounder than ever in a quilted outfit. Hair is freshly curled or else silky smooth. Ginny, the future park ranger, wears a no-nonsense blazer and her husband a vest and bolo tie. Keiko and Michiko run up, out of breath, in identical long dresses. Might they be late? They apologize in unison, *"Ma jumelle et moi nous excusons. . . ."* (My twin sister and I apologize. . . .) Where did they pick up that perfect, formal French?

Faustino's height dominates all, slender as a whip in narrow black slacks and a black silk turtleneck. There are sport coats, a few suits, dress shirts and ties. Rob's tie hangs out of his pocket. Larry, the cowboy type, sports a fringed suede jacket, and Mona, who holds his arm, a prairie skirt and boots. No sweats, shorts or T-shirts in evidence.

Apart from all the others, even walking on the opposite side of the street, comes Dana, whom I haven't been able to find since advisement, in that same black dress she wore in Paris. Good heavens, hasn't she shortened it even more? Several girls, walking up the drive with me, try to draw my attention to it, but I comment, instead, on her pretty earrings.

"Anything goes in France, I guess," remarks someone. "If the police haven't arrested her yet, it's because they won't arrest *anybody*." I studiously ignore this.

"Constance won't come tonight, she wants you to know, because liquor will be served. Anyway, she's busy writing the Chancellor, she said, to report that you *make* us drink," volunteers someone else. "But don't worry, *we* like you," she adds, then takes and squeezes my hand.

"She's writing? Now that's a good one!" exclaims Amanda, shaking her hair, all done up tonight in tiny braids, each ending with a colorful wooden bead. "Believe me, she isn't writing *anybody*! I saw her leaving a while ago with Jean-Luc on his motorcycle. They're out *every* night! It's only *liquor* she objects to," she adds looking at me, trying for an innocent wide-eyed stare. They all laugh, watching to see if I get it—people like me can be dense, they know. I repress a smile, for I couldn't very well seem to laugh at another student behind her back. But they know, oh, they know! We're already becoming friends and women can read other women, no explanations needed.

Our handsome group is scattered on the terrace when the first guests arrive. I shake hands, make introductions, thank everyone for coming. . . . A car roars up the drive and veers to a screeching stop at the foot of the steps. It is a Mehari, one of those two-horsepower jobs Citroën makes this year, with a molded plastic body shaped like a small Jeep, no doors and a canvas top fastened with straps. I've seen them around; they come in candy colors, like orange and yellow. This one is chartreuse. Out jumps a very jazzy young Frenchman, in a white blazer but no shirt, who hands out . . . Parker! Parker in a see-through, unbuttoned blouse with no bra, only adhesive flower cut-outs, strategically placed. By the way, Parker is another one I haven't been able to find all week, she's even missed advisement, but I'll soon know why. Eyes widen to saucer size.

"Hi," she breathes to the assembly at large. "Mind if we park here? Won't stay long, anyway. Just drove back from Saint-Tropez. End of season, but the place is still jumping."

She notices stares fixed on those . . . adhesive flowers.

"Like my outfit? It's from Naf-Naf. You see a lot of those over there." The girls are speechless, and so am I. It has just occurred to me that we had all misread her letter to the General Director, in which she enquired whether Aix was, or was not, a *party* school. She wanted to be sure it *was!*

"This is Thierry, my boyfriend. We met on the first day, didn't we, Thierry?" Thierry smiles, kisses girls, shakes hands.

"Say, Parker," calls out one of the girls who has recovered enough to speak, "your skis are still in the hall at the dorm. Take up a lot of space, they're in the way of the mailboxes. You'll have to move them."

But Parker dismisses the skis.

"Oh, that! I just brought those because I didn't know any better. They're for sale. Any of you want to buy them?

I'll be staying at Thierry's place most of the time and he's got extra pairs." Meanwhile, Thierry is making his rounds, meeting everybody, evaluating the girls, supremely at ease.

Most guests are arriving. I meet professors, male and female, mostly trim and smartly dressed, belying the stereotype of the ratty old professor, and many speak fluent British-accented English. "Sound like Benny Hill or Monty Python," whispers Amanda. One of the men tells me he teaches semiotics. When I saw that course in the catalog, I thought I knew what semiotics is, but for added insurance, I looked up the word. It is, I read, "the science of the signs and symbols—other than language—that define a culture." I ask, because I remember the dictionary entry, which indicates two main orientations of the discipline:

"Are you into pragmatics or syntactics?"

He registers pain: "Pragmatics, of course. I have progressed well beyond syntactics. Terribly limiting, don't you think?" I do my best to indicate that I don't think much of syntactics, either. Conversation is easy because we can talk shop, all of us at ease with academic subjects. That is, until I bring up the matter that has been on my mind all week.

"In our universities, we evaluate units to be attributed to a course on the basis of contact hours. Two hours of class per week make it a two-unit course, for instance. Do you follow the same guidelines?"

That stops the French dead in their tracks.

Finally:

"You Americans flatter us, *Madame la Directrice*," laughs a handsome male professor with a neatly trimmed black beard that makes him look like a pirate, and I mentally arrange a patch over his left eye. "Am I to understand that you expect your students to learn *only* in my presence? That *nothing* but my *bodily proximity* will enable them to absorb the elixir of knowledge? Quite a compliment to my physical powers, even if somewhat undeserved, I fear. . . ."

But I insist:

"Then, how do you assign units to a course?"

They all look at each other, puzzled. Clearly, the concept of *unit* is not seen here as the hard, mathematical, degree-governing measure of intellectual achievement it is for us in the States.

After a moment of confused silence:

"Oh," volunteers the semiotics man, who would like to satisfy me as a fellow pragmatician, I suppose, "we form an . . . an evaluation of the . . . the amount and nature of intellectual expenditure the students would *ideally* invest into the course. But," he adds generously, "you can do with *your* units whatever you want, as far as this is concerned."

Big help, which still leaves me in the dark. But those calculations will have to wait. Liz is tugging at my arm, beaming: the *recteur, en personne,* and his wife are here.

"Never dreamed he would show up! We invite him every year, but he declines each time through his secretary. Must have been curious to see what the first woman director looks like. Others were curious, too, that's why so many people are here."

I hurry down the steps, hand extended in greeting. The *recteur,* tall and angular, horn-rimmed glasses and dark suit, looks stern and calls me Madam Director. His wife is petite, elegant in a short cocoa lace dress. All smiles, she looks around at the assembly:

"How lovely! I am so glad. . . ."

Hélas, we will never know what made her glad because, at that very moment, Truffles and the Monster come bounding out of some bushes, and it happens so fast that I don't even see if they tripped her or whether the Monster tried to leap up on her. Anyway, here she is in her beautiful dress, sitting smack in the middle of a puddle, and not looking glad at all anymore.

Personally, I'd rather die this instant than face the next few minutes . . . and their fallout. Tragedy has struck with the speed of lightning. Doing all that can be done in this disaster, Liz is here, napkin in hand, wiping the mud off the dress—fortunately, mud doesn't show too much on that color. The lady tries to be a good sport and protests weakly that it's nothing, nothing at all. . . . The *recteur* manages a tight-lipped smile, but his thoughts are clear behind the horn-rimmed glasses; *now* he can see how a *woman* director handles responsibility.

All right, let's forget about me, as the first thought of resignation occurs to bring some solace. Yes, I can always resign tomorrow, but more pressingly, these dogs *must* be controlled. We can't have that kind of greeting inflicted on more guests. So, I grab Truffles by the collar and drag her inside, to lock her up in an upstairs bathroom. She has had her fun, and then some, for the evening. Now, *who* will help me get rid of the Monster?

That turns out easier said than done. He cannot be

shooed away and snarls viciously if you approach him. Next thing, he is hurling himself repeatedly at the entrance door, howling for his lady love and rattling the entire house. In his despair, he even ignores proffered tidbits and only steps back to throw himself against the door with renewed fury.

Obviously, we can't let this go on much longer. So, Wayne leaves his place behind the bar, picks up a phone and dials the police. Let them come and deal with the situation, find the owner of this crazed beast, get rid of him, shoot him if they must, for heaven's sakes, anything, but get him out of here, this cannot go on another minute. . . . Oh, but it does, and now he lunges menacingly at Burt who was trying to lead him away.

My disgrace is now total. I am certain that none of the previous directors' receptions featured a commotion like this, topped by a call to the police. Bad luck? Incompetence on my part? Both? Let's face it: the fact is that I am just *not* up to the job, that's all. Resignation is the only way out— under a hail of bullets, yet. But right now, I must hold my despair in check, for I have to meet the police who come roaring up the drive in a Renault minivan that throws up mud and gravel.

Four policemen pile out. Help at last! The Monster is still hurling himself at the door and howling in crescendo.

They'll do something, now, won't they?

Well, they'd like to, only they're afraid to come close to the beast. This is not at all the way the Los Angeles police would handle the matter. By now, there would have been a fusillade, *at least* one dead dog, and probably a few innocent bystanders would, too, be awaiting their body bags. Instead, the four Provence *flics*, cops, try calling out persuasively. Getting no result, they switch to a more severe tone. And finally, they end up throwing out dire threats of the pound. But the Monster ignores their show of authority. "Can't you see my heart is broken?" he howls. "I want my girl, I want her now."

At this point I have nothing to lose, do I? Job ruined, reputation gone . . . to the dogs, getting bitten is the least of my concerns! So I grab the beast in spite of his struggles and growled threats, feel in his fur for a collar. I find it, and a metal bullet that I unscrew. Inside, a rolled-up business card. The owner is Monsieur Amarige, who lives. . . .

"Oh," exclaims a policeman, "I know Amarige! He owns that travel agency on Boulevard des Belges. And he lives . . . why, his home is on the street directly behind this one."

The Renault is dispatched to get the Amariges who ought to be able to control their dog.

The party, meanwhile, in spite of the Monster's assaults, is humming. Trays are passed, students are in conversation with professors and families—in French, or at least some approximation thereof. All is well for them, I think sadly, and I hope they'll like their new director, the one who will replace me, but I must control my tears because now the Renault returns. Out steps Madame Amarige in striped pink pajamas and Monsieur Amarige in a robe tied with a tasseled belt. They had no idea they were coming to retrieve their dog in the middle of a party!

Madame Amarige takes the situation in hand.

"*Scipio, viens là, tout de suite,* come here right away," she commands, ominously not raising her voice. At the familiar sound, the Monster stops so short, you'd think his current was turned off. Then he flattens, belly to the ground and almost crawls, tail wagging apologetically, to come sit on her foot.

"*Méchant chien,* bad dog," scolds Madame Amarige. "*Très méchant. Il sera puni,* he'll be punished." Scipio looks up miserably, the tail wags feebly: "Can't you see how embarrassed I am by my behavior? Forgive me, please." But Madame Amarige will have none of that. "*Très, très méchant,*" she repeats. "*Il ne sortira plus jamais du jardin.* He'll never get out of the garden again." Scipio gazes up imploringly and licks her ankle.

Of course, most of the guests know the Amariges. Their travel agency is the largest in town, and many are its clients. So there's a lot of handshaking, jokes are exchanged about the dog in love.

"Wouldn't swear I behaved any better when I fell in love myself," declares a rotund mayor. "Remember, Monique, that time your father wanted to shoot me? I was trampling the flower beds at 2:00 A.M., throwing pebbles in your window to make you open it and come out?"

The matter resolved, the four policemen are standing there as the chief sums up the facts: "The vagrant canine has been returned to the custody of its owner," he declares. "No property damage, no crime or misdemeanor we could observe. After all," he adds, winking at the crowd, "dogs have the same right to be *amoureux* as humans do. We couldn't very well go around arresting *all* those who act silly because they're in love." Everyone agrees that such police action would indeed severely thin out the population. "No report will be needed," concludes the chief.

No, *they* don't need a report, but *I* will have to write one, recounting all this to the General Director, and preferably before he hears it from other sources. (*Dear Folks, You wouldn't believe what happened here last night. . . .*) I'll include my account of the fray with my letter of resignation, giving, at least, my own version of the events.

Their job is done, but the policemen seem disinclined to leave. Wayne produces a tray of champagne. The Amariges raise their glasses, wishing all those young Americans a happy stay in Provence. The kids cheer. The policemen throw their hats into the Renault and, now out of uniform, each picks up a glass, as their chief proposes a toast to the Fifth French Republic. The kids oblige again, they'd cheer all five if asked! Wayne brings out a dish, fills it with champagne, and Scipio laps it up, feeling that forgiveness is on the way.

But . . . what do I hear? The music is suddenly blaring. It is *Pour un Flirt Avec Toi*, a jumping disco number. Are those kids out of their minds? And to think I trusted Phil! Racy lyrics, yet! Didn't I tell them there could be no dancing until *after* the guests had gone? What am I going to do?

Turn off the damn machine for openers, and let them have a piece of my mind while I am still in charge here—or, at least, ought to be.

Only, I don't have time to do anything because here comes Faustino, yes, supposedly shy Faustino, all gleaming black and bronze under the lights, mannerly and elegant, who bows in front of Madame *Recteur*, offering his arm. She accepts, to the discreet applause of nearby guests.

Faustino, it turns out, could dance Travolta into the dust, and I must say the lady is good, too. At first, students stand around watching as he twirls her and she responds with the grace of a ballerina. She even kicks off her shoes and he lifts her up in a ballet move. Soon, a dozen couples are on the floor: Carola with the son of the Villelaure mayor, Burt with the very staid lady director of the dorms, cowboy Larry who whoopees and does a Western version of disco.

Pour un flirt avec toi	For a flirt with you
Je donnerais n'importe quoi	I would give just anything
Pour un petit tour	Let's say for a turn
Au petit jour	At break of day
Entre tes bras	In your arms
Entre tes draps. . . .	Between your sheets. . . .

Young Professor Féraud is showing how the French group-dance, and his circle includes Keiko and Michiko, Rob and Rebecca. Parker is whirling with Thierry, and I am a little relieved to see the adhesive flowers are still in place. Monsieur Amarige, tassels flying, is doing a lively number, and Madame Amarige, in her striped pajamas, is changing partners. More join in. Do I see Liz dancing with Stan, and a little more slowly than the beat of the song suggests? Dana is on the edge of the floor, twisting all alone, dress to her armpits. Kevin comes to stand in front of her, matches her moves, and they dance away, not touching, she still scowling. Jason is cavorting with the wife of a mayor, and Rosalind discos with the semiotics man. She bounces up and down, squealing—pragmatic signs, I hope, rather than syntactical—loud enough to drown out the music.

Through the ground-floor window, I see that Wayne has liberated Truffles, and, as he refills the dish, both lovers lap up champagne, one on each side.

And now, the chief of the policemen asks me "for the honor." What? Me? Dance? All right, I'll dance, since I see no way to die instead. Well, the guy may be potbellied, but he sure has rhythm. And the next thing I know, the other *flics* are on the floor, too, with our girls. Wayne gives me a thumbs up. Thumbs up? Poor innocent! Doesn't he realize what is really happening? Obviously not, for here he goes, hair tumbling into his eyes, doing one of his crazy numbers with a lady professor who matches him step to step and even does him a few better.

Animation grows with each song. Then, Phil puts on a salsa CD. The beat puzzles the French at first, but the *recteur*, no longer pompous, has removed his coat and tie as Maria leads him through the steps. One must admit that for an academic of his rank, he is pretty smooth. I change partners as another *flic* taps mine on the shoulder, and by now I don't even care anymore. I have botched the job, blown it, whatever. I can understand why the committee at the Chancellor's office never appointed a woman before. Only *men* have the authority to handle this job. As for me, I certainly lack the know-how to run this show. . . . Here, I let the kids, the dogs, whoever tried—and it didn't take much—run all over me. But since I can't resign until tomorrow, I'll dance tonight with tears in my eyes.

Even my midnight curfew has been utterly disregarded. My watch says past 1:00 A.M., and the party is in full swing. They dance in the hall, in the dining room, on the terrace. . . . Jackets are off, ties flying, and I can see our boys giving the French ladies quite a workout. Only Liz and Stan are now sitting off in a corner, quietly talking. I like Liz very much and it hurts to think that, by next week, she'll be showing another director the ropes.

I sway to a slow number with Wayne.

"I am sorry, sorry, sorry," I whimper.

"Sorry? About what?"

"Oh, don't try to be blind! You know this job is over. . . . Didn't last much more than a week, did it? Isn't that sad? My fault, I should never have accepted it when it was offered. At least, I hope the office still has time to appoint someone else."

Wayne acts puzzled:

"Why should they appoint someone else?"

I sigh. He can be that way when I need him the most: Thick. Obtuse. A wall. No communication. I'll have to live through this all alone. The thought makes sobs rise into my throat because I am now feeling sorry for myself, too, instead of just guilty like before.

Well, even the longest night must come to an end. It seems everyone is finally danced out, our kids are practically panting. The guests crowd around me.

"Carola is spending next weekend with us," declares the wife of the Villelaure mayor. "We'll show her *real* Provence."

"Faustino will join our club," this from a music professor. "I'll also get permission for him to practice on the organ in the cathedral. He tells me he's been dreaming of it."

The policemen's hats are on again. "We'll escort the young ladies and make sure they get home safely. Call us again any time you might need us, please. We are *à votre service*."

Monsieur Amarige gathers the kids.

"You are all invited to a *méchoui* at my farm, next Sunday. You don't know what a *méchoui* is? Well, in North Africa, like in Morocco where we used to live, you roast a whole lamb on a spit and. . . ." Cheers let him know they get the idea. "Like lamb barbecue, yeah, man!" shouts Rob. Other invitations are extended by families, accepted by grinning kids. A mayor wants our group to join their youth club for their next affair, another. . . .

The semiotics man shakes my hand.

"There've been other directors of merit," he allows. "But none of them seemed to foster that feeling of *cor-*

dialité, which should, in fact, imbue our intellectual discourse and *intercourse. . . ."* Wow! I am beginning to feel a lot better. I know what you mean, *cher collègue,* only please, don't use that last word with my kids. I don't think they could handle it.

The *recteur* has put his coat and tie back on, rearranged his dignified look.

"Congratulations, Madam Director," he pontificates. "You are creating a positive atmosphere that will open avenues of communication between your students and their host country. This will contribute to the success of their academic endeavors, as well as enhance their appreciation of our French culture. . . ." I smile weakly.

Someone calls out: "I always thought Americans were arrogant asses, but these are okay. Send us more like them!"

You hear that, ambassadors, you hear that? You did your job so well that you even saved me! Thanks to you, maybe I won't have to resign after all. This makes me immensely happy, because I *do* want to stay here with you, and I would hate to turn you over to someone who might not understand and like you the way I do.

Scipio is sleeping off his champagne, snoring loudly, and Madame Amarige has to wake him up to take him home. But next morning, *au petit jour,* at break of day as in the song, he is back to resume his blissful romance with Truffles. During the year, only when we have a reception or expect important visitors do we ask Madame Amarige to come pick him up, and he mopes at home until allowed to join his love again.

A few months after we had returned to the States, the Amariges wrote us a wistful letter: Scipio had died.

> *He was never the same after Truffles left. Only nine years old, the prime of life for a dog, but, although the vet could find nothing organically wrong with him, he stopped eating, lost interest in going out—even for the rides he used to enjoy so much—and just wasted away.*
>
> *We are convinced that he never got over losing the love of his life and simply did not feel like living anymore. We buried him in the garden, under a plaque engraved to read,* 'Ci-gît Scipio, mort d'amour' (Here lies Scipio, who died for love). *Please come and visit next time you are in Provence.*

We did just that, and together with the Amariges, we scattered rose petals over the grave. Truffles sniffed the ground endlessly and finally sat on the plaque, staring at us with sad, questioning eyes. But I am sure she knew.

The fact that both dogs had been neutered, and therefore could only experience the pangs of pure love untainted by carnal desires, makes the story all the more touching. Truffles, who was very young, forgot Scipio, but we didn't. Instead, we think he should be remembered as a role model, an inspiration to lovers with any number of legs. Not that we expect thwarted lovers to waste away and die, of course. But it is nice to know it can still happen, and that the chaste love sung by troubadours of Provence long ago hasn't died with them and still lives on, even if it was in the heart of a dog.

But then, the heraldic colors of Provence, red and gold—red for blood and gold for the sun—tell you that this is a passionate land.

Experience Romance
Be Seduced by a City: Aix-en-Provence

Ville d'Eaux, Ville d'Art
Drawings of a lyre and a fountain announce Aix, "City of Waters, City of Art." Dip your hand into a few of the many fountains, you'll find some cold, others warm, for these are mineral springs. The lyre refers to the world-famous Music Festival (June–July), when the town becomes drenched in music, from concerts in the cathedral cloisters, to open-air opera in the bishop's gardens, to street performers everywhere.

Experience the Cours Mirabeau
On this fabled avenue, in the shade of immense plane trees, cafés spill their terraces onto sidewalks. Sit at leisure to enjoy the passing crowds. Early in the day, order a *grand crème* (or café au lait, a large cup of coffee with hot milk), and later a *noisette* (small coffee with a dash of cream).

At night, become engulfed in the lively Mediterranean street scene with musicians, sidewalk artists and many, many young people from all over the world, for Aix is a university town.

Have lunch or dinner on one of those terraces. My

favorite is Les Deux Garçons (53, Cours Mirabeau; Tel: 04-42-26-00-51; Fax: 04-42-26-74-22), near the top. Founded in 1792, its gold and celadon décor has been freshened, but unchanged.

The Sensory Joys of a Provence Market

(The big Aix market is on Thursday; a more limited version on Tuesday.)

Let colors and fragrances assail your senses. Buy a basket of *fraises des bois*, the tiny, wild strawberries with a musky aroma that defies description, to share as you stroll.

Visit the brocante (in front of the Hall of Justice). *Brocante* fits somewhere between a flea market and an antique fair. You'll discover great buys in silver—bargain for a set of ivory-handled dessert spoons, search among heirloom linens for a pair of pillowcases hand-monogrammed with just *your* initials or come up with six crystal goblets.

Dress Up in Provençal Clothes

Still at the market, the colors of Provence sing in the distinctive bright cotton prints: pink and orange, green and red, yellow and blue or the more sober navy and white. You'll love the tablecloths and napkins, or the place mats, easy to slip in your luggage.

Do not miss the Provençal clothes. They are a fun and chic way to dress, just right for the atmosphere and the climate: Shirts for men, and for women well-cut, narrow stretch pants, tops, flouncy skirts, all in the printed cotton fabrics, show the French flair for style. Wear your new outfit for dinner tonight and you'll feel in tune with Provence.

Dinner: Stylish Romance or Simple Fun
Le Clos de la Violette (10, Avenue de la Violette; Tel: 04-42-23-30-71). A Michelin-starred restaurant. Delicious and perfectly romantic (Villa Galici is the attached hotel, equally delightful). Expensive.

The Ethnic Restaurants in the Old Town
There are dozens of such small, picturesque places with tables spilling into the narrow streets. Try Moroccan, Tunisian, Vietnamese or Caribbean (*Antillais*), for exotic flavors. Inexpensive.

Romantic Places to Stay
Le Pigonnet (5, Avenue le Pigonnet; Tel: 04-42-59-02-90; e-mail: reservation@hotelpigonnet.com; www.hotel pigonnet.com). Right in town, but surrounded by its own park with age-old trees shading the pool. Lovely décor, excellent food.

Le Mas d'Entremont (Route Nationale 7; Tel: 04-42-17-42-42; Fax: 04-42-21-15-83; www.francemarket.com/mas_dentremont; e-mail: masentremont@francemarket.com). Also in a park, but a little outside of town and on a hill. Both food and décor are seductive.

Our Recommendation
A few flowers and a candle or two will turn your hotel room into an intimate bower. If earlier in the day you've bought a box of *calissons*, Aix's specialty, made of almond

paste, pistachios and honey, you'll have a sweet nibble handy, should you wake up hungry at 2:00 A.M.

Simple and Sensuous
An Autumn Dinner *à deux*

If leaves are showing red and gold, and you feel a nip in the evening air, you will enjoy this dinner. The mushrooms infuse it with an aroma of fall; the pears and apples are at their most flavorful this time of year.

Potage aux champignons
Médaillons de porc aux pommes
Linguini au beurre
Tian aux poires

Mushroom Soup
I packet dry porcini mushrooms and I cup hot water
I basket sliced mushrooms
I quart chicken broth
I to 2 tablespoons cornstarch
Light cream, butter
Minced garlic, chopped parsley as garnish

Soak porcini mushrooms in hot water for 10 minutes. Meanwhile, sauté regular mushrooms quickly in very hot pan with a little butter. In saucepan, heat chicken broth. Add drained porcini mushrooms and sautéed mushrooms. Cook for 5 minutes. Purée in blender, saving a few pieces for garnish.

Return to heat. In a cup, mix corn starch with a little cream (or water). Stir in boiling soup to thicken it to light and creamy consistency. Add cream and butter to taste. Adjust seasonings.

Serve in soup bowls, with just a touch of finely minced garlic and chopped parsley.

Pork Loin with Apples
  2 slices pork loin or 2 pork chops
  Olive oil
  1 bunch green onions, chopped
  Salt and pepper to taste
  ¼ cup balsamic vinegar
  Butter
  2 firm apples, cored and sliced, but not peeled

In very hot pan, with just a few drops of olive oil, sauté pork so it browns quickly. Add chopped green onions, sautéing a little longer until pork is done through and onions are wilted and a little browned. Season with salt and pepper. Remove from pan and keep warm. Pour vinegar into pan, scrape brown bits from bottom of pan and allow to cook 2 minutes. Pour this over meat and onions.

In same pan, add a little butter, and sauté apple slices until tender and lightly browned. Set aside and keep warm.

Linguini

Cook al dente in boiling, salted water. Drain, stir in butter and cracked pepper.

On Your Plate

Arrange pork with green onions on top, apples next to it, and pass bowl of linguini.

Pear Tian

In Provence, a *tian* is a shallow, earthenware baking dish. Yours can be round, square, rectangular, it does not matter, but it shouldn't be glass.

I cup sugar, divided in half, plus 3 tablespoons
2 or 3 ripe pears, peeled, cored and sliced
3 eggs
I pint milk

Preheat oven to 450°F. First, make the caramel: In a small saucepan, *without any liquid*, put ½ cup sugar. Over high heat, and shaking pan constantly, watch sugar melt and caramelize. Let it get bubbly. Then, quickly pour it over entire bottom of *tian*. (It will spread out more as it bakes.)

Arrange pear slices in *tian*. In separate bowl, beat eggs, ½ cup sugar and milk. Pour mixture over pears to mostly cover. Place in preheated oven and immediately reduce temperature to 350°F. Check after 15 minutes. *Tian* should be set. If not, bake a little longer.

Remove. Sprinkle with remaining 3 tablespoons of sugar (more if you like). Slide under broiler until top is brown and bubbly. Don't overcook.

Serve lukewarm or cold.

To Drink

Definitely the meal for a Beaujolais. New Beaujolais comes out around the third week in November. Since that particular wine is best drunk fresh, you might hold this menu until then.

Falling in Love
with Provence

"*R*emember me, Bill Hope? We met at your party and I told you I'd call."

Thus began a long friendship with a colorful, offbeat character who introduced me to Provence and whom I came to love dearly.

(I loved him just as much, in fact, after I found out that he was quite mad. So long as Bill took his medication faithfully, he was fine. But should he fail, he would fall into periods of insanity, perhaps gentle, as when he would bring the *Complete Works of Shakespeare* to a blind friend in the hospital, or not so gentle as when he pursued a neighbor lady, brandishing a cane, because she'd dared ask him to lower the volume on his stereo. He was well known to the city's psychiatric services, which welcomed him as a valued return customer.)

I do remember being presented to an American expatriate living in Aix, a "friend of the Program," who occasionally lectures on comparative French and American poetry and also gives readings of the Symbolist poets in translation by Edna Saint-Vincent Millay. At the time, he made me think of a taller version of Truman Capote, with a similar smooth face and a fringe of sandy hair cut across the brow, Roman style. As I commented on his Southern accent, I learned Bill was from Chattanooga, Tennessee, but had chosen to live his adult life in Europe. After a few years in Italy, he'd settled in Aix.

"Well, sugar (pronounced *sugah*)," said the voice on the phone, "how about making good on your promise that you'll come over some evening for a drink? I'll mix some of those Manhattans that have made my reputation in Provence where the natives, though not ignorant about wine, know little about the delights of mixed drinks."

"Oh, yes," exclaimed Liz, when she heard of the call, "he is quite a personality around town, very active in the Summer Music Festival. Some even call him Mr. Aix. He is also somehow connected with the Marseille Opera."

I am delighted to hear from Bill and I say so.

"You are bringing me a whiff of the open world," I laugh. "I haven't had a moment to breathe since arriving here. Never could steal a moment from my desk, always looking after my charges, helping them solve problems, or else on the phone to and from the General Director's office. Visiting with you, and the offer of those Manhattans, sounds like manna from heaven . . . only double, I'd say. I'll come alone, if you don't mind, because my husband is away on an assignment that will keep him for several days. When do you want me?"

"What about tomorrow night? About seven? It is the best time to see my Cézanne. The light should be just right."

"I wasn't worried, or jealous about leaving you alone in Aix," declared Wayne on the phone that night. "But if you are going to pal around with Bill Hope, I'll be even less so. He'll be great company for you."

Bill lives in a fairly central part of town, strangely bypassed by all the traffic and new construction. Several times, I've driven along the busy street he indicates—Avenue Jules-Isaac—but completely missed the stone arch marking the entrance to a narrow road, barely wide enough for a single car, that winds its way up a steep hill, and called—although no sign is in evidence—*Butte des Trois-Moulins*, Three Mill Hill. I will learn, indeed, that until recently (which here may mean a century or more ago) three windmills *did* spread their sails there, slowly revolving in the wind. Now, only vestiges remain, like the wingless, crumbling body of the last one. In an abandoned lot, tall columns rise among a tangle of weeds. Remnants of an ancient temple, or of a demolished house? Hard to tell in Provence, but they give the area the vague air of a savaged Roman forum. . . . And here is Bill, watching for me, making like a semaphore to guide my parking, not too difficult a task, my car being the only one in sight.

A long, low stone building with a roof of pale tile tops the rise. Built in the 17th century, Bill tells me, this is a former monastery, the property of brothers of a teaching order. When the law of separation of church and state was passed in 1905, such orders were no longer allowed to teach, unless they laïcized. These good brothers chose exile instead, sold their building and moved across the border into Spain. There they could continue to operate their school with enough French boys sent them by parents anxious for the strict and competent teaching the order was renowned for. The law had later been amended, but the monastery remained casually remodeled into apartments.

A few steps up a stone staircase leads to Bill's residence, apparently made up of several former cells, small rooms with the elegance of simplicity. I admire the few pieces of antique Provençal furniture.

"Legacy from a former landlady, who remained and died a friend." A vase of desiccated flowers stands on an exquisite table with deer feet. Pieces of massive sterling, a coffee set, multi-branched candelabra, a pair of footed compotes dominate the room, only yellowed by tarnish, they are dulled to dim, brassy tones. I comment on the silver, and refrain from mentioning the need for polishing:

"Wedding gifts to my mother and both my grandmothers. They were all popular debutantes in Chattanooga, very social, members of the Hunt Club, so all three of their weddings made epoch in the society columns of their times. . . ."

"Any of these ladies still alive?" I ask.

"No," replies Bill curtly. Did I see something dark pass into his eyes?

(Much later, I'd learn that Bill's mother, despondent over the onset of intermittent symptoms of insanity, had attempted suicide, but only succeeded in lodging a bullet in her spine, which paralyzed her from the waist down. Bill, a small child then, had known his mother only as a helpless invalid, and, though he never went into details, I could easily guess what the state of her mind—or what was left of it—could have been. What an atmosphere for a child to grow in!)

No Cézanne in sight. But shelves overflow with books, papers, musical scores, and more volumes pile up on the floor. Some must have hastily been removed from the chair I was offered, for they teeter, an unsteady heap, on the edge of a small table. Through a doorless archway, I glimpse another room with piles of records, CDs spilling from the shelves around a state-of-the-art sound system that occupies a good part of the wall. As I sit, I brush a photograph in a silver frame.

"Your mother, Bill?"

Raised eyebrows:

"Indeed, no. My mother was a charming lady, but *this* is Rosa Ponselle, the greatest diva who ever lived. Don't you agree that her voice has remained unmatched? Range, timber, nuance, that high C . . . I *know* you agree. I'll play you some of her arias in a moment."

Barely aware of Miss Ponselle's identity, I only nod in an effort to look wise and informed, but avoid any comment that might betray my ignorance. From another photo in a silver frame—tarnished as well—smiles a young man with a high forehead and luminous eyes.

"Somebody from the opera I should know?"

"Oh, this is Tito, Tito Serebrensky, a lovely, bitching boy, but *volage en diable*, fickle as hell, *hélas!* Yes, he is with the Marseille Opera, the best stage director they'll ever have. Fresh, daring, imaginative. . . . How could one hold his faithlessness against him? You'll see what I mean when I take you to his next production, *Tosca*, that will open the season."

The Manhattans are ready in a crystal decanter, and Bill makes a ceremony of adding ice, stirring, pouring, dropping a maraschino cherry in each glass and then adding a precisely measured teaspoon of the scarlet liquor to the drinks.

"Do you realize that it is virtually impossible to make a true Manhattan in France, because there are no maraschino cherries to be found? Only canned or candied ones, totally unsuitable, of course."

Something else I didn't know.

"How do you get yours, then?"

"Oh, in past years, I befriended a few of the previous Resident Directors—not too dull, most of them—and they send me a jar now and then. You might do the same when you return to the States."

"I'll ship you a *case* of giant jars," I promise earnestly and I am glad to say I kept my word.

We sip the cocktails, which I find perfect, just the right proportion of bourbon and vermouth. Bill keeps looking toward the French doors. Finally:

"Let's take our glasses out on the balcony. The moment has come for my Cézanne."

The balcony, rather part of an encircling stone terrace, looks out over the top of Mediterranean pines that roll down the hill in great green billows. Buildings must huddle under or else perspective hides them, for much of the city teeming below has become invisible. Closing the entire horizon, Mont Sainte-Victoire fills the view.

I have, of course, seen several of the Cézanne paintings inspired by the famous landmark. Born in Aix, he worked most of his life there and seemed fascinated by its overpowering presence. But this is no longer a two-dimensional square of canvas on a museum wall or a distant outline on the horizon. Nothing had prepared me for this gigantic, domineering backdrop to the city and its valley.

From this vantage, the Sainte-Victoire appears as the triangular face of a pyramid. When I know the area better, I'll learn that it is, in fact, the end of a long range, abruptly broken off at some unknown geological era. But now, from this angle, it looks like a free-standing, perfect isosceles triangle, and the evening light brings a translucence to its pale chalkstone. A startling sight.

"By the time we've finished our drinks," comments Bill, "you will see it reflect the blue of twilight skies and you'll swear that it has become transparent, so perfect is the optical illusion. See? See that hint of azure? Now watch it deepen. On stormy nights with dark clouds rolling over it, *then* it turns to purple and indigo."

I believe it, for I have seen how Cézanne rendered those somber, menacing tones. . . . We find it hard to tear ourselves from the sight and remain standing there until darkness sets in, leaving the mountain even more ghostly, as if bathed in an almost phosphorescent glow.

"Nothing like that in Chattanooga, *sugah,*" comments Bill. "And since I don't follow the Hunt. . . ."

We listen to Montserrat Caballé—as a warming exercise to ease me into Rosa Ponselle, I feel. Bill knows Montserrat well and admires her, but with some reservations.

"So . . . Catalan, though, don't you think?" he murmurs, leaving no doubt that, in this case, being Catalan to such a degree isn't a plus. "Still, a rich, pure voice and quite a stage presence. Have you seen her in *Medea?*"

Then with reverent gestures, a Rosa Ponselle recording of an aria from *La Forza del Destino* is dusted with a feather brush and placed on the machine. Finger to his lips, eyes closed, Bill has removed his glasses, and I am touched to see a tear slowly rolling down his cheek. He must have heard this piece a thousand times, and yet it still seems to affect him deeply.

When he opens his eyes, several seconds after the last note has faded away, the same strangely distracted expression I saw a moment ago darkens his even features. Only a passing cloud, though, for an instant later Bill has again become the smooth Southern gentleman.

"Music is my passion, my raison d'être. I am on call at the Marseille Opera as their music consultant. The artistic director—ah, ah! *artistic! director!* Two misnomers for that imbecile. The 'director' then," he sneers, "and forgive me if I gag, is Jacques Karpo, a philistine with a stone ear. Karpo is short for Karpovitch, I understand, but I prefer to call him Karpobitch. More fitting. Formerly with the San Francisco Opera, which he left under a cloud after producing a *Faust* in modern dress that took such liberties with the score that subscribers staged a protest and resigned *en masse*. . . ."

(I will soon discover that Bill's dislikes are just as passionate as his loves, and that when he disapproves of something or someone, his own bitchiness knows no limits. He can then exaggerate so, that the mass protest in San Francisco may, in fact, have been no more than a line of mild criticism in the *Chronicle*'s theater and music review. It also seems that, contrary to Bill's opinion, Karpo is a very competent director.)

"Karpo the Bitch doesn't like me because I can see right through him and his phoniness, but he needs me. Since I am familiar with every interpretation maestros have given of the repertoire in the past, I can guide his orchestra's rendition by comparing it with others, warn him if it veers off into being . . . let's say derivative, to be polite. Or else . . . But I don't want to bore you with details."

"Does the Marseille Opera have its own company?"

"No. For every production—and there are about half a dozen each year—artists are brought from all over the world. I am often able to suggest names. Thus, a production might gather a Russian basso, an Italian tenor, a Swedish or American soprano. They all know the part, but have never met before and rehearsal time is necessarily short. I help homogenize voices and styles. I also work with Tito—we have remained good friends, although he *did* break my heart, but you must show forgiveness to the

talented ones, don't you think?—on matters of perform-
ance and details of staging.

"Which, by the way, reminds me that he *must* do something about that final act of *Tosca*. Last season the way la
Tosca daintily stepped over those battlements, when she is
supposed to be hurling herself to her death, was ridiculous.
Let him put a thick mattress on the other side, or whatever it will take to soften the fall, but a *fall* it must be—or at
least, look like one!"

Later, in the course of the conversation, Bill discovers to
his surprise, because my French sounded so perfect at the
party, that I really don't know France very well and
Provence not at all. I usually dislike dwelling on my life's
history, which seems utterly boring to me, but now I feel
the need to explain.

"I was born in France and spent my growing-up years in
Catholic boarding school. Where? In Angoulême. Yes, the
city that rises on its high plateau and, yes, it is surrounded
by its still intact ramparts. It won't surprise you that, as
soon as I could, I escaped to Paris, where I worked as an
assistant to the painter Jean-Gabriel Domergue and also
posed for him. . . ."

I throw in that last part because I know that posing for
the celebrated painter of women, exclusively women, faces,
busts, nudes, was the least boring phase of my life . . . at
least to listeners. And I must be right because Bill wants to
hear more.

"Domergue's brush could turn *any* woman into an ethereal beauty; that's why his portraits were in such demand.
For his *own* models, he sought, not spectacular girls, but a

certain type, small-boned, with narrow waists. In any case, they served mostly to provide a movement, a shrug, a toss of the head. He'd say, '*Petite*, I want you to bend over, shake your hair, wet your lips and come up with your chin high, smiling.' His talent did the rest. It transformed all into perverse ingenues."

"I wonder what kind of music he used as a background to his work," muses Bill. "I'm thinking Offenbach maybe or . . . why not Stravinsky? *The Rite of Spring*, of course."

"That was only for a few years, and I'd like to spare you the rest, dull as it may seem. But, if you must know, I married an American, moved to California while still quite young, made a life and a career there. Enough? So you see, I do not know France well, except for what I learned in my early years and later in graduate school. But I am eager to discover more, a lot more while I am here."

"Then," said Bill, eyes shining behind his round lenses, "you've come to the right place, *sugah*. Ready for my own life history? I left Chattanooga 30 years ago for a Junior Year in Aix, just like your students. All the time, I harbored only one thought: Return after graduation. Well, circumstances led me first to Florence, where I spent some enchanting years— you'll *have* to meet the contessa, quite mad, but then, aren't we all? Now, where was I? Oh yes, I made it back to Aix, rooming with the same lovely old lady who'd housed me as a student. Shared her place until she died. Yes, it was she who left me those antique pieces. So, you see, I live in Provence out of pure choice, adore it and enjoy nothing more than introducing visitors to it. What are you doing next Sunday?"

Will I be free on Sunday?

By Saturday afternoon, it doesn't look good. Stan hurt his knee playing soccer and, alerted, I take him in great pain to the hospital where he is admitted after a lengthy discussion and the endless filling out of insurance papers. Our compensation forms in English puzzle everybody, and personnel crowds around to wonder at that strange language, unlike what they learned in high school out of a text entitled, I gather, *Tea and Crumpets*. His articulation fearfully swollen, Stan is finally placed in a sort of harness that raises his leg. After painkillers are administered, I leave him resting, more or less comfortably, with a pile of French sports magazines, plus a jug of hot chocolate and a plate of little cakes, brought in by a nurse who informs him that, on other days, he might prefer wine and biscuits to while away the afternoon. I return home, very much reassured about the local hospital system.

No sooner back at the Villa than the phone rings. Dana's voice, so blurred I hardly recognize it, wants me to know she is *dying*. A frantic drive to her place where I find her, indeed, rather incoherent, lying across the bed in an incredibly messy apartment—she has refused to share with a room-mate, like the others do, and her parents have agreed to pay the difference in rent. What in the world has happened?

It seems that, for some reason I cannot quite eluci-date—a misplaced spirit of adventure? A desire to learn about local medical practices? Or more likely out of sim-ple boredom—Dana decided to call a doctor to her bed-side, as French doctors are required by law to make house calls. She complained of violent stomach cramps; finding no cause or symptoms, and nonplussed, I suppose, the physician wrote out a prescription for two different sedatives: One oral for daytime and the other . . . you guessed it, suppositories for nighttime. Encouraged by her success, Dana then called in quick succession two more doctors, repeated her complaint, and acquired two more prescriptions, each for an assortment of sedatives. I find all the packets, vials and tubes open and well dug into, water glasses with traces of powdery medicine . . . Dana has generously sampled all the feel-good stuff.

Should I get her admitted to the hospital for a stomach pump? I hesitate . . . somehow, she doesn't seem that badly off, not passed out, only very groggy and looking cold, I think. So, in spite of her mumbled protests and weak resistance, I pack her off to the Villa, put her to bed in a guest room with extra blankets plus a hot water bottle against her back, then coax her to drink black coffee. She seems to be nodding off again, but when I inform her that I am confiscating the medicine, she recovers enough to accuse me of stealing her personal property. Reassured that she'll be all right, I watch her drift into a peaceful sleep. Let her spend the night here; she'll probably be fine in the morning.

Finally in bed myself, a phrase from my handbook keeps running through my mind: *"Since you are dealing with highly motivated, responsible young adults, your duties will be essentially of an academic nature."* Right.

But the gods of Provence, who'd clearly taken Saturday off, are watching again on Sunday and nothing untoward happens, or at least is brought to my attention. As a bril-

liant September day rises, I find a well-rested Dana, looking pretty without her dark eye make-up, who practically
smiles and mumbles a good morning, the equivalent for
her of outpourings of love and thankfulness. She eats several croissants spread with butter and jam, washed down
with cups of sugary tea with cream. Back at her place, I
trick her into tidying up some, by hanging up clothes in a
way she *has* to correct and asking her how *I* could go about
putting those dishes away.

A quick look-in at the hospital, where I find a smiling
Stan with a much less swollen knee, Liz doing needlepoint
at his bedside, obviously settled for the day. She has
brought books, candy, flowers. Sunshine streams in
through a tall window. I am clearly not needed, and I drive
away to meet Bill with a clear conscience.

Bill starts off by scolding me because I haven't seen
much of the town yet. I beg forgiveness: As soon as everyone has settled in and classes have begun, which will keep
my charges out of mischief, I'll . . .

"Am I to understand that you haven't even sat at a terrace on the Cours Mirabeau in this dappled, September
shade of the plane trees? Not had lunch at the Deux
Garçons? Not peeked inside at their authentic Directoire
décor? Then, sensuous Aix is wasted on you, *sugah*."

I promise to start what will surely be a love affair with
the city very soon. Like tomorrow, Monday.

"I vow that, no matter what, I'll get away for lunch at the
Deux Garçons. With you as my guest, I hope," I assure him
as a peace offering. "But today, please, let's get out of town.

If we don't, I'm sure to run into some of my students, and I'll feel guilty if they seem unhappy, bored or out of sorts, so I'll have to stay and try to take care of them. . . . But I *do* need this day away from it all, so I'll let them fend for themselves this afternoon."

Several miles out of the city, Bill points to a low range barring the horizon.

"These are the Luberon Mountains, the real heart of Provence, the magical, mysterious Luberon where legends abound because of the springs that surge on its slopes. Folks here have always associated fountains with supernatural beings. You'll find the Luberon dotted with ancient villages, built on hilltops or hillsides. These are the fabled perched villages, so arrestingly picturesque that some have won the prestigious award 'Most Beautiful Village of France,' granted by the Ministry of Culture.

"Right now, though, we are entering Pertuis—pay no attention here. This is just a shopping *bourg*, so smug in its prosperity that the city fathers have let it go to pot. . . . Still you should see the Friday market here! What am I saying? Not just this one, for heaven's sake! All the markets of Provence assail you like . . . like an orchestra for the senses."

A sign indicates Ansouis, seven kilometers ahead, and directly across the way another reads "Château d'Ansouis, 8 kilometers." At the intersection down the block, two more signs facing each other point this time in opposite directions, showing the way (which one?) to the same Ansouis, which has now backed out to nine kilometers. Is this some mythical place that, as water in a mirage, recedes as you approach it? A Camelot of Provence? A Brigadoon visible only once a century? The very name has its own different ring among all the other place names on signs that sing with a Provençal accent: Lourmarin, Bastidonne, Manosque, La Tour d'Aygue. But Ansouis?

"To begin with, one doesn't pronounce the final *s*. The name must be of Greek origin, older than all those other names which are derived from Latin," says Bill. He adds, after a pause: "I know the area well, but I've never been there. Seen pictures, I believe. Seem to remember a perched village with its castle on top. However, you should know, these villages may look good from a distance, but many of them are in ruins today. Young people leave to build in the valleys."

I listen absently, unaware that Ansouis will, some day, become the center of a new life for me, a new home, and that I will find peace and *loves* in the embracing shelter of its weathered stones.

Lourmarin, one of the "Most Beautiful Villages . . ." does not seduce me at first. Flat, undistinguished, a foothill sort of a place, I think disdainfully and wonder why the award.

"It may have nothing to do with it, but Albert Camus, the existentialist writer, had a home here and when he was killed in a car accident, still quite young and just after receiving the Nobel Prize for literature, they buried him here."

I insist on visiting the tomb, and Bill reluctantly stops at the small cemetery gate. I circle around twice before I locate Camus' resting place, a simple stone slab devoured by yellow lichens. One has to push away the rank over-growth of rosemary bushes to read the engraved name and dates, 1913–1960. Nobody to look after such a famous grave?

"His wife still resides in the village, but when he died, he had been living with that actress, Maria Casarès. So maybe Madame Camus holds a grudge," muses Bill. "Who cares?" Try as I might, he won't evince the slightest interest in the author of *The Stranger* and *The Fall.*

"Not cosmic in the least," sneers Bill.

"What about the *Myth of Sisyphus*, then? That rock forever rolling down the hill that must be pushed back by man? Camus gives the legend a new twist because, instead of a cause for despair, he sees the situation as the only possible source of happiness, since man has no recourse, between birth and death, but action. That's not cosmic?"

"Cosmically boring, then. Only dry intellectual concerns. That constant reminder of the tragedy of *existing*, that obsession with the uselessness of it all. Mind, intellect, yes, but no heart, no soul. These guys have never watched a sunset or heard an opera. No sensuality whatever."

"Why did Camus move in with the fiery Casarès, then, instead of just pushing his rock uphill?" I wonder. But Bill will not budge: "Probably to bore her with his philosophy." He concludes, *"Lasciale riposar in pace,"* for he is fond of sprinkling his conversation with Italian and German phrases, mostly drawn from librettos.

With the narrow, winding streets of Lourmarin, its tiny squares with cafés and fountains, its château framed by square towers, shops with bouquets of lavender and dried herbs pinned to open *volets*, shutters, the displays of blue, green and yellow faience, an image of Provence begins to emerge. I pick up a green baking dish and learn that this is a *tian*. Anything baked in such an earthenware dish takes its name and becomes a *tian* in turn. "Do you like to bake *tians* of lamb with *aubergines*, eggplant?" asks the saleslady. My mouth waters, but I shake my head regretfully, as I put down the *tian*. "I am afraid I won't be doing much cooking in the coming months," I confess. "At least, you must have a good café au lait for breakfast. You need a *bol* to drink it from," she insists. The *bol* would hold enough café au lait for several breakfasts, but its veined, pale green glaze enchants me, so, thinking of Wayne's return in a few days, I buy two. "*Bon après-midi et bonne promenade*," smiles the lady, handing me my purchase.

From the doorway of a boutique, a dog pushes his face into my hand and licks it vigorously.

"*Eh, voyez, madame*," exclaims its owner. "*Il aime les jolies dames*, he likes pretty ladies! Am I going to punish him when I feel just the same?" I laugh and stop to pet the dog. Within minutes, I know his name, *Voyou*, Rascal, his life story and a good bit of that of the owner. Laughter peals from a café terrace, the Provençal accent sings. . . . Why do I feel happier, suddenly no longer harassed? Why do I want to laugh, too, slow down and enjoy moment and place? Sit at that terrace and stay there . . . how long? Like forever, maybe? But Bill has other plans.

Beyond Lourmarin, we drive into the Combe, the low pass that divides the *Grand* Luberon from the *Petit* Luberon. It winds its way along a narrow valley, following the meanders of l'Ayguebrun, "a trickle now, but a torrent after the spring snow melts, for the Luberon can get quite snowy," comments Bill. When the road climbs again, fields appear on a plateau, long rows of neatly trimmed round shapes, not unlike endless lineups of well-disciplined porcupines. "Lavender fields," explains Bill. "They're pruned for the winter now, but they bloom in July and they're a sight then when these rows become painterly strokes of unimaginable blues and violet. Then, *sugah*, the aroma intoxicates you like . . . like some passages in Rimsky-Korsakov when he rises above being a wimp. It has to be experienced." By then I know that somehow, someday, and not too far in the future, I will see and *experience* those lavender fields in July, regardless of previous schedules.

"Brace yourself for the sight of Bonnieux, it is a heart-stopper. We're just coming to it after this curve." Bill slows and stops as the village comes into view and I gasp.

Bonnieux spills down the steep slope of a high promontory, backed against the mountain and topped by the slender arrow of a steeple emerging from a nest of cypresses. The afternoon sun etches every angle, glows on pale blue and green shutters and washes pink on faded ocher walls that cascade all the way down into the valley below.

"The lower part is a little more recent, wasn't built until after safety from the pirates' raids had been insured. But isn't it amazing, when you think that defense was the only purpose, and that beauty wasn't sought, only occurred as an accidental byproduct? Bonnieux is often called the Saint-Michel of Provence because its pyramidal shape makes it resemble a land-bound Mont Saint-Michel."

I remain lost in contemplation, moved almost to tears by a feeling I strive to explain: Is it recognition of a long-lost home where another I lived centuries ago? Longing for that other, unattainable identity? For this is more, much more than architecture. It is life. Life in stone, life *in fact*, an accretion, centuries in the making, created by generation after generation, of the kind one could compare to that of a coral reef. And now all there, displayed, offered to me drenched in sunshine, as some incredibly generous revelation, a gift even.

When Bill reaches over to release the hand brake, I put my hand over his.

"Just a moment more, please."

He looks at me searchingly, smiles:

"*Sugah*, you are falling in love with Provence. Watch it! This is a land of passion. I love it myself more all the time, so I never tire of watching newcomers succumb to its spell."

In the distance, jagged ruins crown another hillside village. "Lacoste, and the castle you see—or what's left of it—belonged to the Sade family, a noble and perfectly respectable one, until that naughty marquis came along to disgrace it in the eyes of posterity. For these are misguided times we live in, don't you think? I grant that Sade might have gone astray, but what a dear boy he must have been . . . wrong influences, I suppose."

As we draw near: "The château was dismantled at the end of the Revolution. The ruins, passed through the hands of a succession of owners and finally abandoned, were purchased by a young teacher in a nearby *lycée*, named Bauer. The fact that he could afford it gives an idea of the price! Bauer spent his life and all his resources working on restoration projects." As we walk right up to the foot of the walls, it is clear that an awful lot remains to do, judging from the gaping doorways, towers left with only two walls standing, loose rocks cascading everywhere. Still, some rebuilt terraces appear and one wing shows several restored rooms. Bless Monsieur Bauer, and now that he has died, who will come along to fall in love with that place and project, just as he did decades ago?

Underneath the castle spreads a quarry from which great rectangular blocks of limestone used to be cut. No longer in operation, there remains something like a gigantic, monolithic room, ghostly white, all surrounded by strange, geometric steps, an oversized cubist décor carved out by the removal of blocks. With its great acoustics and year-round even temperature, it is often used for concerts of all kinds. Now, workers are setting up chairs for the next one.

"These are for older people who like their comfort. Younger ones prefer to climb onto those niches you see all around and sit or lie there, deep in the shadows. Some bring candles with little paper shades, and it makes for quite a sight. Some also bring bottles, and I've been here a few times when the smoke wafting out of those recesses wasn't from tobacco."

When, a few weeks later, armed with my newly acquired knowledge, I take my group past the view of Lacoste and its jagged ruins on one of their weekly outings, I hesitate:

Should I point out the home of the infamous marquis or just forget about it? What will I get myself into? Recklessly, I decide that these students' education should win over any prudishness.

"See, over there? On top of the hill? Those are the ruins of the castle of the Marquis de Sade."

A few heads turn but interest is mild. The castle of who?

"The Marquis de Sade. The word *sadism* was coined from the philosophy he exposed in his writings."

"Didn't he, like, write stuff more like porn?" asks someone.

"Well, yes, you could call it that, although there was a definite philosophical intent. He was a free-thinker of the Revolutionary period, felt there is no such thing as morals, no right or wrong. . . . Therefore, inflicting pain was not a bad, but an indifferent act."

"Wasn't he into, like, kinky sex, whips and bondage and stuff?" insists the same voice.

Interest has been aroused. Rob elbows his seatmate who removes the earplugs of his Walkman. "Listen, this ought to be good," he mouths.

My duty as an educator is leading me down a strange path. Still, it has to be fulfilled. Always build upon existing knowledge.

"I suppose you could call it that. As a matter of fact, I do not believe Sade ever describes a single, normal sex act."

This gives the group food for thought, apparently, for silence follows this information. Not for long, however. Rob turns the bill of his baseball cap from backwards to sideways:

"What do *you* call a normal sex act?" he asks, as inno-cently as he can, elbowing his seatmate again.

Every question should be answered, even this one.

"I don't doubt you know quite well, and probably even better than me, what that is," I reply, perfectly aware that this is not the end of it.

Sure enough, a chorus of protests arises from which I understand that, flatteringly enough, they feel I am not *that* old and couldn't have forgotten. . . . A suggestion to help refresh my memory is even voiced from the back of the bus.

I distract them by pointing to the bridge we are about to cross.

"This is the Pont Julien, built by the Romans almost two thousand years ago and still in use. Want to get out and see the clever system that allowed water to rush through in time of flood?" But the bridge meets with lim-ited interest. Only a few—Phil, of course, a born engineer, among them—get out to examine the open stonework dis-guised as decoration that, above and between the arches, allows torrential waters to flow through. Earplugs are back in place, Walkmans turned on again.

Bill and I have crossed the Pont Julien after a precipitous descent into a wide plain to reach National 100, the road formerly known as the Via Domitia, built to connect Rome with its new province, the Provincia Romana, hence the name Provence. In places, the original paving stones have been left exposed to remind one of the sandals of the Roman legions and the chariot wheels that traveled them, long before blacktop was poured to obliterate their well-hewn design.

Then, the landscape changes, becomes much more rocky. Walls of dry stone, alternating layers artfully laid out in a zigzag pattern, line the sides of the road as it climbs to Gordes and its ancient *oppidum*, for dry-stone construction is Gordes' signature. More lavender fields, with their armies of porcupines, climb high slopes, as Bill points out the first *borie*:

"See this rounded structure, entirely of dry stone, no mortar whatever, with its small door, no window and arch-ed roof, also of the same stone? This is a *borie*. They dot the region around Gordes, but are found nowhere else. Old? Rather. I'd say about two thousand years, like most everything around here, it seems. Later, you'll see a whole village of them. And then I have another *borie* surprise for you. No, no, don't ask. I won't tell you. You'll see, *sugah*, you'll see."

If Bonnieux startled and enchanted me, what can I say about Gordes? It is the same, only not the same at all. Another personality, a different light, another color stone. . . . Here, the castle, intact, still crowns the top, and the almost vertical cliff is laced with cypress-lined walks leading to splendidly restored homes with swimming pools dug out like grottoes into the face of the rock, and many others still in ruins, awaiting their rebirth. Gordes is more upscale, or soon will be, and it is as perched as perched can be. Now, an even lower sun gilds façades, casts long shadows and backlights the Luberon range into the darkest blue.

Why would my heart beat faster as I gaze upon the proud cascading profile of the ancient *oppidum*? What can the appeal of those hilltop and hillside dwellings be to someone like me, surrounded in real life by a world of what I've come to call "California Functional?" Yet, there must be a romantic side to my nature: haven't I chosen to reside in Malibu in a beach home acquired through some feat of juggling mortgage versus salary, feasible only because, then, beach living was still regarded with suspicion as a little too bohemian. Pilings sunk into shifting sands, a flimsy structure teetering on those wooden poles, exposed to every whim of the Pacific, which would either lick its feet or rattle it in the anger of its storms. Earthquakes, yet, to add to uninsurable insecurity! So, it was probably inevitable that the next impractical sort of real estate should dry my throat with uncontrolled longing.

Bill is watching me again.

"The pangs of love, *sugah*. You must learn to close your eyes to the wiles of Provence, otherwise, you'll be lost without return, unable to find happiness elsewhere. Others have been. I know, I am one of them."

He takes my arm.

"Let's drive a bit down the road, and I mean *down*. Almost headfirst, in fact. There's another experience there for you." And that is how we descend upon the Abbey of Senanque nestled way down in the valley, snug in its setting of more lavender fields, one of the many houses of the Cistercian monastic order of Saint Bernard, which came to dot Europe in the Middle Ages.

The saint preached poverty and humility, which is why his monasteries must avoid pridefully elevated locales and remain confined to modest vales. Ignoring Bill's insistent glances at his watch, I demand we park and at least walk *through* the buildings.

First, we step into the cemetery, a simple plot where small, black wooden crosses show only the name in religion of the defunct brother with his dates of birth and death. Most of these monks surprisingly lived to an advanced age, even into their hundreds, at a time when human life span was decidedly shorter than today. Yet the buildings bear witness to a stark life. Signs guide the visitor to a dormitory, where monks slept on the floor, wrapped in their homespun robes and never for more than three hours at a time—slumber interrupted by nighttime services that included filing into the cemetery, where each dug out a shovelful of earth from his future grave as a reminder of his own mortality. Then to the chapel, completely unadorned, nave and transept intersecting to form a simple cross. I imagine the procession of ghostly figures marching in, long before daybreak, heads bent under their cowls. Then, in the dark, lit perhaps by a single candle, heavenly voices rising in Gregorian chant.

The rule of silence endured in the refectory, where, under high arches, meals served twice a day out of wooden bowls consisted essentially of black bread, dried figs, a little cheese and lukewarm water—not cold, to avoid the sinful pleasure of a cup of cool water running down a parched throat. A small goblet of wine marked Christmas and Easter.

Long before modern medicine recognized that caloric deprivation stands as the only certain way to life extension, the severe Saint Bernard's rule achieved the same result by demanding that his followers remain forever hungry. In addition, they must have been sleep-deprived and cold most of the time.

When we cross the chapel on our way out, a German madrigal group is tuning up beneath its vault.

"Each of these Cistercian chapels is said to resonate in a different key," the leader tells a few visitors gathered around him. "We have sung in several of them and found this to be true. Yet, they were supposedly built by pious, but untrained monks, assisted only by the occasional local stonemason. Don't you find this hard to believe?"

"By whom, then?" someone wants to know.

"A mystery. One of many because so much remains unknown about the real state of knowledge in the Middle Ages."

Entranced, as ethereal voices rise once again in song under the resonating vaults, I find it hard to leave all this for the world of comfort, plentiful sleep and food, which these monks willingly abandoned in a quest for the salvation of their eternal souls.

"Too much for you, *sugah*?" teases Bill. "Take a few deep breaths and return to this world. Wipe that sainted look off your face, too; you wouldn't have lasted a *day* in a place like this, so quit grieving over your lack of spirituality."

Nothing is far in Provence, and Bill is in a hurry because he has, apparently, a rendezvous later. *Le Village Noir* where he takes me next, but only for minutes, he keeps repeating, has recently been excavated from the engulfing growth of Mediterranean oaks rising out of thickets of bramble and thyme. How old? Signs admit that nobody knows, but venture the opinion that it was occupied until the fourth or fifth century of our era. Among the *bories* huddled inside a dry-stone wall enclosure, archeologists have identified a common baking house with its large oven, a storeroom where dregs of olive oil still cling to the bottom of earthenware jars, a mill, its grindstone in place, plus a dozen habitations. All seems so well preserved that I find myself searching for ancient footprints among visitors' tennis shoe tracks. But Bill turns threatening and the distracted look that passes again behind his eyes brings me to my *own* senses. It is time to go, way past, he claims, and he is angry at me for ruining his carefully staged program.

"We have a date with the sunset. And if we miss it from the place where I am taking you now, the whole day will have been a complete waste, all for absolutely *nothing*," he fumes in perfect bad faith. So, I now hurry, trying weakly to apologize for being entranced by all he has shown me, but he isn't listening.

Bill isn't listening, for he can barely contain his excitement: We have reached the crowning moment of *his* tour of Provence, and he loves to stage-direct a show.

"I am a whore," he says delightedly. "A real, shameless whore. I make you fall in love and now I'll show you the grand finale of passion. You'll never forgive me for I am ruining your life for years to come. Forever, I hope," he adds smugly.

By now, we are sitting on the terrace of Les Bories, the hotel and restaurant built on a core of ancient *bories* that form a warren of small rooms under their narrow arches.

It faces the setting sun, where a grandiose show is in progress, spreading gold, scarlet and carnelian across the entire Western skies. In the left foreground Gordes etches its cascading profile, castle windows aflame. The darkened face of the Luberon bars the horizon where the sun descends in a blaze that reflects red light on the stones of the *bories* and paints with gold the oak forest around us.

"Now," says Bill, "we shall hold hands and think cosmic thoughts in worship of this spectacle offered to us." And hold hands we do, abandoning for a moment our kirs, which turn into glowing garnets that cast quivering pink halos upon the tablecloth.

"I wonder," murmurs Bill dreamily, "I wonder if they still have that lovely boy who used to work here as a bartender. Doe-eyed, with long, feathery lashes . . . I always thought he was in love with me, and those sidelong glances made Tito *quite* jealous one night. . . . I'll take a look inside." But the sexy bartender is now working somewhere on the Riviera, sighs a disappointed Bill when he returns.

The glow lingers long after the sun has disappeared, and the castle's windows remain incandescent, even as the sky turns into strata of sulfur and coral.

Hard to think of food after the spiritual experience of the monastery and the cosmic one of the sunset? Not at all, we are famished and inhale the plate of *amuse-gueule*, taste teasers, that arrives, no questions asked: A jar of tapenade, pink radishes, slices of mountain sausage. A small crock of *pâté de grives*, pâté of thrush, is devoured without a thought of pity for those thrushes caught, says the hand-written label, after they fall dead drunk in the vineyards from eating fermenting grapes left on vines after the harvest. "Serves 'em right," growls Bill, munching ferociously. If Wayne were here, I am not sure some sort of memorial service for those thrushes wouldn't be in order.

"Food here is simple, but perfect. One orders the *bourride*, without ifs and buts," directs Bill. Does he fear I'll start asking for hamburgers? Fried chicken? Pie à la mode? "And," he declares, "there'll be no argument about the wine. It *must* be a flinty white, a Bandol preferably. They happen to have just the right one."

This is how I discover *bourride*, at least this one version, for there are, it seems, several, each with its committed champions. A heavenly fish dish, and the evidence of my delight pleases the chef when he comes to make his rounds, so he outlines the recipe:

"Poach *lotte*, monkfish, which tastes something like lobster, with the same firm flesh, in well-seasoned white wine. Then, set the fish aside but keep it warm while you make the custard—yes, a custard—using that white wine, egg yolks and crème fraîche. Stir in a little saffron, and pour this sauce over the fish in heated plates. Don't forget a few lightly steamed potatoes. Ah, but they must, of course, be the *ratte*, a small, elongated tuber that grows only near Pertuis, with a nutty flavor like no other. Simple, no? Except that, *madame*, your dish will be ruined if you do not use *fleur de sel de Camargue* instead of ordinary salt."

"What in the world is *fleur de sel*? How special can it be? Aren't all salts alike?"

"Madame, I pity you if that's what you think," scolds the chef. "The crystals that form on the surface of water in evaporating flats, on windless moonlit nights, are *fleur de sel*. Camargue is the delta of the great Rhône. There, experienced *sauniers*, salt men, and there are very few of them left today, gather those fragile crystals with such expert care that each gets to sign the little jars he has collected."

I understand: This isn't salt at all we are speaking of. It is something precious stolen from the sea on those rare nights when, lulled by moonlight and seeking its shimmering caress, it carelessly allows its soul to rise to the surface.

(Back in the U.S.: "How French," exclaims a friend to whom I tell the story as I present him with such an autographed little jar. "They know how to find enchantment and a sensuous thrill even in their *salt*! I wonder whether French women transfer that same elusive talent to their lovemaking?")

For the life of me, I cannot recall dessert, only that Bill starts humming Schubert's *Die Forelle*, The Trout, a bravura piece and a fish one, fitting with our menu after all, I think drowsily as I make noble efforts to keep my head more or less straight. When he finishes, discreet applause from the next table startles me, and Bill looks modest, but pleased.

"The French are a physically aware, a visual people, a nation of painters and lovers, but not musicians. . . . So, I am surprised these people here seem to appreciate Schubert. Could it be the inhabitants of this divine country are not as tone-deaf as I sometimes think?"

Much too sleepy to call him a snob, I let it go at that. "*Sogni d'oro,*" he sings softly as I rest my head on the back of my seat in the car and close my eyes.

Back at the Villa, I find no sign that disaster has struck in my absence. On the contrary, a note from Faustino, slipped into the mail slot, informs me that he has, this very morning, practiced on the great organ of the cathedral during the early morning hours.

"The sun had just risen and its rays were slanting through the stained-glass windows, painting patterns on the stone floor. The splendor of the moment carried me away so that I broke into Beethoven's *Ode to Joy* and it rolled, in great waves of music mixed with the colored lights under those soaring arches. I experienced bliss I never knew before. This is the spiritual enlightenment I sought, and I do not want to leave this country. *Ever.*"

You and me both, Faustino, I think, pushing the *traversin* away so I can sleep flat, lying on my stomach as I like to do. You are right: It is a glow, a wash of gold on life. What was mere existence before becomes joy. I am so glad that you, too, found what Provence has to offer.

Experience Romance
Feast Your Senses in the Luberon

Wear your Provençal clothes, plus a pair of espadrilles you've picked up at a market, and, hand in hand, explore the Luberon.

What Is the Luberon?

It is a modestly elevated mountain range and its surrounding area, studded with picturesque, historical villages. Since it forms the French equivalent of a state park, development is strictly controlled, so you'll find there all the charm and ambiance you're looking for. In the past 20 years, the Luberon has been "discovered" by European intelligentsia and well-heeled foreigners, Americans among them, and a rush to ruin has been followed by a plethora of splendidly restored homes.

Most Beautiful Village Award

This award is granted to villages that meet exacting standards of beauty, architectural authenticity, charm and impeccable municipal management. Of the hundred or so that have qualified nationwide, several are in the Luberon. You'll see panels: *"Plus beau village de France"* as you enter these.

Play House: Rent a Home in the Luberon

You'll find many homes for lease by the week or month, although they are not, strictly speaking, rental houses.

They belong to owners, often Americans, who rent them out in their absence. Most are elegantly restored former ruins, furnished with antiques, well appointed, with pools and terraces.

Once settled into your own home (for a week or a month), you can buy all those tempting fruits and vegetables, cook Provence-accented meals, sip aperitif on your own terrace and share in the life of the village. Escaping your daily reality, play house as you did when you were a child, with a Luberon moon watching over your sleep.

How to find such a place: Terry Avery, of Greenwich, Connecticut, owns and rents his home, and also rents those of his friends! Visit his Web site at: www.myhomeinfrance. com (Tel: 203-861-0811; Fax: 203-861-0837). On the site you will see interior and exterior pictures of these homes, with detailed descriptions and conditions for rental.

The Fabled Markets of the Luberon

They are held mornings, until 1:00 PM. They sell all sorts of foods, fruits and vegetables, but also Provençal fabrics and clothes, souvenirs, and so forth. Let their color, fragrance and sensuousness envelop you.

Monday:	Cadenet
Tuesday:	La Tour d'Aygue
Wednesday:	Cucuron
Thursday:	Ansouis
Friday:	Pertuis
Saturday:	Apt
Sunday:	L'Isle-sur-la-Sorgue

Romantic Places to Eat and Stay

These are my favorite places, and they range from simple and inexpensive to elegant and pricey.

Ansouis. L'Olive Bleue: Friendly, informal, inexpensive. Serves home-cooked-style Provençal dishes. (Tel: 04-90-09-86-84).

Lourmarin. Two very different places: *La Récréation:* Informal. Sit on the terrace for *déjeuner* almost year-round, or by the fire in winter. Excellent selection of Provençal dishes. Moderate. (Tel: 04-90-68-06-69; Fax: 04-90-68-01-60).

Le Moulin de Lourmarin: Elegant and expensive. An ancient olive-oil mill morphed into a romantic, elegant restaurant. "Poetic" cuisine, a succession of small, exquisite courses, each served on its own set of colorful ceramics. A place to hold hands by candlelight. Lovely rooms. Pricey. (Tel: 04-90-68-06-69; Fax: 04-90-68-31-76; www.francemarket. com/lourmarin; e-mail: lourmarin@francemarket.com).

Bonnieux. La Bastide de Capelongue: Beautiful. Romantic décor in shades of white, with great chandeliers. Apéritif time on the terrace as the sun sets over Bonnieux is an unforgettable moment. Rooms are poetry itself. Fairly expensive. (Tel: 04-90-75-89-78; Fax: 04-90-75-93-03; www.francemarket.com/capelongue; e-mail: bastide@ francemarket.com).

Roussillon. David: Scenic view. Your table will face the ocher cliffs that have made Roussillon famous. Enjoy the show when the cliffs light up at night. Excellent Provençal food. Moderate prices. (Tel: 04-90-05-60-13; Fax: 04-90-05-75-80).

Simple and Sensuous
A Cold Night Dinner *à deux*

It is cold tonight, and you're glad to be home! You need comfort food to warm you up and there's no better way to start than with this hearty, stick-to-the-ribs soup, prepared almost instantly.

As for the chicken, what makes it aphrodisiac—beyond its great flavor—is the fact that it takes so little time to prepare, leaving a lot for other pursuits.

Dessert? Just watch it flame.

Soupe haricots tomate
Poulet aphrodisiaque
Purée de pommes de terre
Bananes flambées

Bean and Tomato Soup

    1 16-ounce can cannelli beans, drained
    1 16-ounce can diced, Italian-style tomatoes, drained
    Bouillon cube
    Chicken broth
    Worcestershire sauce
    Salt, pepper, butter, thyme

In blender, purée beans and tomatoes with bouillon cube, adding a little chicken broth to desired consistency. Add dash of Worcestershire sauce. Remove to saucepan. Heat to boiling. Adjust seasonings.

Serve in bowls with a sprinkle of thyme and a pat of butter melting in the center.

Aphrodisiac Chicken

    ½ cup balsamic vinegar
    Olive oil
    6 to 8 shallots, peeled and coarsely chopped
    ½ fully cooked, barbecued chicken
    1 small can tomato sauce

In very small pan, cook vinegar until reduced by half. In skillet, heat a little olive oil and cook shallots until transparent. Remove visible bones (like ribs and spine) and extra skin from chicken. Lay it in skillet, *skin side up*, over the shallots. Add tomato sauce and vinegar reduction. Cover and cook for 10 minutes over medium heat. Adjust seasonings.

Mashed Potatoes

    Peel two medium-size baking potatoes and cook in
    chicken broth; mash with salt, pepper and butter to
    taste.

On Your Plate

Divide chicken between two plates. Spoon sauce over it, and place next to it a mound of potatoes. Sprinkle lightly with nutmeg, if you like nutmeg.

Flambéed Bananas
  ¼ stick butter
  2 firm bananas
  4 tablespoons peach or apricot preserves
  ½ cup rum

Melt and heat butter in skillet. Peel bananas, cut them in half crosswise and split them lengthwise. Cook in butter until soft and a little browned. Turn with spatula and cook other side.

Add preserves and stir around bananas to melt to a syrupy consistency, making a sauce.

In a very small pan, quickly heat rum without boiling. Prepare a long match. Turn lights low. Ignite rum in pan and pour flaming over the bananas as you bring to the table.

Shake pan to keep flames burning.

To Drink
White wine with white meat is not a hard and fast rule. So, unless you insist on a Sauvignon blanc, I'd see a hearty red tonight.

A big pillar candle with bits of greenery
around the base would be nice.

Loving the Legionnaires

*M*any will be surprised to hear that men from the French Foreign Legion, *the Légion étrangère*, cut quite a swath among the ladies of Provence.

The ladies of Provence? But aren't these men stationed in Africa, where they ride dromedaries, bare feet resting on the animal's neck to guide its course, white cape billowing in the sirocco, the scorching desert wind? True, and one cannot dispute the immortal image that Gary Cooper created of the Legion and the legionnaires in the now classic movie, *Beau Geste*. Thanks to it, the Legion remains forever associated with the searing breath of the Sahara, romantic gallops over rippling dunes and great feats of heroism against countless adversaries, thirst not the least of them, while blood and sweat seep into the arid sand.

And then, there was Edith Piaf's immensely popular song, *Mon Légionnaire*, a sensuous, heart-wrenching cry of passion:

Il était mince, il était beau
   (He was slender, he was handsome)
Il sentait bon le sable chaud,
   (With the fragrance of desert sand,)
Mon Légionnaire. . . .
   (My legionnaire. . . .)

See? Even Piaf, who knew a thing or two about men, at least in her songs, could not dissociate legionnaires from the Sahara's burning wastes. Her guy was no slouch in bed, but fell quite short on staying power:

Il m'a aimée toute la nuit
   (He made love to me through the night)
Et me laissant à mon destin,
   (But leaving me to destiny,)
Il est parti dans le matin,
   (Left me in the early morning)
Plein de lumière. . . .
   (Bathed in sunlight. . . .)

The song's pathetic ending is consistent with the easily imagined destiny of those men—adventurers, mercenaries, often desperate—who fled their own country for the anonymity of the Legion:

On l'a trouvé dans le désert,
   (When he was found in the desert,)
Il avait les yeux grands ouverts. . . .
   (His eyes had remained wide open. . . .)

Thirst? An enemy bullet? Settlement of some private feud? Suicide? Whatever. One did not expect legionnaires to settle down and die of old age.

All this *was* true when France still possessed her colonial empire, mostly in West Africa. The Legion, an elite, impeccably disciplined, superbly trained corps, won many battles of conquest there. Later it fought, in what was then called Indochina, an endless conflict that turned into the U.S.-Vietnam War. On Bastille Day, during the great military parade on the Champs-Élysées, throats tightened when a slow pounding and familiar beat heralded the Legion, which does not march, but slowly swaggers in waves of white képis and sand-colored uniforms, set off by the trademark red-fringed epaulets and the wide black cinch that girds lean hips. The *Mehari*, the Dromedary Corps, followed, bare feet indeed, nape protectors fastened to képis and white capes flowing, the stately pace of the great beasts underscored by the muffled roll of the drums.

But France no longer occupies a colonial empire, and the countries that composed it stand now as independent nations with their own armed forces. The Legion is still active—it was recently posted on a peace-keeping mission to Kosovo—but it has lost its exotic home, and only a small contingent remains in Djibouti, on the Horn of Africa. The main body has retreated to the metropolis (well, a few are in Corsica, which *is* France, but not *really* the metropolis) to make its home in Provence with headquarters in Aubagne and small detachments elsewhere in the area. The dromedaries, *hélas*, remained behind as motorized equipment replaced them.

Aubagne, you said? Never heard of it. Where is that?

Aubagne is near Marseille. It was identified as the quintessential Provence when two of Marcel Pagnol's most popular films, *Jean de Florette* and *Manon des Sources*, were filmed there. It was country then, a sleepy village, where the hub of activity revolved around the *boule* grounds shaded by ancient plane trees. But all this has changed, so much so that the recent remake of both films had to find new locations in the Luberon. Today, with the big city spreading evermore, Aubagne finds itself imbedded in the greater *banlieue*, the suburbs of Marseille. One of its claims to fame is the *Centre Commercial*, anchored by the *Auchan Hypermarché*, a staggering place, where more than a hundred cashiers line up. Girls on roller-blades, in short red-and-blue skater's dress, patrol the aisles, informing customers, servicing cashiers, occasionally reuniting a lost kid with parents. The variety of foods and their displays are mind-boggling: cases offering *entremets*—yogurts of every description, flans, creams, soufflés, crème brûlée, crème caramel and other assorted milk-based desserts—must be a hundred feet long. A fisherman's bark, draped in fishnet and fresh seaweed, anchors the seafood section, while an authentic thatched shepherd's hut, surrounded by alpine rocks with an occasional sheep or goat grazing on its pocket-sized lawn, serves as focal point of the cheese division.

Anything else we should know before we come to Aubagne's real claim to fame, the Legion?

Well, those fond of couscous, the spicy African stew of lamb and vegetables with chickpeas, will be glad to learn that it is traditionally served in Aubagne on Thursdays by several restaurants. Placards in windows announce that Mohammed, Larbi, Ali or Mamadou is cooking his special couscous today, and the name of the chef tells initiates whether it will be the Algerian, the Moroccan or one of the West African versions.

But above all, one should know that Aubagne, properly pronounced Au-ba-gn*e*, with the local accent that stresses the mute *e*, is nowadays the home of the Foreign Legion.

The fabled Legion was founded more than a century and a half ago—for those fond of dates, it was 1831—after the conquest of Algeria by France opened the way to more inroads into West Africa. Louis-Philippe, last of the Bourbon kings, and for that matter last of all French kings *so far*, approved the project, advanced by the military, for a force that would enlist foreigners as well as Frenchmen to be stationed outside France proper on colonial lands. The motto *Legio Patria Nostra*, The Legion is Our Homeland, summarized the allegiance, not to country, but to the Legion itself.

It seems that no prying questions were asked as to past activities, and that even the name a recruit proffers is accepted as a matter of fact. I heard that these recruits are on their honor to reveal any criminal past that might render them unfit for service in the prestigious corps, and one assumes they live up to these expectations. Once inducted into the Legion, troops must accept relentless training, iron discipline and sometimes dangerous duty for the duration of their enlistment.

But then, there are free evenings and days of leave, when the legionnaires descend upon Aubagne and its neighboring villages, seeking . . .

Seeking, one supposes, what single, red-blooded young men, in top physical condition, would seek: Sex, of the whatever and however varieties. But sex isn't all. Absence of wives and families spells, of course, loneliness, and for many of these men, the quest runs beyond simple sex to the longing for a home and the comforts of a hearth. So, while some are satisfied with the relationships Piaf wails about in her song, love that ends with the morning light, others look for, and sometimes find, some sort of commitment. A few, *hélas*, are not even satisfied with tender loving care and will not stop at scamming naïve, unsuspecting ladies. Others fall prey themselves to callous women in a reversal of the classic situation. And there are even the rare ones who, unable to find any of the above, resort to sheer violence and rape. . . . We even know of one legionnaire story with a happy ending.

When the end of their five-year term of enlistment draws near, which will leave them stranded with no home, no job and little cash, some will resort to any measure and trade their muscular bodies and masculine presence for whatever they can get in exchange.

During our stay in Aix, we saw examples of most of the above.

Housework, at the Villa, was the domain of our cleaning lady who answered to the mellow name of Madame Bon. Madame? The French aren't fond of using first names. Theirs is a culture where respect and consideration are prized over friendliness, which is often seen as patronizing, or unduly familiar. That is why we Americans are often puzzled by the constant *monsieur, madame* and *made-*

moiselle that punctuate conversations. *Bonjour, monsieur* is preferable to a simple *Bonjour*. Children are taught to say, "*Merci, madame,*" and the saleslady will ask your 12-year-old daughter, "*Et avec ça, mademoiselle?*" (Will that be all, miss?) Many see no reason to address their help differently. Therefore, Madame Bon she was, and Madame Bon she remained. I do not believe I ever knew the lady's first name. As for Bon, it was simply a name of Italian origin, perhaps, she thought, a shortened form of Bono or Bonino.

Madame Bon was in her late 40s, a small woman, wiry, kept trim by a life of hard labor. The defunct Monsieur Bon, recalled by his Maker a few years earlier—as is the custom with defective products, only, generally, after the worst has happened—had been a thorough *vaurien*, a good-for-nothing scoundrel, a drunk, a wife-beater, who bestowed nine children upon her, together with full responsibility for their care and feeding. She managed that bravely, cleaning houses, scrubbing floors, and washing clothes every day of the week. Now, her brood grown and all gainfully employed, rid of her reprobate husband, her life had taken a turn for the better, and she even dyed her hair an unlikely shade of orangey auburn. Her work schedule now reduced, she worked one day a week in Liz's house, and gave us three days at the Villa. I would have liked more, but Madame Bon was adamant: She must reserve Tuesdays and Wednesdays for herself.

I was curious.

"What do you do on those days?" I wanted to know.

"Tuesday is my cemetery day. I couldn't miss it."

"Whom do you visit there, Madame Bon?"

"*Hélas*, madame, it is my poor departed husband. Don't

I owe him one little visit a week, lonely as he is out there without his wife and dear children?"

I was dumbstruck for I'd heard, and from Madame Bon herself, about the horrors inflicted upon her by the dear departed: stealing her hoard of coins to buy drink so the children would go to bed crying in hunger, this followed by bouts of drunken violence that ended in punches that threw her to the floor, where he would then proceed to kick her, endangering whatever new child she happened to be pregnant with. . . . He even set fire, from a carelessly tossed cigarette butt, to the shack they were living in, so that she and her brood, barely escaping with their lives, had to be given shelter in the basement of city hall, without heat, running water or even bedding.

After all *that*, she would grieve and devote her free days to visiting his grave? Now, this was fortitude and forgiveness beyond any duty I could imagine. All right: *try* to forgive and forget, if you are able to, *that* I can see. But a weekly visit to comfort that evil man's spirit? Way too much. Let him look for company in hell if he is lonely.

"And where is the dear man buried?"

"In Aubagne, that's where he came from. His folks have a tomb there, and I felt he'd want to be with them. . . . Anyway, I had no money to buy a plot, so that's where he rests. Besides, it is so *hard* to be dead, don't you think, one feels better in the company of their own people."

I do not know how hard it is to be dead, having had, as yet, no personal experience. But I do know that, in Madame Bon's place, I'd greatly rejoice at the thought that being dead might just be somewhat unpleasant to Mr. Bon.

"And how does one get to Aubagne?"

"Oh, it's not difficult. First, I take the bus to Marseille. There, I catch a train connection to Aubagne. It takes a little over two hours and then I only have to walk a couple of miles to the cemetery which is on the other side of town. It works the same to return."

My admiration for brave little Madame Bon knows no bounds: Including the walk, probably along some dusty road with cars whizzing by, and in a broiling sun, this would be, *at the very least*, a five-hour round trip. The woman is heroic.

"And what do you do when you get there?"

"I know one should remain kneeling upon the grave, but I am tired, my knees hurt sometimes. . . . So, instead, I sit on a bench across the way—I hope he doesn't mind—and I talk to him. I tell him how well the children are doing, and how we all miss him and speak of him often. I pray, too: I recite a whole rosary with fifty Hail Marys. . . . And then I feel so sad, madame, you see, that I cry. I cry a lot."

I am almost crying too, at such unheard of devotion.

"All I can say is that you are a dear, forgiving, loving woman. I am sure you make him feel a great deal better! And a whole rosary yet! Prayers certainly help him, too."

There is still that endless return trip.

"And then, you walk back to the bus?"

"Oh no, not right away. After crying so, I feel faint, so I wouldn't try walking just yet. I must recover for a while, get a little pick-me-up. . . . So, I go to that small café around the corner. A real nice place, too. Most times, I meet other ladies there who've come to visit tombs: husbands, parents, relatives, friends. . . ."

I visualize that café as some sort of an annex to a funeral parlor: somber, depressing as hell, with all these women in mourning.

I must have thought aloud because Madame Bon protests:

"Oh, no, madame, it is not that depressing. The music cheers you up. People dance. . . ."

People dance? These fainting widows, these bereaved, orphaned ladies *dance?* Did I hear right? And whom do they dance with, for God's sake?

"With the legionnaires, madame, of course! Lots of them frequent that café when they're off duty. Real gentlemen, too, polite, generous and all to the ladies! A pleasure to meet some *messieurs* like those! Sometimes, one or another buys me a drink or two, and we talk. They're so understanding! We dance, even, but not *every* time."

Now, that's a new twist on the situation. The little café transforms itself and, instead of a mourning chamber, where a dirge might be softly piped in the gloom, it morphs into a brightly lit, lively place, dance music playing, handsome legionnaires leaning over the billiards table, drinking beer at the bar, evaluating the charms of the ladies in black, or chatting them up at marble-topped tables. Couples sway to waltzes, perhaps even rock to more rhythmic numbers. I try, and fail, to conceive of Madame Bon in her little black coat, rocking in the arms of Gary Cooper, or at least someone resembling him, in the same pale, sand-colored uniform, with the red-fringed epaulets.

"So you'll have a few drinks?"

"I was never a big drinker, like some, madame. I'll only have *quelques petits coups de blanc.*" (The French word *coup* means "a hit." A few little hits of white wine, and it says admirably well what it means.) "That's enough for me. . . . Even after that, I get sort of light-headed, so I don't like to set out alone. Accidents are so quick to happen, you better be careful."

"*Alors?*"

"*Alors*, usually, one of these gentlemen offers to accompany me home. . . . Real caring and attentive, wouldn't you say? Even insists on paying my fare, too! The least I can do is cook him dinner, and it would be hard to send him away after that; buses stop running early."

Slow thinker that I am, a picture begins to emerge in my mind: Grieving Madame Bon uses her weekly trips to the cemetery to pick up some legionnaire, take him home and. . . . Propriety forbids delving farther into the matter. The man will leave in the morning, stay the day perhaps, if he is off duty. That is why she needs her Wednesdays off, in addition to Tuesdays.

"And wouldn't you know, they are so handy, most of them!" enthuses Madame Bon. "They'll fix a wobbly chair, repair a broken outlet, clean the carburetor of my moped. . . ."

Let's put morals aside for a moment, shall we? You have to admire the deft way in which Madame Bon telescopes her perceived duty to the dead with pleasure for the living into a single outing, paying respects to her late husband, and in the same stroke insuring herself a varied—and I hope satisfactory—sex life, while maintaining her home in good repair. I think, more power to her, after all. Here's a woman who can fight back, however poor the cards she was dealt in the first place.

Later in the year, Madame Bon's schedule changes.

"I don't mind working on Tuesdays and Wednesdays, now. I only visit the cemetery now and then, and *we* go on weekends."

I know that none of her children feels the slightest duty to the soul of their late father and despise the very thought of him.

"Who goes with you?"

"*Mon ami*, of course. He doesn't mind going, feels not a bit jealous, he says."

Mon ami, in that context and without qualification, as for instance *mon vieil ami*, my old friend, or *mon meilleur ami*, my best friend, means my boyfriend. It seems that particular *ami* has moved in with Madame Bon, in her small apartment in the *HLM*, the projects.

"A legionnaire, I suppose?"

"Oh yes, and such a fine man! He is crazy about me, and I have to say I don't mind him one bit. He is from . . . I can never remember the name of the country he came from, but he is a Serb, that much I know, and proud of it. Handsome devil, too, dark, piercing eyes, and a mustache he's growing now that he's left the service."

"When did he finish his enlistment?"

"Just a month ago. And now, everything is taking a turn for the better. He wants us to get married as soon as we can get all the papers together. He tells me he had some savings, and then they paid him money, quite a bit, I understand, when he left the Legion, some back pay and a severance allocation, too, with extra for good behavior. As for me, Social Security owed me some because my widow's pension went up last year, but the difference wasn't paid until now, so it came in a lump sum. I also have a little something set aside in the *Caisse d'Épargne*, the Savings Bank. So, Bora says the smartest thing we can do is make a down payment on a house. Then, he's sure to get a job, and he can meet the monthlies."

I clasp my hands in delight.

"So, you'll have a nice husband for a change, and you'll be living in your own home. How wonderful! I am so glad for you!" I know Madame Bon is unhappy in the rundown, noisy projects where thievery is rampant.

A week later she is beaming.

"I can't believe our luck! A friend of Bora is selling his house in Célony, just outside town on the road to Avignon. "Here's a picture Bora gave me. Look! A real villa, madame, with a little garden in front and a garage in back. We don't have a car yet, but Bora says it won't be long. . . ."

Madame Bon has entrusted all her money to Bora, even cashed in her modest savings. He's added it to his own, he told her, to put a suitable down payment on the house, and is only just a little short. The happy fiancée now sports a diamond ring that she keeps rubbing to make it shine. It may look more like glass to me, and does leave a black mark on her finger, but so what? Happiness isn't measured in carats. She floats through her work, humming the Piaf song.

A few days later:

"You have to hand it to that man! He's got those ideas, like stuff you see in the movies. Can you imagine he won't even let me *see* the house? He wants it to be a surprise when he brings me there to stay. He says it is beautifully furnished with a TV in the bedroom and a red sofa in the living room. We won't need to bring anything. So, I'm selling my fridge, my bed, the kitchen table and chairs to help him complete the down payment. We're moving in next Sunday, and then we'll get married."

I heartily rejoice with her.

All proceeds according to plan, up to and including the surprise.

Bora leaves the apartment on Saturday, taking all his personal belongings to the new house to spend the night there and prepare everything for her. He'll return on Sunday morning and bring her, almost a bride, to her new home, all dusted and ready, with champagne and a festive lunch waiting.

So, on Sunday, she gets up early, goes—for the first time in her life—to a beauty salon, opened just for her, returns home, puts on a brand new red suit bought for the occasion, with an artificial rose on the lapel, and waits for Bora to appear.

And waits, and waits, and waits.

When it becomes obvious that Bora isn't going to show up, she turns frantic: all her money gone, even her furniture! But what to do? She knows only Bora's first name and isn't at all sure of what his last name could be. Outside of the snapshot she carries in her purse, she's never seen the house, or any papers connected with the sale. Where is it? In Célony, Bora said, but she has no idea of the address. It was all to be a surprise, she keeps repeating . . . and it is. A surprise it turned out to be indeed!

Alone, in tears, in her now empty apartment, she can think of only one recourse: call Liz.

Liz is kindness and efficiency personified. So, she goes into action, not even wasting time to scold poor Madame Bon for her foolishness. First, of course, she calls the police.

When they arrive, and hear the full story, the policemen shake their heads. What do they have to go on? A description given by a distraught woman of a man who looks more evil with each recounting? A first name, probably made up, and a last name she isn't positive about. "I know it ends in *ich*" is all she is certain about. What else? The house? They seriously doubt it even exists. The photo she shows them? All right, it *is* a picture of *a* house, and so what? There are thousands just like it in the working class suburbs, *les quartiers ouvriers* of Aix.

Although Liz, by now, shares the policemen's opinion that Madame Bon has been had, scammed on an elegant scale, she gamely tries the only other avenue and calls on the commanding officer of the Legion in Aubagne.

A spare, stern major next in command receives her, standing in his office, sympathizes curtly with Madame Bon's plight, but:

"There's nothing I can do to help your employee, madame. To begin with, our rosters do not show any individual by the first name of Bora, so, whatever his real name might be, he gave her a different one. Secondly, if the man was, in fact, released at the expiration of his term of enlistment, we'd have lost all jurisdiction over him, and, should we be able to identify him, could take no legal action. Only the police could, and you tell me they are at a loss. Your Madame Bon has behaved in an incredibly foolish and naïve manner by entrusting all she owned to a practical stranger. I fear she'll have to bear the consequences of her imprudence. All I can do is hope that she'll see this episode as a hard-learned lesson for the future."

So, Liz and I do our best to help Madame Bon furnish her apartment anew from the *Pèlerins d'Emmaüs*, France's equivalent of Goodwill, and give her an advance on her salary, together with a little purse, chipped in by us and the students.

But in the days that follow, I watch her suddenly look older, the spring gone from her step, her hair color faded, and an inch of gray growing out at the roots. I feel immensely sorry for this poor woman, a basically good person, brave in adversity, whom bad luck has pursued so tenaciously. Only the diamond ring, completely tarnished by now, remains on her finger.

This, sadly, goes on for several weeks. No doubt a gloom had descended upon the Villa. Even the students tiptoe when she is around. But then, one day, I notice her hair has returned to its brilliant orangey tones. Another week passes, and she asks:

"I would like to take Tuesdays and Wednesdays off

again the way I used to do. I feel my husband is missing me, so I should go back and visit him. It's not right to abandon him just because he is *dead*. Dead people have feelings, don't you think, just the same as we do?"

Four years later, I am again serving as Resident Director of the International Program, much more self-assured this time, armed as I am with previous experience. The Villa has been sold, so now Directors live in nondescript apartments and therefore have much less contact with the students than when the Villa served as a gathering center. Only by now, Wayne and I have bought a house in a village 20 minutes north of Aix, and I commute to the office every day. But I try to keep as much contact as possible and invite the kids to visit on weekends. Many come and become valued friends we have kept to this day.

The big, upcoming event this fall is to be the Thanksgiving dinner. The other Directors and I have had negative experiences with restaurant banquets, where the menu served bore little resemblance to what had been ordered, and too few servers were hired for our large group. Worse, much worse, a total absence of traditional foods made the kids nostalgic and homesick. "*Lamb* for Thanksgiving?" So, I have planned that we will hold the dinner in our village home, in the *voûtes*, the large, medieval, partly troglodytic rooms that form the lower level. The same blue bus will bring the group and take all back to Aix afterwards. Only now, Jean-Luc is no longer the driver. He has been replaced by a burly, gruff native of Camargue.

Since I have learned the hard way, on my first tour of duty, that it is impossible to procure *real* Thanksgiving foods in France, I came prepared this time. Planning ahead, I have shipped, along with equipment and other belongings, a foot-locker crammed with cans of cranberry sauce—two kinds, jellied and whole berry—sweet potatoes, pumpkin pie filling, boxes of pie crust mix, others of bread stuffing, bags of marshmallows and, for good measure, a case of Jell-O in green, red and orange flavors. We should, therefore, be able to turn out a decent Thanksgiving dinner.

The day before the event, three of the girls volunteer to come help and march into the village bakery to instruct the baker about the making of pumpkin pies. *"Pumpkin pies? Sounds terrible,"* says the man, scratching his head as he examines the boxes of pie crust and cans of pumpkin. But the girls stand firm, and they, themselves, while the baker and his wife watch in disbelief, knead the crust and mix the pumpkin filling with eggs and condensed milk in just the proper way.

"Make a few extra ones, there's stuff left," suggests Shawna to the baker.

"Extra ones? Whatever for?"

"For yourself, your family. To *eat*, you know."

"You mean, we should *eat* that?"

But under the young ladies' competent direction, the pies come out beautifully golden. Six turkeys have been procured, and we make the stuffing with celery, onions, walnuts and Mrs. Cubbison's seasoned bread stuffing. Wayne takes them to Pertuis for baking in the caterer's oven. That lady also makes vats of mashed potatoes and, unasked, adds a giant *tian* of *gratin de cardons*, cardoons, the winter vegetable that looks like two-foot-long, whitish ribs of celery, but tastes like artichoke, a seasonal delicacy in France. She balks when I insist on dotting the *tians* of sweet potatoes with pink and green marshmallows, but as I insist, she gives up, shrugs and slips them, too, into her ovens. The red, green and orange Jell-O, which I feel should be entrusted to no one, we prepare in my own kitchen in large glass bowls loaned by the same caterer. There it glows, like gaudy jewels, improbable and incongruous, among the old stone walls and weathered beams.

The *voirie*, which handles village services, delivers tables and folding chairs from the city hall storeroom. Shawna and her two friends create tablecloths and napkins out of orange and black paper, then decorate the tables with fall foliage and red hawthorn berries. They whisper to me that a group has secretly written, and is rehearsing, a skit to explain Thanksgiving to our guests.

For there will be guests. I thought we should at least invite the mayor and his wife, a few village notables as well, and the families who have already hosted our students. A few of the kids have asked for permission to bring a French friend, so there will be a fair sprinkling of non-initiates among us. I have even sent an invitation to the *duke!* The duke, with his mother the duchess, owns the castle just above, but lives in Paris most of the time and looks (gasp!) just like Robert Redford. He has responded that, should he be in the village at the time, he'll be glad to attend and meet, as he puts it, "the flower of American youth."

At six—an outlandish time for dinner—did we *really* mean six? Not eight or nine, like civilized people?—the French contingent arrives, led by our sweet mayor and his motherly wife, brave, but extremely apprehensive at the prospect of eating an *entire* American meal. The sight of the food laid out, buffet style, puzzles them, but they try, gingerly, to follow the kids' example and pile *everything* on their plates, everything *at once*, at the risk of mingling unrelated flavors.

The salad dressing strikes the first wrong note: "Much too sweet! Do you put *sugar* in your dressing? And—no, it couldn't, or could it be—*cream*? Do you *always* serve salad first?"

The turkey is all right, almost. But why did we overcook it so? The stuffing remains untouched. "Celery? Bread? Inside a turkey? *Quelle idée!*" The sweet potatoes with their melted marshmallow topping surprise, but not pleasantly. "Sweet stuff like that? It might do for dessert, but with turkey? *Une autre idée bizarre. . . .*" Only the mashed potatoes are okay. In spite of explanations that cranberries are not a *confiture*, jam, nobody will touch the red jelly. "I was served something like that in Sweden, once. Lingonberries, they call it, and they pour it over venison," says the mayor. There are shudders. All fall, however, on the *gratin de cardons*. Something familiar at last; therefore, something *good*.

Just as dessert is going to be served, the duke arrives,

mistaken at first by several of the girls for Robert Redford himself. He greets everybody, sits down, but makes a point of changing seats several times during the rest of the evening, so he will meet as many of the students as possible, he says, although I notice that he always seems to land next to the most attractive girls.

Dessert turns out to be even more problematic than the entree. Pumpkin pie, *tarte à la citrouille*, is politely tasted, but declared another *idée bizarre*. *Citrouille* counts as a vegetable, no? Used in soups mostly, isn't it? Why sweeten it and . . . Better forget it and don't remind us of it. As for the Jell-O, it becomes the centerpiece of wonderment. That wobbly stuff in lurid colors tastes of . . . well, it tastes just as it looks: *chemical*, not remotely related in flavor or color to any fruit anyone has ever seen. And then, like everything else tonight, *much* too sweet. Jell-O will remain in village lore as a paradigm of American food, never to be forgotten, and the mayor, now retired, still mentions it every time we meet on the street.

The duke, tactfully, chooses that moment to give a little speech: He is glad that these *voûtes*, which for centuries served as a village dump and even housed goats and a donkey, have been restored and brought back to such vibrant life. He welcomes these beautiful young people to the village where his own ancestors have resided for more than a thousand years, and thanks them for their hospitality tonight. He hopes they'll meet again, he adds meaningfully, casting a few glances around. The girls swoon.

Now, do we have here a group of starved, unhappy, dispirited guests? *Not in the least.* They've come expecting the worst, and they're not disappointed. Americans are well meaning, friendly people once you get to know them. As for those kids, it would be hard not to like them, not all that different—are they?—from our own children. It was nice to be invited to share one of those American holidays one reads about in magazines, wine was good—local of course. But they are now confirmed in what they've always believed: Americans don't know a thing about *good* food, put sugar into everything and are hopeless when it comes to *gastronomie.* All these young people here need to be fed a few real meals to make up for years of Jell-O and pumpkin pie. So, invitations rain upon our bemused kids, who accept willingly, all the while refilling their plates from the *idée bizarre* dishes.

The skit, after coffee is served—French coffee, for heaven's sake, not the watery, American kind!—meets with great success. It tells the story of the Plymouth landing, famine, the growing of corn and *citrouille* and finally festivities with the Indians. The guests are delighted by it—whatever they can understand—especially when the Indians run in, in war paint and headdresses of feathers saved from the plucking of our turkeys.

Everyone parts in great good cheer, girls crowding around the duke who bends low over their hands. Rosalind declares that she will not, ever, wash that hand that the duke *almost* kissed. A lot of hugging, handshaking and *bises* accompany promises of gourmet meals that will show these poor kids what the word *food* really means. I smile inwardly at the thought that *foie-gras,* truffles, *andouillettes,* escargots, tripes and calf brains, together with other assorted French delicacies will, in turn, puzzle the kids and confirm *them* in the idea that, thank God, America holds an exclusive patent on what's really *good* to eat. Cultural exchange? Well, yes. They're learning about each other, and who knows? Some might even learn to *like* what they're discovering. Finally, the bus takes the kids back to Aix.

None of us has any idea that, during our festive evening, something somber has taken place in the village, involving another young woman of just about their age.

Early next morning, the mayor is knocking on our door but in his official capacity, this time. While we were banqueting on our *bizarre* foods, all has not gone well in the lower village, and a Canadian girl has been raped.

Some years earlier, a house there was purchased by a Canadian man, who only partially restored it and seldom comes to visit. We heard of him, but never met him. He's loaned it, this fall, to three young women, who are apparently spending a few months of what they'd hoped would be a footloose and fancy-free time in France. But the place is unheated, barely livable; they don't speak a word of French, and the neighbors feel they can't be too happy there.

"Ah, it's misfortune that would have it," sighs the mayor, wiping his brow in spite of the cold morning. "I don't know what it's like in Canada or in the United States, but here, unescorted girls don't go to bars at night; they don't let men buy them drinks and dance with them. If they did, they'd have to expect the worst. . . ." It seems that the youngest of the three, maybe twenty-two or so, probably seeking some sort of entertainment and social life, had taken to frequenting the only bar in the village and spent her evenings there. She would perch on a barstool in her miniskirt, long fair hair spilling against her cheek. Men would indeed buy her drinks and when someone put a tape on the deck, she'd dance with this one or that one. There were some coarse jokes that she totally missed, but as long as she fooled around only with the local guys, she was safe from rougher treatment. Everything gets known here, and these Lotharios all have mothers or wives, or both, not to mention the occasional mother-in-law, to answer to. Only, as bad luck would have it, last night three legionnaires walked into the Bar des Sports.

This was a rare event, for legionnaires seldom venture that far from Aubagne. But these were returning from the Legion's hospital somewhere up north in the Alpes de Haute-Provence and stopped to visit a friend, a local no-good guy named Théophile. So, all four staked stools at the café and saw the unexpected presence of a blonde for-eign girl, presumably looking for adventure, as a thought-ful gift placed there for their solace and enjoyment by whatever god looks after the comfort of legionnaires.

The kid knew nothing of the reputation—deserved or not—that surrounds legionnaires. Impressed, perhaps, by the glamorous, pale uniform, the red epaulets and white képi, she accepted numerous *"coups"* of white wine into which the men slipped jiggers of *gnole*, a rotgut brandy, danced suggestive dances, even held up her miniskirt in an imitation of cancan, laughed, let the men squeeze her waist, and run their hands up her leg, sang along with the tapes and, probably more than half drunk, had a jolly good time, totally unaware of the company's intentions.

When she announced she was going home, they offered—and she accepted—a ride in their car.

However, instead of taking her home, less than five minutes away, they drove to the *pinède*, the pine-tree forest that covers a hill overlooking the village, and there, one, perhaps two, apparently forced themselves upon her. *Then*, they delivered her home, oblivious to the fact that their behavior was not only reprehensible, but *criminal*, and promised to return the next day for some more of this good, clean fun. The older girls put the victim to bed, sick to her stomach, sobbing and bruised. Then, they summoned the gendarmes, who in turn spoke to the mayor, who decided to call on us.

"Perhaps you can help her, poor thing, she breaks your heart, so sad, with scratches on her face and," he adds modestly, "elsewhere, too, I understand. It's so cold in that barn of a house, and I am not sure they have much food to eat or money to spend, either. Perhaps you can visit, bring her some of that American stuff you served last night. It would make her feel better to eat sweet food like that, and she'd enjoy talking to you in English. Poor kid! Of course, the police are out looking for these scoundrels, and they've staked out Théophile's house, but he seems to have left with them."

My heart bleeds for the girl. Would things have been different at home? Perhaps there she'd understand better which are, and are not, safe places for a young woman. On the other hand, political correctness affirms that women have a *right* to go anywhere they *want*, dressed any way they *want* and behave there any way they *want*. Sure, they do, and no one would dispute that. Only, should rape occur—and let's hope it is not murder—even if the offenders are caught and severely punished, these women are, and *remain*, raped. No prison term can change that; so, perhaps, it is better to choose not to exercise every right, or at least do it wisely.

We find poor Sabrina lying in bed in that cold house, with tear-stained cheeks and a few scratches drying on her neck. We've brought a basket of turkey and stuffing, sweet potatoes, a whole pumpkin pie and a great bowl of Jell-O. All three girls dig gratefully into the food, and when we make ready to leave, Sabrina is recovering a little and thinking of returning home to Toronto.

Wayne and I feel terrible: If only we had known of the presence of these women in the village, we wouldn't have failed to invite them to our Thanksgiving dinner, and the dark events of last night would have been avoided! But strangely enough, in a place where no secrets—what am I saying: *secrets?*—where any *bit* of information is instantly passed around, nobody dreamed of telling us. "I thought you knew them, for sure," later says Madame Oraison, who lives across the street. "With Canada so close to America, you couldn't fail to know each other! Don't you speak the same language, after all?"

Just as we are about to return to our house, a commotion at the door startles everyone: The three legionnaires and their good friend Théophile are there, knocking festively, making good on their promise to return for more of the same brand of fun. The older women show great presence of mind by letting them in and allowing Wayne to slip out to alert the gendarmes. Then, they lock the door while the men are not looking.

In no time, the gendarmes are here, handcuffs are slipped on four pairs of wrists, in spite of protests by three of the group that they only stood around smoking cigarettes and never touched the girl, while the fourth one insists that it has all been shared enjoyment. And then: They bought her drinks, didn't they? Danced with her? Fooled around with her? What is a gentleman to expect in cases like that? Men will be men and have every right to be, even those gendarmes should agree, they're men, too, after all! But, imperturbable, the gendarmes load all in their minivan and take them to Pertuis for booking. The following summer, we will learn that they remain in the Carpentras jail, serving a long prison term.

Two days later, Wayne takes the three ladies to the airport, as they have decided to cut short their France caper and return home to safety in Canada.

Only months after the Thanksgiving events, another legionnaire-connected episode shakes the village.

A few years ago, a woman named Réata purchased the home of our erstwhile housekeeper Mélanie in the lower village and moved there. Is some kind of a wicked spirit ensconced in that place that imparts meanness and a viper tongue to its residents? The new woman displays the same charm as Mélanie. She constantly calls the gendarmes on her neighbors if their radio plays after hours, throws mud and refuse on cars parked close to her door and is always quick with some attack or insulting remark. She comes from some undetermined country: Syria? Turkey? Or could it be Iran? No? Macedonia, perhaps? Some whisper that she might be a gypsy and are a little afraid of her. Her looks complete her personality: small, dark head, out of proportion with a heavy body and massive legs. With the best good will in the world, Réata could not be called attractive.

"Did you see Réata's new boyfriend?" asks Dolores, our pretty, smiling housekeeper. "I can't believe it! Never had a man before, and this one is really good-looking. Manners, too. Always greets everybody, polite, helpful! Pushes a stalled car, helps bring in firewood, teaches a kid how to ride a bike. . . . He is living with her, but nobody can understand why he puts up with her and the way she treats him. People don't know the story."

"Do you know where he comes from?"

"He talked some with my husband, who likes him. He said he was a legionnaire, recently released from the service. He met Réata when she was visiting in Aubagne, and they . . . connected. Madame, these men have no place to go, no families, they need time to find a job and a place to live. Réata has a home, so he went with her. People say she's crazy about him, but we all hope it won't last. Just let him get on his feet, and *psst!* He'll be gone. Will it ever serve her right! You should see what that man has to endure."

Walking down the Rue des Remparts that afternoon, I

do meet the man, busy painting Réata's house a hideous color between khaki and brown. He greets me and explains, with a slight German accent:

"She picked that color, and it's *her* house, so that's the way it will be. Ladies can be strong-minded, sometimes. . . . I'll see if I can talk her into something more cheerful for the shutters. . . ." But Réata's angry voice calls from inside:

"Hey, you, stop wasting your time out there. You still have a load of wood to chop today."

So he smiles sheepishly, salutes and resumes his work.

After a few weeks, Réata's house has been repainted inside and out, new *volets* installed and flower boxes now brighten the khaki façade. Her car sparkles like new. Evenings, she walks him around the village, holding firmly onto his arm, stopping to inform onlookers that he is down and out, a good-for-nothing, living on her charity and lucky she is so generous. People gag but say nothing, and fervently hope that time will correct the situation.

Wayne and I have occasion to chat with the man, whose name is Manfred, on those rare occasions when Réata isn't watching. We find him well spoken and surprisingly literate.

"Have you read Doris Lessing?" he asks once. "I read her in English some years ago. Great insight into various cultures!" I am dumbfounded. No, I haven't read Doris Lessing, but certainly will on his recommendation. He speaks admiringly of Frank Lloyd Wright and Le Corbusier.

"Back in Germany, I was an architecture student at the University of Göttingen. Almost finished my degree when. . . . But that's a chapter I'd better leave untold. Anyway, five years in the Legion and here I am."

Réata's mistreatment continues, and the whole village hopes for a severe retribution. Only, *when* will it come?

A few doors away from Réata lives Annette, an attractive young widow whose husband has been killed in a motorcycle accident. A slim brunette with arresting periwinkle eyes, she owns and operates a beauty salon in Pertuis. Pert and smart, she has long been Réata's *bête noire*, who harasses her with insults, complaining to the gendarmes that Annette's firewood sticks out in the street, that her cat prowls neighbors' roofs and her car is parked in the wrong places. She spreads lurid stories in which poor Annette entertains men at all hours, drinking and playing loud music that keeps honest people awake. You only need look at her short dresses on slender legs and low-cut necklines to get an idea of the kind of woman Annette is, *n'est-ce pas?* Cautious, the village nods, waiting. It will come, oh, it will. . . . There has to be *somebody* up there to set those things straight.

Well, it turns out there is.

Nobody had an inkling that anything was going on, but one day, while Réata is out shopping, Manfred simply gathers his clothes and moves in with Annette. In spite of their efforts to keep the matter discreet, the village knows of it in no time and rejoices *en masse*, in a low-key but heartfelt celebration.

I run into Manfred and Annette one Friday, shortly after the event, at the Pertuis weekly market, where you'll sooner or later meet everybody. They make an attractive couple:

he, tall and blond, she petite and dark-haired with those bluer-than-blue eyes. They carry a basket between them and laugh as they walk. I feel good on Manfred's account and Annette's, too. The same day, I learn he has secured a job with a nearby city hall in the office of the architectural commission where restoration permits are delivered. In spite of odds one can only conjecture, here's a man who's apparently rebuilding his life with a job and a nice lady.

But that isn't the end of it. First, enraged, Réata hounds the couple, vandalizes their car, steals their mail, breaks the windows of their house and even tries to set fire to it—but fortunately a downpour puts out the blaze she had started in an adjacent woodshed. Unable to stand the abuse any longer, Manfred and Annette find other lodgings and simply move away.

Far from calming down, Réata goes instead into hysterics of such violence that alerted neighbors call the doctor. It takes a great deal of sedation before the paramedics can finally strap her to a gurney, which they load onto the ambulance that takes her to the hospital. There she spends several weeks undergoing treatment that includes, confides a neighbor lady, shock therapy.

When at last she returns, somewhat gaunt, but at the same time just as massive and heavy-legged, she becomes a recluse for a time and will leave her house only in the early morning hours or else late at night, when few will be abroad. The village continues rejoicing: justice has, at last, been done to Réata! The gendarmes relax, no longer called to her street at all hours, and life goes on, free from the vile gossip that had poisoned it.

I hear that Manfred and Annette are building a home with bright blue shutters and that he is taking university courses toward a degree in architecture, a happy man, finally free of his past, in the company of a good woman, one legionnaire at least who, successfully if not quite painlessly, has returned to civilian life.

Experience Romance
The Lure of the Legion

The Legion, originally destined to serve only *outside* the continental limits of France, that is to say in the French colonies, is now stationed in the metropolis (with the exception of small detachments in Corsica and Djibouti). In addition to the main base in Aubagne, there is another one in Saint-Christol.

At the Legion Museum in Aubagne, Buy a White Képi
Visit the *Musée de la Légion*, which preserves the history of the corps with documents, displays of weapons, uniforms, scenes of battle and so forth.

In the boutique, you can buy books, documents and objects stamped with the Legion's emblem of képi, epaulets and the 13-flame grenade. These include key rings, portfolios, wallets, desk accessories and more. You can even buy the white képi of the Legionnaires. How about getting one to wear in private, when you wish to evoke *Beau Geste* and Piaf's glamorous lover in *Mon Légionnaire*?

Musée de la Légion: Route de la Thuilière, 13400 Aubagne; Tel: 04-42-18-82-41.

Visit the Auchan Hypermarché

You'll find all sorts of products not available in the U.S. And don't pass up the chocolate section: So many varieties will make it difficult to choose. But it will be easier if you agree with me that Belgian chocolates are the best and Côte-d'Or the top among those.

Experience Couscous

On Thursdays, look for a couscous déjeuner. A special spice, or rather a mixture of pungent spices, called *ras-el-hanout* ("best in the store" in Arabic), imparts that lamb stew with an unforgettable flavor. The red *harissa* condiment served on the side is hot, so use it sparingly until you've determined how much heat you can stand.

Meet the Legionnaires

Late afternoon, you'll see legionnaires enjoying a beer in the many cafés. If not in uniform, they're recognizable from their shaved (or at least closely barbered) heads. There are a few Americans in the Legion; otherwise half are French and the rest from dozens of other countries. Legionnaires usually welcome conversation with visitors.

A Romantic Drive to Saint-Christol

On a high plateau near Saint-Christol, while the Cold War lasted, rockets used to lie, deep in their underground silos, guarded by troops stationed in the village. Today, the silos are empty, but the caserns are occupied by a regiment of the Legion.

Saint-Christol is in the eastern part of the Vaucluse. You'll drive through Apt, and you must stop to enjoy this lovely, very Provençal town, whose main industry is the making of candied fruit. Ask in the confiseries, where it is sold, about visiting one of the factories (active in summer), and do not fail to buy some of the tender, flavorful *fruits confits* to nibble on.

Translucent, glowing like jewels especially when presented on frosted glass shelves with underneath lighting, you'll find them irresistible. The *fruits confits* of Apt have nothing in common with the chopped, mixed and dried-up kind we use to make fruitcake.

There, the whole fruit—pear, peach, apricot, cherry, fig, even an entire peeled cantaloupe—is treated in a succession of vats and comes out tender, shiny, distilling the essence of the fruit.

Confiserie Le Coulon, 24 Quai de la Liberté, 84440 Apt; Tel: 04-90-74-21-90.

Lunch in Apt? I love L'Auberge du Lubéron, overlooking the Coulon, the torrent that flows through the town. Sit on the vine-covered terrace and enjoy Provençal dishes prepared with local produce.

L'Auberge du Lubéron, 17 Quai Léon-Sagy; Tel: 04-90-74-12-50; Fax: 04-90-04-79-49; www.auberge-luberon-peuzin.com; e-mail: contact@auberge-luberon-peuzin.com.

As you continue, direction Rustrel, you'll see signs to Le Colorado Provençal. These are vast ocher quarries in activity and a uniquely colorful sight. Your camera will have a field day recording those sulphur yellow, chartreuse green, orange, magenta crags, cliffs and pinnacles. In the little shop you might buy packets of different colored ochers to use imaginatively or present as a gift to an artist friend.

In Saint-Christol

As in Aubagne, you'll meet legionnaires relaxing in the village bistros. Here, too, they are friendly and, in my experience, happy to chat with visitors. Inquire from them—or in the village—if there might be a ceremony, such as a change of command (called *une prise d'armes*) to which visitors would be admitted.

There is an informal atmosphere in Saint-Christol. Officers are French, and married ones reside nearby with their families, so wives and children come to watch parades. As for the legionnaires, they must remain single for the period of their enlistment, but many establish relationships with local ladies.

Simple and Sensuous
An Exotic Dinner *à deux*

A couscous dinner, the traditional dish of North Africa, is often associated with the Legion. It takes a little while to cook, so plan on about one hour of cooking time.

Couscous is very easy to make, but you'll need two specific spices: *ras-el-hanout*, a pungent but mild mix, and *harissa*, a red, hot one (in a pinch you could replace *harissa* with a mixture of cayenne pepper and paprika). You'll find both *ras-el-hanout* and *harissa* in Middle-Eastern food stores.

Couscous marocain
Salade de fruits exotiques

Couscous is actually two dishes: The stew and the grain.

The Stew
   1 pound lean lamb, cubed
   Olive oil
   1 yellow onion, coarsely chopped
   ½ small head of cabbage, chopped
   1 8-ounce can diced tomatoes
   1 small can artichoke bottoms, drained
   3 tablespoons raisins
   1 quart chicken broth

2 small green zucchini
2 or 3 tablespoons *ras-el-hanout*
1 teaspoon *harissa*
Salt and pepper

Brown lamb quickly in a skillet with a little olive oil. Add onion and cabbage and cook until limp. Remove to heavy saucepan. Add tomatoes, chicken broth, artichoke bottoms and *ras-el-hanout*. After it has cooked a while, adjust seasonings, add salt and pepper (*ras* is not salty). Cook until meat is fork tender. About 10 minutes before serving, add raisins and whole, very lightly peeled zucchini (leave green underskin). Cook until zucchini is done through but still firm. Adjust seasonings once more, adding more *ras* if you like.

The Grain

1 box instant couscous, plain
1 16-ounce can of garbanzo beans (chick peas),
  drained and rinsed. Save 2 tablespoons for *harissa*
1 pint boiling water

Stir couscous in boiling water and keep stirring as it swells. Add garbanzos. Moisten with broth from stew to consistency of fluffy rice. (Couscous takes only a few minutes.)

Harissa condiment: Mash 2 tablespoons garbanzos in small bowl. Add 1 teaspoon *harissa* spice, mix and stir in enough broth from stew to make a paste of mustard consistency.

On Your Plate
Make a well in a mound of couscous grain. Ladle in the stew. Place a whole zucchini on top. Pass the bowl of *harissa* to add to taste.

Exotic Fruit Salad
Mix any or all exotic fruit, fresh, canned or frozen, in any combination: pineapple, mango, lichee, guava, mandarin sections, banana, papaya. Spike with rum (or *Malibu*, a coconut-flavored rum). Top with grated sweetened coconut. Decorate with slices of starfruit.

To Drink
In North Africa, you'd be offered glasses of hot, sweetened mint tea, a surprisingly cooling drink to complement the pungent couscous and hot *harissa*.

A single exotic bloom surrounded with greenery
resting on the table will look perfect.

The Great Lovers
of Provence

*P*rovence is a land of lovers. Golden skinned, utterly feminine, from slim ankles to narrow, rounded waists and high breasts, the women of Provence are not hard to fall in love with. Quite aware of their allure, they acknowledge male interest with laughing eyes and a toss of the head. The men, for their part, not only desire the women, as they do anywhere else, but sincerely *like* them, and both sexes recognize that flirting can be enjoyed in a hundred exciting and delicious ways.

At parties back home in the States, men will congregate to discuss basketball scores, the stock market or the latest advances in computer technology. Women, then, reduced to the company of other women and usually intimidated by some holier-than-thou character among them, remain confined to a discussion of child-rearing, cooking tips and problems with household help. But not in Provence.

There, instead, at social gatherings a man will seek out a woman he finds attractive and, after a moment of smiling banter, will often bring a drink to share. Afraid of transmissible diseases, you say? If that's the way you feel, by all means, refuse that drink. But please, do not discourage others from that subtle, next-best-thing-to-a-kiss game.

For flirting is just that, a game, ambiguous perhaps, but a game you must know how to play. It's a game in which sarcasm, heavy mockery or smart-alecky jibes have little place if you are older than 16. It is played with laughter and almost tender gestures. He will attempt to decipher the inscription on your pendant or examine the pin on your shoulder. Identify your perfume, perhaps. Meanwhile, you touch his watch, admire his tie, brush an imaginary speck from his lapel, all indicating physical interest. Compliments are, of course, a part of flirting, and you can expect to be told *why* you are attractive. For, whatever arguments may rage as to what is, or is not, the most erotic organ, the French maintain that it is the ear. They may well be right. Otherwise, why would the simple words, "I love you," have such an electrifying effect?

When a man playfully takes her hand and turns it over to kiss the palm, all the while looking straight into her eyes, a Provençal woman's thoughts are not of sexual harassment, and calling a lawyer is *not* what enters her mind. And suppose an attractive Provençal guy flirts with you with that accent that sounds more like singing, singing in the sunshine? He might say something like, "Should you wish to make advances, *je ne me défendrais que mollement*, I'd only oppose token resistance." See? He's told you that it is strictly up to *you*, the game will be played according to *your* rules. *You* decide how far things should go, but whatever the outcome, there'll be no hard feelings. Only, don't be smart or biting. Delicately acknowledge the compliment paid to you, for it is flattering to be found beautiful and desirable—even if you do not reciprocate the feeling.

When the lights are low, and after a few shared kirs royal, you might hear him whisper, "I'd love to let you make love to me." A lazy lover? Not at all. . . . Provençal men have never been accused of *that*. It is only a gentle way to keep the ball in your court, while, at the same time, paying a deft tribute to the lovemaking skills he credits you with. So you should be angry? Feel insulted? Then I am afraid Provence is not the land for you. You might prefer the sort of place where blood runs cooler and where sexual innuendoes are liable to end up as evidence in some courtroom.

It is no wonder, then, that Provence—from Marseille to Aix and Avignon—is the land of some of the most passionate and celebrated lovers, although their love wasn't always fulfilled. The poet Petrarch may even hold the record for the longest and most dedicated flirt: If we are to believe him—and my group of students seems to raise serious doubts—his anguished love for Laure lasted for 21 years and wasn't rewarded by the slightest little kiss.

It all started in Avignon, the most poetic city of Provence, still girded by its fortifications, every crenellation intact, that glow pink as the sun sets over the great Rhône river. There, the massive Palace of the Popes still stands, austere but ready to welcome the pontiff again, should he decide to abandon Rome and return to this ancient papal domain.

The popes resided in Avignon in the 14th century. Seven popes ruled Christianity from there and built both palace and fortifications. Italian civil wars raged: think of Romeo and Juliet, victims of such a clan feud that divided their families. Refugees came in droves to Avignon, where Italian clergy abounded, Italian was the most commonly heard language and they were assured of finding both a welcome and the chance to earn a living in the fast-growing city.

Among them came the notary Petrarco de Parenzi with his family, which included a son, Francesco. Born in 1304, the latter would be known to us as the poet Petrarch who would one day receive the ultimate honor, the crown of the greatest poet of his time. Widely admired by his contemporaries, not many today read his verse, which admittedly loses much to the passage of centuries as well as translation.

However, the course on Petrarch at the university is popular with our students, perhaps because it is taught by the man I met at our party, whose neatly trimmed beard makes him look like a pirate and who is named Bugatti, just like the famous car.

Professor Bugatti enjoys a glamorous reputation: Residing in Paris, quite a distance from Aix, he has scheduled all his classes during a single week each month. Leaving wife and family behind, he then lives in a carefree, bachelor style here for that week, say the kids, reporting rumors they've

heard. But he seems to motivate his students with methods
that stress individual research and a manner that convinces
the girls he is flirting with them. He cuts quite a dashing
figure in his black velvet blazer and white cashmere vest.

Haunting the library, students learn that the name of
Petrarch will always be pronounced in the same breath as
that of Laure, his lady love, with whom he carried on that
lifelong, platonic affair. Encouraged to read, in addition to
the verse, which bores them, letters and memoirs of the
time, they discover that, at 23, Petrarch was a dandy, who
singed his hair by curling it too often with a hot iron and
bruised his feet by wearing too narrow shoes, when he saw
Laure for the first time.

"You don't go around in that get-up," reason the guys,
"just to look for *platonic* love." The girls chime in, "I would-
n't get all fixed up that way, either, to *look* at somebody
from a distance." "He wanted *action*," concludes Rob, "and
I bet he got some."

Laure appeared to him on the steps of a church and,
although he didn't come near her that day, he was seduced
by her flowing golden hair and dark, laughing eyes.
Hoping to meet her again, he looked for her at social gatherings and made discreet inquiries. He learned that her
health was delicate and that she resided with her parents
some distance from town. He was glad to hear that she
knew and loved Italian. And thus did Petrarch's destiny as
a poet take flight under the inspiration of his growing love.

"But who was Laure?" asks Professor Bugatti. "Can you
find out?"

Petrarch himself always remained secretive and never revealed more than his beloved's first name. So, scholars were left to conjecture.

First, students check the *Larousse Dictionary*, under "Petrarch." The entry states that the poet wrote in honor of "Laure de Noves." But Professor Bugatti shrugs and prods them to further research: "Don't believe *every* entry in a dictionary. Find out for yourselves."

Thus, they discover that a Laure de Noves did exist, a daughter of the house of Sade, married to the Lord of Noves near Avignon. *That* Laure, however, bore eleven children during the period Petrarch celebrates her as a chaste, pure and youthful maiden.

The students don't go along with the hypothesis. "A *mom!*" they say. "How would anybody be in love with a *mom?*" I suggest, "Your dad, maybe, with *your* mom?" But they dismiss the thought. Their *father* in love? Like, with their mom? Oh, come on now, man!

Then, says Professor Bugatti—who won't be able to make it to class next time, that is to say, next month—you should look further. Have you checked the archives of the great Provençal houses in the library? So, the best of our sleuths triumphantly digs up a rare work by Hilaire Enjoubert, a medieval Provence specialist. Enjoubert suspects that the Sade-Noves identity was put forward by the Sade family, perhaps in order to attract attention to another relative, one more chastely attractive than the infamous marquis.

There lived, at the time, he postulates, a Laure de Sabran, daughter of a powerful lord, whose extended family possessed enormous land holdings and several castles in the area. The family endures today, still living and prospering in their château of Ansouis. There even exists a current Laure de Sabran, a very attractive young lady, residing in Paris.

Laure lived in Caumont, a village then, now a suburb of Avignon, the locale of the airport. Her parents' castle, in ruins today, guarded the narrow Durance valley. Her age at the time of the meeting has never been firmly established: She could have been as young as 12, as old as 16, either one a marriageable age at a time when life was short and must be lived fast.

But marriage with a commoner such as Francesco, a foreigner who possessed neither estates, title nor family connections, was, of course, out of the question.

"But the guy wasn't, like, thinking of getting married," protests Jason, who has shaved his beard, revealing neat features and high cheekbones. "He just wanted to have *fun!*" The girls agree, "She wanted some fun, too, like go out on dates, get to meet more guys. . . ." They have no idea, of course, of how different things were there and then from what they know in California.

Laure could read, not a common skill in those days, especially among women. She was an avid reader, often seen with a book in hand, a handwritten one, for printing would not be invented for another century. As befitted her position, an entourage of young ladies would usually accompany her, making meetings difficult. Petrarch, passion growing in his heart, was bold enough to write her a sonnet. How would she receive it? He waited anxiously.

Finally, during one of those long summer twilights of Provence, there she was, walking along a lane, when he least expected her, with two attendants. Seized with a vertigo, he lowered his eyes. When he raised them, he found she was alone and smiling at him.

"Smiling? That's all? Come on, man! She told her girl-friends to get lost, that's what she did. She wanted to be *alone* with him." Everybody agrees that this is when they kissed. But there is disagreement: Did *he* kiss her? Or did she, tired of his dilly-dallying, grab him and kiss *him*? "I think *she* kissed him," ventures Phil, clearly thinking of Pomme.

During the following months, Petrarch saw his beloved a few times: once near an old chapel where she went to pray; another time as he walked along the banks of the Durance river. Finally, in the course of the winter months her family spent in town, he met her at a social event, and they exchanged a few words. The poet was entranced by the sound of her voice he was hearing for the first time.

"What, for the first time, he says? Man, like they've been *dating* all along! Only, he's afraid she'll get into trouble, so he's being careful." "Near a *chapel*, they met?" giggles Rosalind. "I know all about dates in church, like with that guy who sang in my choir, and we always stayed late to lock up, *we said*."

Surprisingly, we see the young poet agree, shortly after-wards, to accompany his friend, Bishop Colonna—who was about his age—to his new see in the Pyrenees moun-tains. Why would he wander so far from his ladylove? Yet he seems happy; she has asked him not to try and see her again until fall, and *then* they can meet again.

Enjoubert—as well as other scholars whose works the students have dug up in those archives—theorizes that Laure was getting married. An arranged marriage, to be sure, where love had no place, only the advantage of two families. There would be endless festivities of betrothal, wedding, followed by jousts and tournaments, enough to fill her time until summer was over. Then she could resume the . . . flirt?

But the kids don't go along with that. In spite of their freewheeling ways where romance and sex are concerned, they are imbued with respect for marriage. You can fool around until then, but after *that*, the fun is over. You settle down, start thinking of a home, a mortgage and becoming mom and dad.

"It was just, like, she was going on vacation with her folks, I bet," suggests Amanda. "Maybe she'd met another guy she liked. So, she'd want to see how things would turn out with that one," offers someone else. "Were they even going *steady*, like?" another wonders.

In any case, they met again in the fall and Petrarch admits that now, for the first time, she extended her hand to him. He took it, rendered mute by the intensity of his passion. But he felt that, while she returned his love, she was uneasy, prey to a vague fear.

"He'd touched a lot more than her *hand*, if you want to know," is the general consensus. But: "You have to hand it to the man, though," interjects Carola, "he doesn't blab everything to his buddies. I like that. Some guys we know could take a lesson from him."

They also don't see how, from a handshake, he could have detected her deeper emotions: "I bet they spent a lot of time together that day. Like in *bed*, don't you think?"

Petrarch, who was by now acquiring quite a reputation as a poet, resided at that point in the opulent Colonna establishment in the center of Avignon. Elegance had reached such a height that a council was convened in the nearby city of Apt to repress abuses. "Young men," complained one of the articles, "resemble ladies with their curled hair and ribbon-laden tunics." It went on to enjoin severely, "These tunics are much too short and shall be lengthened as *much* as modesty demands." We can only hope that our poet's dress conformed to the rules of modesty when, at a gala featuring singers, harp, flute and tambourine players, he saw Laure appear in a green dress adorned with stones that sparkled like diamonds. She looked quite petite next to her father, the Lord of Sabran, who stood tall with a chiseled face and a shock of white hair. Francesco kept a distance, trying to conceal his emotion, but at one point, walking past him, she let drop her glove "woven of silk and gold threads." He picked it up, returned it, and was thanked with a gracious smile. He wrote yet another sonnet:

> *Dear sweet glove, an object most blessed*
> *To have covered such ivory and fresh roses*
> *Who in the world ever picked up such a treasure?*

They met several more times in the garden of his friend Senuccio. He admits to a few conversations there. And then, one day, Laure stole behind him and covered his eyes in a playful, familiar gesture.

"She was getting tired of all the pussyfooting around," conclude the students. "They've been going together now how long? Wow! Time to go public. All that poetry is fine, but there's more to *life!*"

But instead, something the poet claims not to understand happens: Was she scolded for her familiarity? Was a jealous husband watching? Or had she been promised to some lord of the vicinity and must refrain from marks of affection to Francesco? All we know is the sonnet of bewildered despair Petrarch addressed to Senuccio:

> *Senuccio, let me tell you how I am treated*
> *A moment ago sweet, now I see her prideful*
> *She's become rebellious, a friend turned to foe*
> *She was chaste and modest, now she's scornful and haughty.*

"Okay, so they had a fight. And now he goes bitching to his buddy. Man, let that guy Sen go talk to her, then!"

A friend loaned Petrarch a modest house near Fontaine-de-Vaucluse, a few miles south of Avignon. At the students' request, we include that charming village in our next weekend tour, looking for memories of the poet.

In contrast to the rocky Provençal landscape where water is rare, the village of Fontaine-de-Vaucluse (the name is *never* shortened to *Fontaine*) is alive with a wide, swiftly running stream, the Sorgue River, where weave those long, green, ribbon-like aquatic grasses called *cheveux de sorcière*, witch's hair, to discourage little children from leaning too low over the bank, for then, the witch might reach out with her hook and . . . Just stay *away* from the edge, you hear?

The river does not originate from a spring. Instead, it surges, boiling and churning, at the foot of a high cliff, a *resurgence*, a phenomenon by which water, absorbed by a limestone plateau, will reappear, sometimes quite a distance away, to give birth to a torrent.

A lovely walk of less than a mile, shaded by trees leaning over the water and lined with romantic little restaurants built on pilings, leads from the village to the *"fontaine,"* which is most spectacular after heavy spring rains. There, at a late dinner, Wayne and I once enjoyed the most overbaked, deliciously crusty and caramelized stuffed tomatoes, as I trailed my hand into the icy river.

On a peak overlooking the river still stand the jagged ruins of a castle that belonged to Petrarch's friend, Philippe de Cabassole. A plaque affixed to a rock reminds you that the poet visited there often, and it is easy to imagine him trudging up the steep slope, casting downward glances in the hope of discovering Laure, perchance strolling on the path below.

He admits to seeing her several times there. Once, he watched for a long time as she sat at the foot of a chestnut tree, weaving daisies and buttercups into a garland, while moving shadows of branches alternately darkened and illuminated her face. . . .

But my group is more interested in the precise implications than in the poetry of the image.

"See? They're dating again! It was just a fight they had,

like everyone will. . . . So she comes to visit him in his little house. Wow! That must have been nice. Like lying in bed with the river running by. Wonder if they already had all these little restaurants?" (If not, I suspect they'd think of pizza delivery. . . .)

But soon, Laure's health, always fragile, declined suddenly. Petrarch would catch a glimpse of her one day and be struck by her appearance, her eyes seeming larger in her emaciated face. She had fallen behind her companions and stopped to catch her breath, leaning against a tree. Soon, he was told that she had taken to her bed, too weak now for even the shortest walk.

In despair, he accepted a mission to Italy. There, he was received with great honors and granted by King Robert the title of "Grand Poet and Grand Historian." With the title went the right to wear at all times a laurel crown and "poet's garb." One wonders if he wore that crown over still singed hair and hopes the poet's garb, whatever it was, reached a length sufficient to satisfy the modesty requirements of the Apt edict.

It was there that he learned the tragic news: death had claimed Laure on the 21st anniversary of their first meeting. Dazed with sorrow, unable to cry, he lived cruel hours and wrote on the blank endpaper of his *Virgil* the famous epitaph:

> *Laure, illustrious for her virtues and long sung in my verse, appeared to my eyes for the first time in the year of Our Lord 1327, on the sixth day of the month of April, in the Sainte-Claire church in Avignon. It was in the same*

*month, on the sixth day, at the same morning hour in the
year 1348 that she was ravished to the light of day while
I was in Italy, unaware, alas, of my tragic misfortune. I
learned the sad news in the month of May, on the 19th day.
I am certain that her soul has returned to the Heaven
whence she came.*

Thus ended one of the most famous, best-sung loves, per-
petuated in sonnets which, says Professor Bugatti, "heralded the Italian Renaissance." Did Laure, in fact, really exist?
Was she only a figment of the poet's imagination, as some
have thought? Or, if she existed, was this the pure, uncon-
summated, 21-year affair Petrarch tells us about—and the
students strongly doubt? It doesn't matter because Laure
will live on as the symbol of pure, never-ending passion.

Was she the beauty of roses, pearl and ivory the poet
sings? Perhaps. But, as Bugatti editorializes, "The intensity and the quality of love has little to do with its object.
Instead, it depends upon the one who loves, his or her
power of passion and, in this case, of *expression.*"

The kids are saddened by Laure's death. But: "She was
old, though, by then, wasn't she?" Someone does the
math: "Between thirty-three and thirty-seven." Heads
nod. Not *that* old, but still. . . . "And what about *him*? He
must have been what? Forty-four?" And then Amanda
cries out: "Forty-four? Yikes! Just like my dad!"

Now that Christmas is drawing near, we often hear the
famous tune called in America *The March of the Kings.* Students hum it, and they've even learned the lyrics:

De bon matin
   (Early in the morning)
J'ai rencontré le train
   (I met the train)
De trois grands rois qui
   (Of three great kings)
partaient en voyage. . . .
   (Leaving on a voyage. . . .)

They are surprised when Liz tells them, "This *is* a French tune! The overture of Bizet's *L'Arlésienne.*" This piques Faustino's interest: "Bizet? Who composed *Carmen?* Was he from Arles?" They have been to Arles and loved the place, in spite of a disappointing Thanksgiving dinner there. "Bizet was not from Arles, but this is a tragic story that owes nothing to fiction. He heard about it from a Provençal friend."

It all began in 1862. (I love dates, don't you? They pinpoint an event, let you know what was and was not possible in the climate of the time.) While Alphonse Daudet, author of the classic *Lettres de mon Moulin*, was visiting his friend, the Provençal poet Mistral, he was taken on a sort of pilgrimage to a nearby farm, a *mas*, belonging to Mistral's relatives. There, a few months earlier, the son of the house had committed suicide, jumping from the top story of the *magnanerie*, where silkworms are kept, to crash upon a stone table below. Daudet shuddered at the bloodstains still visible there.

He recounted the simple episode in a brief story, included in the *Lettres*: The boy, Frédéri, had fallen in love with a girl from Arles, an *Arlésienne*, with a passion that brooked no reasoning. The young lady wasn't quite suitable, being from the city and from an unknown family. However, seeing Frédéri unredeemably in love, his parents reluctantly agreed to the marriage. "He is all of 20 years old," said the father, "and languishing to put those to good use!" But, just as plans for the wedding progressed, a man appeared who revealed that the girl, far from being the innocent maiden one imagined, had been his passionate— and not even faithful—mistress for two years. All doubt that he might not be telling the truth was removed when he produced letters she had written him.

So now, a matter of honor arose. This was grassroots Provence, where tradition dies hard and honor was held dearer than life. Marriage to such a woman, now that the truth was known, meant dishonor to the family, who forbade the union—impossible, under the law, without parental consent.

But the boy's despair proved so overwhelming that, eventually, the parents relented. "Let him have his *Arlésienne*," sighed the father, "he might die if he doesn't," as the mother smiled through her tears. So now, outwardly, the boy seemed happy, even danced at the village fair, but it was all pretense for, later that night, unable to choose between lost honor and lost love, he ended his life by jumping through the window of the top floor of the *magnanerie*.

When the composer Georges Bizet heard the story, he was seduced by the fact that, "You speak of the *Arlésienne*, you dream of her, you love her, you die for her, but you

never see her." And he composed the melodrama whose overture has become a Christmastime standby.

The term "melodrama" was later given a disparaging
meaning, but its original one meant simply "a theatrical
production accompanied by song and orchestral music to
fit the action." Sort of an opera, where actors speak, rather
than sing. Beethoven's famous *Egmont* is a melodrama, for
instance.

In the piece, when Frédéri hears of the *Arlésienne's*
betrayal, chords come crashing with a sense of doom. To
his despair Bizet adds that of Vivette, who, in love with
Frédéri, sees him lost to another woman, then her hopes
raised when, pretending to have forgotten his *Arlésienne*, he
asks her to marry him. Tremulous music then underscores
Vivette's trembling, uneasy happiness, as she wonders,
"Has he *really* given her up?"

At the village fair, Frédéri dances with her and, come
early morning, leads the farandole that snakes through the
village, following flute and tambourine players. His mother stands among the crowd, timid hope in her heart: could
the boy be cured? But, not reassured, when she returns
home she decides to sleep in a room close to his, on the
pretext the silkworms on the floor above might need some
attention during the night.

It all happens, however, too fast for her: A moment later
Frédéri runs out, climbs the stairs to the attic and, once
inside, pushes the bolt that secures the door, deaf to his
mother's cries, as she runs after him calling out his name.

Only a dull thud answers her. And the curtain falls on
the image of the woman, tears streaking her face, sitting on

the ground, holding in her arms her son's broken body. Needless to say the orchestra rises to the occasion with chords of mourning and lost hope.

The students remain lost in thought for a moment. But: "That was crazy," says one. "Okay, so that Arles girl had another boyfriend? So what? He couldn't expect to be the only one if she was *that* cute!" Kevin continues, "She'd made her choice, she was dumping the other guy to marry him. So why bother with that tattling dude, just a sore loser, I bet!" There are nods of agreement. Family honor? What are we talking about? That stuff concerns the principals and nobody else. They have no idea of the mores of Provence a century ago, and picture the world, past and present, as an image of California and its codes. "He shouldn't have paid attention to what anybody said, and go off with the girl he loved," affirms Steve. "He couldn't marry her? Wasn't there some place they could *elope* to? No? Well, then, just *live* together!"

Someone concludes, "As soon as they'd have a kid, the parents would have come around and everything would have been fine!"

Vive la Californie!

The group has learned that Picasso is buried near Aix.

"Yes, in Vauvenargues, at the foot of the Sainte-Victoire," I tell them, for I was there recently in the company of Bill, who, by the way, loathes Picasso ("Obsessed with sex but not *sensuous,*" is his kindest verdict). "It is not far from here." So it is decided to make the visit part of our next weekend outing.

Everybody ohs and ahs at the lovely turreted castle nestled in the foothills of the famous mountain. Both castle and grounds are hermetically closed to visitors, so we can only gaze from a distance and wonder in which part of the park lies Picasso. The winter sun shines bright, but the wind blows cutting and cold, and the discovery of a pizza truck cheers everybody up. Those trucks seem to be a Provence specialty: pizzas are baked over a wood fire, blazing right over what must be the gas tank. The kids love the idea. "Bet the fire department back home would go nuts!"

The pizzas—clearly charbroiled, even a little carbonized around the edges, with lots of cheese, plenty of wrinkled black olives and generously sprinkled from a bottle of fiery *pimentée* oil—are a success. We sit, well protected from the wind, but in full view of the castle, as we eat and discuss Picasso, what they know of his work and his life. His life? He shared it with a long list of women, didn't he?

"Wasn't he married to that Jacqueline he painted so much when he was old?" Yes, the last chapter of Picasso's life stands out among the great love stories of Provence.

The aging Picasso lived in Vallauris, on the Mediterranean coast, when he broke up with Françoise Gilot, the mother of his children Claude and Paloma. Although the relationship had been stormy, her departure with the children left him at loose ends, depressed, for he found it impossible to live without a woman.

Vallauris, when Picasso first moved there, had been a decrepit, half-abandoned pottery center. But the artist, who discovered media for his creativity where others saw only debris—think of his famous *Goat*, later cast in bronze, with a palm leaf for the spine, a wicker basket for the belly and broken jugs for the udders—immediately set out to explore the potential of ceramics.

His presence there and his creations brought renewed life to the town and pottery shops reopened. The Madura business in particular, owned by the Ramié couple, developed a thriving trade, selling reproductions of Picasso's plates and decorative objects.

Working for the Ramiés as a saleslady was their cousin, Jacqueline Roque, about 26 at the time. She was the divorced wife of a minor French official stationed in Ouagadougou, capital of Burkina Faso in West Africa. Tired of colonial life, or of her husband, or both, she had returned to France with her small daughter Cathy, and sought a job at Madura.

A small, dark-haired woman with olive skin and a classical profile—Picasso's type—and, most important it developed, an unquenchable capacity for adoration and self-sacrifice, it was fate that placed her in the artist's path, even if some will claim that Madame Ramié's maneuvering did much to foster the romance. . . . The first of the myriad portraits Picasso would paint of Jacqueline, entitled *Madame Z.* (from the name of her modest villa, *Le Ziquet*), dates from that period.

Now came a long, and for Jacqueline, harrowing time during which she stoically endured all the whims, cruelties and humiliations the 74-year-old man would inflict upon her, as in some initiation rite of passage. Would she become his *maîtresse en titre*, the titular, live-in companion?

How would she prove herself worthy of that supreme honor? For Picasso, who needed women both in his art and his life, also harbored ambivalent feelings toward them, an atavistic mixture of desire, worship and resentful hostility.

Jacqueline accepted all. She took to calling him *"monseigneur,"* my lord, kissing his hands and addressing him in the third person of servile respect: "Will it be the pleasure of *monseigneur* to come to the table now?" Then came a particularly trying trip to Perpignan, in the company of Picasso's daughter Maya and several friends—among them Picasso's future biographer, John Richardson, who recounts the event. The group stayed at the home of a couple, with the wife suspected of being Picasso's mistress. After a frightful row, he kicked out Jacqueline and moved into his daughter Maya's room.

Jacqueline, meanwhile, disconsolately set out to drive back to Provence, stopping on the road every hour or so to call. Halfway, she turned around and returned to Perpignan.

"Monseigneur told me to do as I pleased," she explained. "It pleased me to return, so I did."

Had she passed a last and final test? When they repaired to Provence, Jacqueline had won the place she coveted so single-mindedly. "She entered his home and life, mistress of all," writes Richardson.

Now, Picasso wasn't the marrying kind. After coming to France from his native Spain, he'd shared years of poverty with Fernande, then Eva, who died young. Yet, when he met Olga Kokhlova, a dancer with the Diaghilev ballet company, he did marry her, and a son, Paulo, was born. The couple separated shortly afterwards, but were never divorced, and Olga would live to an advanced age.

That marriage would save him for years to come. "How *could* I marry you?" he'd ask women who bore him children: Marie-Thérèse Walther, the mother of Maya; and Françoise Gilot, the mother of Claude and Paloma. "I am married already!" Although the very opposite of a religious man, he'd call on his Spanish Catholic heritage: once married, married forever in the eyes of God, as long as both live. And Olga lived on, comfortably ensconced in Normandy, while her son Paulo, "an amiable young man of limited aspirations," served his father as a chauffeur.

Not uxorious, Picasso was not, either, of a faithful nature. From the beginning of his affair with Françoise Gilot, when she was twenty and he in his sixties, he started *another* liaison with an even younger woman, Geneviève Laporte, the threads of which run like a filigree throughout the Gilot years and the early ones of Jacqueline's tenure. He did several portraits of Geneviève. One of them, an erotically explicit nude, remained hanging in his bedroom until Jacqueline felt firmly established enough to present it as a gift to art collector friends.

Thus, it took several years, even after Olga finally died, for Picasso either to feel free from the bonds of that union, or to gather his nerve to enter another one. At last, presumably with a clear Christian conscience, he married Jacqueline in 1961 when he was 80 and she 34. But the Geneviève Laporte affair still had not died.

Laporte herself recounts her last visit.

The couple had moved from Vallauris to a splendid villa in Cannes, *La Californie*, where she went to call on him. She was shown into a vast salon with painted ceilings, sculptures, mirrored doors and a bare, highly polished parquet floor. Furnishings consisted solely of a couch, easels holding some of the master's works and canvasses stacked against the walls. Jacqueline and Picasso received her, but Jacqueline tactfully excused herself after a few strained words.

Suddenly, Yan, the boxer dog, burst into the room, carrying in his mouth a scrap of wood that he dropped at the visitor's feet. She picked it up and slid it across the floor, as the dog ran after it barking happily.

"One does not play with a dog in a room like this," Picasso remarked icily.

It was, says Laporte, as if the man she'd known and loved had died. The bohemian artist, the self-proclaimed communist, who crushed his cigarette butts underfoot in his Paris studio, was no more, replaced by a stranger, a bourgeois, who valued a polished floor. She would never see her former lover again. One cannot refrain from thinking that Jacqueline must have looked with renewed pleasure at the empty rectangle left on the bedroom wall by the anatomically detailed nude.

When encroaching constructions stole the sea view from the luxurious villa, the Picassos moved to another in nearby Mougins, the backcountry of the Riviera. The name of the house, *Notre-Dame-de-Vie*, after a neighboring chapel, must have appealed to the aging artist, who harbored a terror of death and banned any reference to it. They moved in with the pride of newlyweds, Jacqueline reigning over a household both bourgeois—her own touch—and hopelessly cluttered, not only with the accumulated works of the master but with ever growing piles of assorted junk he kept amassing as possible elements of future inspiration. She never departed from her adoration and humble service, even in the face of his tactless jokes.

As when he decided that only an alliance with royalty would represent a suitable match for him, and he offered to send his friends Cooper and Richardson as ambassadors to Queen Elizabeth, asking for the hand of her sister, Princess Margaret. He even whipped up ambassadorial regalia of cardboard crowns and ties, and designed an impressive scroll made of torn paper, according to Richardson.

"But where would that marriage leave Jacqueline?" he mused. "She'd have to retire to a convent, then! How would you like that, Jacqueline?" "Non, *monseigneur*," she replied. "I would *not* like that at all." (When Princess Margaret heard the story years later, she was not amused and found the joke in poor taste.)

When Jacqueline fell ill with some serious female ailment, doctors recommended surgery. But she refused. Why? She told friends that, when Picasso was young, his sister had fallen gravely ill. He then made a vow to God that, were she saved, he'd never paint again. She died, so he went on painting. By the same token, Jacqueline felt she was now the designated sacrificial victim, who should give up her own life so the master could continue his work. Unfeelingly, during that period, Picasso painted portraits of her pain-ravaged face and complained, "Oh, women! They're always sick. . . ." It was only when she collapsed in excruciating pain that her doctor took matters in hand. The necessary surgery was performed, and Jacqueline, after a long convalescence, finally recovered. Picasso grumbled, but admitted grudgingly that, while she was away, he'd perhaps missed her.

During the Jacqueline years, the friendship between photographer Lucien Clergue, his wife Yolande and the Picassos flourished. The master, at his own insistence, served as godfather to the Clergues' daughter, Olivia. Their frequent visits are recorded on the images of Clergue's famous book, *Picasso, mon Ami*. However, one day Picasso came in holding a small bronze figure of a bull he had just cast. The animal was endowed with a huge organ the master fingered while looking beautiful Yolande straight in the eye. Finally, handing her the bronze as a gift, he held onto her hand suggestively. Jacqueline said nothing, but from that day on, Yolande never felt welcome in the house. She told me the story, the little bull resting on her table, as we sat in a room whose walls are lined with Picasso drawings.

Yet, Jacqueline's devotion never flagged, and she remained obedient to every whim of *monseigneur*. However, she wove an invisible fence around him, and while accepting visits from his son Paulo, she firmly excluded his other children, and fanned the fires of Picasso's anger when Françoise Gilot published her memoirs, depicting herself as an innocent victim, helpless in the power of a ruthless master. . . .

There are consequences to such an obsessive passion and to the obvious difficulties of living with such a man. Although she seemed to recover from her illness, Jacqueline soon began showing signs of nervous troubles, suffering bouts of depression that led her to find solace in drink. She rallied for a while, when Picasso purchased the château of Vauvenargues, where they spent months at a time in the sparsely furnished yet cluttered rooms, hallmark of all Picasso's residences. The portraits he painted there, some entitled *Jacqueline of Vauvenargues*, show some serenity, but the eyes remain haunted.

Picasso's fear of death was such that he'd always resisted making a will. "I'd die the next day," he used to say. He knew that, under French law, his estate would be divided equally between his widow and his only legitimate son, Paulo, after the state had subtracted its own, considerable cut. Nothing at all would accrue to Maya, Claude and Paloma. So, when he finally died in 1974—a belated victim of decades of chain-smoking—it was left to Jacqueline to deal with the problems of such a gigantic and complicated succession.

The inheritance tax must be paid. However, selling the large number of works that would meet its figure was out of the question: so many Picassos suddenly on the block could not fail to collapse the art market. So, instead, it was decided the state would appropriate a number of choice pieces, and these today form the nucleus of the collection shown in what became the Musée Picasso in Paris, incongruously housed in a 17th-century town home, the Hôtel Salé.

One of the most pathetic images I will ever retain is the photo by Lucien Clergue of Jacqueline, standing disconsolately in front of the atelier in Mougins, looking much older than her years, surrounded by the ghostly, white-wrapped forms of the sculptures ready for shipment.

By special permission, because burial on private property is not allowed in France, Picasso was interred in Vauvenargues on the castle grounds. But Jacqueline never accepted the fact of his death, bowing and greeting *monseigneur* each time she passed his great portrait in the hall. "Picasso is *not* dead," she'd tell visitors, interrupting conversations for a trip to the kitchen and her bottle, as drinking problems grew with isolation.

Nevertheless, she did her best to face the endless formalities, and even the lawsuits brought, inevitably, by the three dispossessed children. But she lived as a recluse, repeating she longed to be with *monseigneur* again, and more and more dependent on the support of alcohol and her faithful maid, Doris.

She made one more public appearance, recounts Richardson who accompanied her, and that was for the great retrospective exhibit at the Museum of Modern Art in New York. Coifed and dressed up, she seemed, nevertheless, only in tenuous control of herself. When at a party, some woman exclaimed loudly: "I *know* Madame Picasso. This one is an *imposter!*" she flinched, and when later, the same woman approached her, gushing endless apologies and declaring herself a painter of hands, who wished to paint Madame Picasso's "beautiful" hands, it was too much. Those broad and stubby-fingered hands, unflatteringly drawn by Picasso, had been a source of his mockery and a sensitive point for Jacqueline. She fled and was not seen again at public functions. Soon, she began to resemble "those terrifying late images Picasso had painted of her," according again to Richardson, who was one of her last visitors before she was confined to a clinic.

A year or so later, she seemed better, had the living room repainted, even went to a bullfight, the only one since Picasso's death. But these were ominous signs. . . . Every month, she visited Vauvenargues on the day of Picasso's passing. Ready to join him now, his legacy organized to the best of her abilities, she shot herself, aged 59, just before what would have been Picasso's 105th birthday.

She was buried in the same tomb, he underneath, she on top, in a dismal ceremony, which, for Richardson, evoked the Hindu ritual of *suttee*, in which a widow will throw herself upon her husband's funeral pyre. Meanwhile, French officials in attendance kept their sight narrowed on her daughter Catherine, now sole inheritor of that enormous treasure trove of Picasso's works.

"I never believed she *really* loved that old man," says Maria, sitting there in Vauvenargues. "I thought it was all an act she put on because he was so *rich*. But if she shot herself. . . ."

"How could you be in love with an *old* man?" asks Dana, a changed Dana, who no longer charcoals her eyes and doesn't seem to leave Kevin's side. But Kevin shakes his head, where hair is growing back in short curls: "Love is a matter of *chemistry*, not age. You can be in love, or be loved, at any age." But I can see many are not convinced: love and age just don't go together.

"Why do these love stories *all* have a sad ending?" someone wants to know. "Aren't there any with a happy one?"

But Carola is wise: "Only *fairy tales* end well, like they married and had many children. Only *these* stories are *not* fairy tales. They're for real, so people die at the end." A few wistful moments. . . . Not for long though:

"But dying is such a long time away," concludes someone, "like *almost* forever, right? So, like, there's plenty of time to be happy."

Experience Romance
Antiquing with the Great Lovers

This is the perfect trip for a Sunday, if you make a fairly early start.

Antiquing in Petrarch's Territory
Did you say Sunday? When everything is closed?

Not *everything!* This is the best day to go to L'Isle-sur-la-Sorgue, the city of antiques and antique dealers, very close to Fontaine-de-Vaucluse, the famed Petrarch stomping grounds. The shops are open only on weekends, and furthermore, Sunday is market day. Literally, hundreds of *bro-*

cante stalls line the picturesque quays of the lively Sorgue river. (Remember *brocante*, halfway between flea market and genuine antique fair?)

Antique dealers are everywhere. Many are grouped in large buildings where each occupies a space. My favorite is *Le Village des Antiquaires de la Gare* (2bis, Avenue de l'Égalité—opposite the railways station—www.villagegare.com).

To give you an idea, here is what I recently found there: A pair of Louix XV–style armchairs (probably 19th-century reproductions) in perfect condition, gilt and newly upholstered in just the right fabric. Another day, it was two low chairs, same style, also freshly upholstered. Either pair cost less than fabric and labor to recover would have. My latest find was a charming little cabinet to hold phone and phone books, with drawers for pens and pads. (All at Denis Bourguignolle. Tel: 04-90-03-22-94 or 06-03-24-22-68.)

Didier Luttenbacher sells world-class antiques, but is a trained clockmaker as well who restores clocks to perfection. (Atelier D.L. Tel: 04-90-22-27-94.)

Some of the dealers want you to bargain in reverse. It goes like this:

"How much would you give me for this chair?"

"Ah . . . two thousand francs?"

"Oh, no!"

"Three thousand?"

"Nnno. . . ."

"Three thousand five hundred?"

"It's yours."

All dealers have facilities for shipping and will arrange for delivery to your home address in the States.

The Brocante

I could not begin to list all I purchased there: Silverware, even a set with the lucky find of my own initial, and other pieces with the coat of arms of some noble family; dishes, antique linens, including a *bouti*, the rare, all-white Provençal quilt. (I saw a similar one in a Beverly Hills boutique for $5,000. Mine cost $300.)

Take your time, look around, bargain, leave and return. Finally, in victory, walk away with your prize.

A Perfect Place for Lunch

Le Jardin (right in the courtyard of *Le Village des Antiquaires du Quai de la Gare*). Reserve when you arrive, as it tends to get crowded by lunchtime. Mingle with dealers, sitting among flower beds under shade trees in summer, or indoors on those rare winter days when it is too cold for outdoors. (*Le Jardin* is not listed in guidebooks, and is little known outside the antique-dealer crowd. It is excellent.)

On the Trail of Petrarch

Now, having satisfied your appetite for antiques and tasty, Provençal food, you are ready to drive a few miles to Fontaine-de-Vaucluse. Look up at the ruins of Philippe de Cabassol's castle, looming on a peak just above the Sorgue. Conjure up images of lovely Laure strolling along this very path, under her lover's adoring gaze.

For a Romantic Dinner (and Night)

In Fontaine-de-Vaucluse, *Philip* (Tel: 04-90-20-31-81; Fax: 04-90-20-28-63) leans over the water, at the foot of the cascades. Lovely, good and inexpensive.

Hostellerie de la Bastide des 5 Lys (on N100, in Les Beaumettes, Gordes; Tel: 04-90-72-38-38; Fax: 04-90-72-29-90; www.bastide-des-5-lys.fr; *e-mail:* info@bastide-des-5-lys.fr). For something elegant as well as romantic, drive a few miles on N100, direction Apt, to this *bastide*, a former mill, in a delightful country setting. In summer, you are served under a single, immense tree; in winter in the refined dining room. The imaginative cuisine will delight you.

Should you not feel like driving tonight, the rooms are charming, and the cicadas' melody will lull you to sleep.

Simple and Sensuous
A Birthday Dinner *à deux*

Surprise him or her with this festive dinner.

Cocktail de crevettes
Filet mignon aux champignons (flambé?)
Pommes sautées au fenouil
Gâteau minute au chocolat

Shrimp Cocktail
½ cup small shrimp
½ cup finely chopped celery
6 large cooked shrimp

Cocktail sauce

1 lemon

In a bowl, mix small shrimp, celery and cocktail sauce. Squeeze in a little lemon juice. Serve in footed glasses with large shrimp over the sides. Decorate with a slice of lemon.

Filet Mignon with Mushrooms

2 beautiful slices of filet mignon

2 tablespoons butter

1 box brown mushrooms, quartered or halved

Cracked pepper and salt

¼ cup brandy (optional)

In dry pan, over very high heat, sprinkle cracked pepper and grill filets until brown. Turn over, continue grilling until done to your taste. Season with salt. Remove and keep warm.

In same pan, add butter and, over high heat, sauté mushrooms until browned and lightly crisp, not limp. Season with salt and pepper.

If you wish to flambé (and this adds a wonderful flavor): Quickly warm up brandy. Return meat to pan with mushrooms. Prepare match. Turn lights low and bring pan flaming to the table, or you could remove to a heated, heatproof dish if you prefer. Shake gently until flame dies out.

Potatoes Sautéed with Fennel (Sweet Anise) Root

2 or 3 Yukon Gold potatoes, peeled and sliced

½ fennel root, sliced

Olive oil

Salt and pepper

In a little olive oil, sauté potatoes and fennel until tender and lightly browned. Season with salt and pepper.

On Your Plate
Arrange filet with mushrooms on top and sides. Garnish with potatoes and fennel.

Instant Chocolate Cake
   3 tablespoons sugar / ¼ cup warm water
   ¼ cup rum
   I box (16 ounce) German semisweet chocolate
      squares
   I dozen ladyfingers
   ½ stick of butter, cut into pieces
   I small jar raspberry jelly
   Whipped cream bomb and maraschino cherries
      (optional)

Dissolve sugar in warm water. Add rum. Melt chocolate over hot water, stir in butter. Mash jelly with a fork.

   Dip four ladyfingers in rum mixture, but do not let them soak. Lay them side by side on a plate. Spread jelly over, then pour enough chocolate to barely cover. Repeat operation twice, until you've used all 12 ladyfingers. Pour rest of chocolate over cake to cover. Place in freezer for a few minutes to firm chocolate.

   Decorate with whipped cream, maraschino cherries, etc.

   With a spatula, remove to a *large* plate and place cake on paper doily. Write HAPPY BIRTHDAY around plate with whipped cream and lay a fresh flower on the side. Candle on top, of course.

To Drink

A glass of champagne as an aperitif, followed by an elegant red Burgundy. Or else, champagne all the way through.

This is the night for flowers, cards, gifts and candles.

The Rougher Shores
of Love

*T*he insistent ringing of the doorbell jostles me
awake. It is dark outside and raining hard. Morning, already? What time could it be? Six, says the night-
table clock. And this is. . . . Let's think. Sunday, of course!
No need to emerge from the night, we don't have to be up
yet. That sound must have been a dream. . . . Wayne, who
arrived late last night, exhausted after a long, practically
non-stop drive from Brussels, has been deep in sleep, lightly snoring, curled into a fetal position. Still, he must have
heard the noise, too, because he grunts, reaches out and
pulls the blankets over his head.

But the bell rings again, a prolonged 30-second thrill
that sends me jumping out of bed and running barefoot
across the room. I lean out the window to see a figure

standing down there in the slanting rain. My heart skips a beat: now what?

"*Qu'est-ce qu'il y a?*" I call out, "What's the matter?"

A face peers up from beneath the hood of a raincoat and the night bulb over the front door throws just enough light for me to recognize Frances, one of our students.

"Fran! Is something wrong?"

"Well, there might be," replies Frances. "As a matter of fact, I realized last night that we only have six weeks left to turn in our next year's schedule to our home campus. I worried most of the night that mine might not be ready for the deadline, so I came here to discuss it with you."

All right. I know Frances: superconscientious, always early, constantly worried about not doing things *just* right, having missed a *word* out of a lecture, or perhaps failed to *quite* understand an assignment. She is a tall, rangy girl, hair cut boyishly short, who walks with a long, determined stride. At rare times, her freckled face will light up with the sweetest, most innocent grin, revealing dazzling teeth. I know that after graduation she intends to join the army and obtain a commission as an officer. Her record shows she was an outstanding ROTC cadet on her home campus. Forsaking her budding military training for a full year abroad has been a wrenching decision, but she's been informed that good working knowledge of a foreign language would be a plus in the army and, therefore, encouraged to go.

"Don't worry, Frances. You know we have meetings scheduled just for that. I'll be there to advise you, and you can fill out all those forms for your next year's program.

There was no need, really, to get up *this* early! You have *plenty* of time. So why not just go back to bed now?"

Still looking up, wiping off rain that runs into her eyes:

"Oh, I didn't get up early at all! I *know* this is Sunday! Nobody wants to be up early today. Me? I am usually up *much* earlier than this! Every weekday morning, I run to get croissants for the other girls, and I like to be there when the bakery opens at 5:00 A.M."

I see. In the army, no doubt, Frances will be the one who, in full, impeccable uniform, marches into the barracks at 4:00 A.M. to wake up the sleeping, exhausted recruits. Yet, at the same time, I am touched by her thoughtfulness: Of course, she is by nature an early-morning person, but still. . . . Who else would, in cold and rain, stand waiting for that bakery to raise its metal curtain, just so others can find warm croissants on their doorstep? I bet that, while she wouldn't let her trainees sleep an extra second, she'd find little ways to make their life nicer.

"Just wait a sec, Fran. My husband is coming downstairs to let you in. Meanwhile, do step inside the doorway to keep out of this rain. I'll be down in no time, and we'll all have breakfast while you and I look at your campus catalog to see how the courses you wish to take would work toward your degree requirements."

A rumbling sound from under the blankets. Wayne is growling:

"I am going to *kill* that girl. I swear I am going to *murder* her this moment. Tell her to go away, get lost, don't come back." And a hand springs out, grabs a pillow, pushes it down over his head. Unimpressed, I throw the pillow away.

"What you *are* going to do is wake up. Wake up, get up and put on a robe. Then, you'll go downstairs, bring her in and start making breakfast."

As consciousness slowly seeps in, Wayne now refines his previously inchoate thought.

"I'll *strangle* her," he yells, "that's what I'll do. Strangle her, and then hit her over the head to make her shut up. Oh, and tell her I'll *shoot* her, too."

But I know, through long experience, that when Wayne is tired and rudely awakened, he'll display all the grace of a grizzly disturbed from hibernation. The less attention is paid, the sooner he'll calm down.

I shake him hard.

"Please, get up *now*. You know *I* do not want to appear *en déshabillé* before the students. On the other hand, *you'll* be fine in your new green robe. So, be a good guy, put it on and let Frances in. Then, start coffee, slip some bread in the toaster and set the table for breakfast. We have eggs, and there should be some slices of *jambon*, too. *Confiture* and butter are in the fridge's door. I'll be down as soon as I'm dressed and presentable."

Wayne is now viciously kicking the blankets away, roaring:

"Yes, I'll get up! Yes, I'll go downstairs and *then* I'll murder her! Kill her dead, that's what I'll do. That way, she won't wake me up again. Damn right, I'll get up, and she'll be sorry."

When he tells the story later to our friend Bill, this is how it comes out:

"I wanted to murder that girl who came to wake us up

at six on Sunday, but Yvone—you know her—said I should make her breakfast, instead."

"You murdered her anyway?" asks Bill hopefully.

"Well, stubborn as she is, I *never* give in to Yvone. I *always* hold out for a compromise, that's the only way to deal with her. So that's what I did. I compromised. . . . If I made breakfast, it was only because I *wanted* to."

Bill still looks smug: He, at least, has safely avoided marriage. No one to make him get up at six on a Sunday. He'll never have to hold out for a compromise, either.

Breakfast over, as Wayne refills coffee cups once more, Frances and I have pored over her campus catalog, decided on her courses for next year and filled out the forms. I signed them and they'll go out with tomorrow's mail. Finally, I can see her relaxing, and the smile that transforms her lights up her face:

"I should tell you something," she begins shyly. "It's not really official yet, but. . . ."

She hesitates. Finally reaches for a chain that disappears into her crewneck sweater, pulls out the pendant and shows it to me: it is a ring, a Naval Academy ring.

"Matt is an ensign in the navy, and we decided to get married after I graduate, but my parents think we should wait until I return to the States before making a formal announcement. He'll give me my real engagement ring then. This one is only a promise, but we're both very serious about it."

"This is wonderful news! Congratulations, Frances. I am happy *with* you and *for* you. Where is Matt now?"

"That's just it, you see. His ship is making port in

Marseille next Thursday. It will stay for a week, and Matt will have liberty. So, he thinks we can spend time together. But," she frowns, "that schedule to be filled out and mailed would have weighed on my mind and spoiled our reunion."

So, that is why the frantic rush to fill out the damn form! She had to be sure that nothing remained to be taken care of, so she could surrender, in total peace of mind, to her private moments. Wayne, standing by the coffee maker, is spellbound by her story and no longer thinking of murder. Instead:

"You and Matt will need a car while he is here, won't you?"

"Yes, I looked into renting one, but it is *so* expensive! I suppose we can do without."

"You can have one of ours, since I'm going to stay here for a while. It will be much better, if you are to show that man of yours some of Provence! Just tell me when you want it and it's yours."

Frances blushes, protests, refuses, but at Wayne's insistence finally accepts. "We'd thought of taking a train to the Riviera, but a car would make it so much nicer! How long a drive is it?"

So Wayne produces a map, guidebooks, brochures. . . . Frances is very happy, she beams, but cannot stay any longer. She still has much to do, extensive reading, a paper. . . . Neither is due until two weeks *after* the ship leaves, but we know Frances and, frankly, I admire her. As I open the door, I can see the rain has stopped and a wet sun peers between clouds. So she walks out into bright light, her long stride practically dancing. I watch her go: would that I'd be that well organized myself. . . .

As the morning light glistens on every drop that studs the leaves of the plane trees, I smile inwardly: Several hours of peace and quiet lie ahead to enjoy that feeling of being at home, enhanced by Wayne's rare presence. Only later this afternoon do I have an important appointment to keep.

Home is the *Villa du Rocher du Dragon*. Dragon Rock Villa? No rock in evidence, and no dragon, either, but out in what used to be a vast back garden, now sadly neglected, I discovered a fountain fed by a spring and surrounded by tall weeds. Water seeps out of the cracked *bassin*, tracing a lushly green path of watercress that snakes among the drying grass. On the margin sits a large stone, carved into the primitive semblance of a . . . a crocodile, maybe? The Villa was built around the turn of the century, over what must have been a much older residence, as evidenced by the imposing vaulted stone cellars. As for the "dragon," it obviously harks back to a distant past.

The street is named Avenue Henri-Pontier, in homage to Pontier, who erected the Villa on what was then his family farm. Most of the land around has since been sold, and today, a large apartment complex and a school have replaced fields and vineyards. Pontier served as curator of Aix's Municipal Museum, as an admired painter and sculptor. Today, though, he is remembered mostly for his feud with Cézanne, which led to an oath, unfortunately kept, that no Cézanne work would sully the walls of the museum. He never married, and at his death, cousins inherited the house. Their descendant, today's owner, is a single lady residing in town.

She is represented by the manager of her estate, Monsieur Adhémar, an elderly gentleman. He has been here a few times, driven by his daughter, herself a lady of no uncertain years. Together, we verified the inventory of furnishings, for the house has been left practically as it was at Pontier's death, the Program only adding those incongruous plastic chairs and turning two of the bedrooms into offices.

We ritually checked the French insurance policies against our California ones to ascertain that every eventuality is covered. I learned that the rent must be paid monthly—not quarterly as we would prefer—and by the director *en personne* to the owner herself. This is apparently her wish and a condition of the rental. Furthermore, payment *must* be made on a Sunday, the one closest to the first of the month, specifies M. Adhémar.

"You are favored," comments Liz. "M. Adhémar must have given a good report on you. Previous directors had to go, too, but were only allowed to slip the check through the lady's mail slot."

One cannot ignore Sunday in a French town. Although the population is, by and large, not religiously oriented, the bells of every church will ring mass and peal at different times from nine to noon. Businesses are closed with the exception of restaurants gearing up for *déjeuner*, bakeries and pastry shops. Traffic is light; passersby, dressed up, carry home the *déjeuner's tarte aux fruits* or *millefeuille* in its crisp white paper wrapping, delicately held by the loop of a gold string.

Wayne has gone back to sleep, *volets coffrés*, the wooden shutters held three-quarters closed by their iron hook, so that only a narrow bar of sunlight bisects the darkened room. No question of a *déjeuner* after that massive breakfast, and it is soon time for me to examine my small closet and try to decide on the outfit best suited to the image of official business that I must project this afternoon. I decide that my navy blazer and pleated plaid skirt will be best. The skirt is a bit short, but I see no need to turn downright dowdy. After all, I'll be meeting our landlady, who may be a very stylish person herself. My zipped leather portfolio to carry check and receipt, plus a copy of the lease, should we need to refer to it, will suffice; a regular briefcase would be overdoing it.

It is far easier to walk than to bother with a car, for parking is nearly impossible in the old town, where the lady lives in a building, I learned, that she owns as part of the estate. I find the address without any trouble and am soon standing in front of one of those 18th-century *hôtels particuliers*, town homes, actually small, towerless châteaus, with a carriage entrance courtyard, the main residence surrounded by what used to be service buildings. They abound in Aix.

Aristocrats built those when, after the death of Louis XIV, they were at last able to leave Versailles and return to their provinces. But many spurned their long-abandoned castles in favor of life in town and improved comfort.

Most of these town homes have been restored, turned into apartment buildings, sandblasted to their original pale stone. This one, however, is still untouched; two centuries of grime mar its façade and tarnish the grillwork of the balconies. Left of the sculpted portals, I ring the bell with the lady's name next to it—the only one, in fact—and push the massive door. It resists but finally creaks open, just enough to grudgingly admit me into a circular, imposing but dingy hall paved in black and white marble that could use some serious sweeping. I find the light switch. It is a *minuterie*, a timer, something the thrifty French install to avoid waste of electric current, so I have only a few minutes—perhaps seconds—of light to find the apartment on the second floor. Better hurry up the majestically curving staircase with its elaborate ironwork banister. Just as I reach the landing, the light goes off as, in sudden semi-darkness, I step carefully, feeling the floor with my toe—would there be, perchance, another step?—searching for the switch. But before I can find it, a door opens a crack and someone peers out. I ask:

"Is this the home of Madame? . . . I am with the International Program. . . ."

The door opens a bit wider. The first thing I notice, in spite of the gloom, is that the lady stands beneath a large, dark umbrella. She beckons me in and closes the door behind me.

"Come in quick, dear, quick. Here, stand with me under the umbrella. It is safer this way. You might want to bring your own next time, only be sure it is a large one."

She is such a small person that my five-foot-three towers over her, as we huddle under the umbrella's protection. Together we walk the length of her hall, and I become aware of a fringed shawl, droopy ruffles, flouncy skirts hanging one over the other and gloves. Yes, white crocheted gloves, mittens rather, with cut off fingertips, hold the handle. As we enter a vast drawing room, I can see her hair is a bird's nest of gray frizz with a faded auburn hairpiece sitting on top, the whole thing held in place with a dozen combs and barrettes, while a nosegay of limp artificial flowers leans coquettishly over one ear.

As she faces the window, and in spite of the dim light filtered through thick curtains, I can see her face, wrinkled as a *pomme reinette*, those overwintering apples that become all wrinkled and sweeter after the frosts. But her expression remains youthful, and I can conjure up the features of the pretty girl of her early years, with large gray, guileless eyes, now in their cradle of fine lines, a rounded chin and what must have been a mass of softly curled hair. She smells— the whole place, in fact, smells—of dusty lavender that would also have gone musty.

Now she leads me to a sofa piled with odds and ends— empty paper sacks, raveled skeins of yarn, torn pillows, old letters, a ragged doll—pushes the stuff away and seats me next to her, still holding the umbrella over both our heads.

"I am glad you came over, my dear. You see, we don't entertain as much as we did when mama and papa were alive."

I have no trouble believing that she does *not* entertain a lot. . . . The umbrella alone would make it difficult. I estimate her age about 90, so I figure her parents must have been dead for *some* time. No need to inquire, for she continues:

"They died . . . oh, during the war. And I will always blame myself. Papa repeated I was such a bad girl, I'd be the death of them."

During the war? World War II, no doubt. Well, that was almost half a century ago. Enough time to regroup, since, you'd think. The lady rushes on:

"But I feel it is my duty to my parents to meet with those foreigners like you who occupy their house. That is, when they speak enough French that I can understand, and M. Adhémar told me you did. However, one has to be careful in this place, and I wish the dear man had told you of the . . . the danger here."

No doubt M. Adhémar was derelict there. I wish, too, that he'd told me a little more about this situation, like that umbrella business, for instance. So I venture:

"Please tell me, madame. . . ."

But she interrupts:

"Oh no, not *madame!* It is *mademoiselle.* I was never married, good heavens! Papa wouldn't have allowed it! *He was too young. . . .*"

Her *father* was too young? Is my head beginning to spin? Let's get back on track, if we can:

"Could you tell me, mademoiselle, what the problem is? Leaks in the ceiling? Or plaster falling?"

She laughs, a short little laugh like the tinkle of a cracked china cup:

"If only! *This* is a great deal more bothersome than a

few drips or a little plaster in one's hair! It is that *man*, you see. . . ."

"Which man?"

"That wicked man who lives upstairs. He wants to marry me, but he is much too young, and poor, too. That's the problem. So he sends rays."

I am now completely at sea. *Rays?*

"How does he send those rays?"

"With his eyes, of course, with his eyes, those big brown eyes. He stares at the floor and sends rays that traverse my ceiling."

"And how do you *know* he sends those rays?" The lady laughs the same cracked little tinkle:

"How do I know? It is not hard, believe me! Those rays simply pop the stays in my corset, that's what they do. Most bothersome, I must say. They would pop yours, too, if you strayed from beneath the umbrella."

Now, I think I get the idea. The dear soul is a little mad, harmless, no doubt. I try to reassure her on my behalf: personally, I have nothing to fear since I do not wear a corset with stays—or any other kind for that matter.

"Oh, you think that, but you are wrong! Then, he'll untie your shoelaces or even," she shudders, leans to whisper in my ear, "do *things* to your underwear. A friend of mine used to visit occasionally, but every time the lace of her drawers would rip and the elastic band would snap while she was here. So you can understand why she stopped coming. . . . Please, hold the umbrella over our heads while I get the tea things."

Trying to match my step to her mouse-like shuffle, we walk to the kitchen where a tray is waiting.

"I thought you were due last month. I mean last Sunday, wasn't it? So I prepared it then. But M. Adhémar reminded me it was today."

Is it a mouse dropping, that dark speck on the yellowed lace tray liner? Better not wonder. The biscuits on a plate and the few candied fruit are not getting any fresher, and it seems to me at this point that the sooner they're eaten, the better. Still under the umbrella, and each holding one side of the tray—she's obviously forgotten about the tea—we make our way back to the sofa.

After we settle down again, I still holding the umbrella with one hand and a broken piece of stale biscuit in the other, she leans over confidentially:

"You see, papa says I could *never* marry him. Too young for me. Ladies do not marry younger men, now, do they? A foreigner, yet! Yes, from Spain. And poor. Poor as a church mouse, mama says. So he came to live upstairs and he persecutes me now. He does not understand I can *never*, never, return to the barn. . . ."

Let's forget about that barn for a moment. But her parents. . . . Let's see . . . they've been dead for nearly half a century, so they couldn't very well have forbidden anything for *quite* some time. She is obviously mixing periods and people, too. How *young* can that man be? Clearly, she is confusing the *now* with something that happened a long time ago. Feeling that I shouldn't linger, I unzip my folio and draw out the prepared check. When I hand it to her, she looks puzzled, as though totally unaware of the purpose of my visit and drops it in the general direction of the plate that holds the broken biscuits and rock-hard candied cherries and apricots. No point asking for a receipt. I'll settle that later with M. Adhémar.

She returns to the matter of her concern.

"You *must* marry a man who's *at least* five years older than yourself, didn't you know? Otherwise, people will think badly of you and your parents, and shaming her parents is the worst a girl can do. It will kill them, you see."

News to me. This isn't a rule in California, where anything goes. In fact, women now age more slowly than men, as evidenced by the staggering number of widows one sees around, so marrying an older man might not be such a good idea. But this is apparently what was drummed into her by her parents, whom she keeps referring to.

"You should have a look at him," she whispers. "So handsome! Dark and proud-looking. Haughty, even. A Spaniard, of course, he would be. But he only works in our vineyards, a hired hand, and nothing more. . . . And then, he is so *young!* Papa says he is 10 years younger than me. And *that* is shameful. . . ."

Then, eyes shining, she cups her hand near her lips and leans over so her words will not stray:

"'We are lovers, he tells me. Yes, that's what it is called. Like married,'" he says.

A picture is beginning to emerge out of the fog: None of this is happening *now*, of course, she is speaking of events from a distant past, mixing them all up. But I get the idea.

"Do you see that man who lives upstairs?"

"Oh no, papa and mama would never allow it! They sent me away when they found out we meet at night. . . ."

"You *meet* at night? You mean, you *met*."

She clasps her hands in dismay or delight, impossible to tell; both, perhaps, and shakes her head.

"Oh yes, we do. I am such a bad girl, if you must know! I climb out my bedroom window and join him in the barn where he sleeps. I know I shouldn't but it is so, so very . . . nice! He kisses me and he'll undo my stays and touch me where it feels so *good*. . . . So *good* . . . better even than singing in church. When he does what married people do, I can't even *think* of mama and papa anymore. . . . It is like heaven. He says we should marry soon, because. . . ." She shudders violently. "But I can't see him again, *ever*. Mama would cry terribly, like she did that night and she would die. All through my fault."

She clasps the fingers of both hands over her mouth. . . . After a moment she shakes her head, takes my hand.

"It was that night. Oh, that *night!*"

"What happened that night?" In spite of my efforts to remain grounded in reality, I am getting involved in the drama of this romance.

"My dear, I was never so frightened in my life! All of a sudden, the barn door crashes open, there's a light, my father rushes in, holding a lantern high and brandishing a pitchfork. He threatened André—his name was Andrès but we called him André—right there and then. He'd run him through, he shouted, unless André ran away and never came back."

"So, did André leave?"

"Oh, he was brave and in spite of the pitchfork at his throat, he did try to protect me. But when he said he wanted to marry me, my father became even more enraged and yelled he'd kill me, too. All André could do was run."

"Now, you were left alone with your father. Was he as angry with you as he'd been with André? And how old were you anyway when that happened?"

Too many questions disorient her.

"How old? Oh . . . older than now, I think. . . . Yes, he was just as angry. He dragged me to the house all undone. My mama was sitting in the parlor, sobbing. I tried to throw myself at her feet, the way I always did when she had to forgive me for something bad I did, like when I broke a plate. . . . But she pushed me away with her foot and sent me sprawling. 'You are a bad, a wicked, a sinful girl!' she shouted. 'The devil himself possesses you. We are going to send you away, far away. . . . We can't keep you here, you have disgraced us!'"

"So you went away?" I ask breathlessly, caught up in the story. But she suddenly looks vague. Is the memory getting dimmer? Or rather too painfully clear that she cannot bear to remember?

"More tea?" she asks, although there is no teapot in evidence, no cups, either, only saucers and, unaccountably, two large bone-handled knives. Only I cannot abandon the drama, which is getting clearer by the moment.

"But you came back?" I insist.

"Oh yes, my dear, I did, but not for a long, long time. . . . You know, I couldn't be *seen* for months, and after . . . *after* I had to look . . . well, right. But yes, I did, I came back after papa had died. Then, mama made me stay in my room, and she locked the door. She'd let me out on Saturdays to take me to confession, and then to Mass on Sundays so I could ask for God's forgiveness. Sometimes, relatives came to visit after the services, and there were times I was allowed in the parlor for a while. But I must never speak to them, only nod, like this." And she nods a few times, lips pressed together. "Sunday is the day to ask for forgiveness and the day for visits, too."

I am indignant at the treatment that this poor girl—woman—had to endure and try to reassure her:

"But you don't have anything to be forgiven for! Your parents were cruel! They treated you in an unfair, despicable way. And why? In the name of principles that have no meaning at all!"

She isn't listening. Her eyes, raised, now stare at the ceiling. She gestures, hush, finger to her lips, points up, whispering:

"He came back, don't you know? That's him upstairs! My papa would be so angry if he knew. . . . You must promise not to tell him." Then: "Come, I'll show you pictures. Follow me and keep the umbrella straight."

I have understood what must have happened, and now she scurries about the room, like a Beatrix Potter character, searching in drawers, hunting for photos. She cannot see well enough and hands me cracked snapshots of people clearly dead a long time that I examine with feigned interest. But wait, here is one of her, a studio portrait, in which she leans against a prop balustrade, unsmiling as they posed you then, and looking soulfully over her shoulder.

Yes, she *was* a pretty young woman, I guessed right when I first saw her: combs could barely control the mass of her curly hair.

Next, she insists I have some of that candied fruit.

"It comes from Apt," she confides. "The factory belongs to some relatives and they always send me a box for my birthday." But candied fruit dries up fast and these cherries and apricots must have been resting on their little pleated cups for *months*.

"When is your birthday, mademoiselle?"

She frowns, tries to remember, but finally waves airily:

"Oh, most years, I think. No, no, I mean, most months."

She must have made a tremendous effort for this visit because I see her looking suddenly absent, eyes unfocused. Too much remembering has exhausted her. So, I plead a multitude of tasks waiting for me and take leave, thanking her for her hospitality. But she grabs my hand, not the one holding the umbrella, which I am trying to hand over to her, and asks, suddenly earnest:

"You will come back on Sunday, next year, won't you?"

I know she means next month, but time has lost meaning for her.

"Of course, mademoiselle, I'll come back." And I take her small, bony hand with tissue-paper skin in mine, like a fragile, precious object. . . .

Back in the sunlight, I shake my head to clear the confused events I just heard and try to rearrange them into some sort of sequence. A few deep breaths expel the last of the musty, dusty lavender perfume. Where is reality?

Here, in this busy street with people strolling, sitting on café terraces while music plays somewhere? Or behind those closed windows I can see as I look up, where a life—no, an existence—is running its aimless course?

"So, you met the lady?" asks Liz when she arrives next morning. "Quite an experience, isn't it? I didn't warn you, because I thought you should get the full impact."

"I haven't, in fact, quite recovered yet. I think I understand what happened, but I'd like to know the rest of the story. Have you heard it?"

"M. Adhémar told me, a few years ago. Her parents bought the Villa from the Pontier's heirs. The land around it was still farmed; there were barns and vineyards where you see those apartment buildings. This is where she grew up. As a matter of fact, she tried to paint like Pontier did; there are a few of her daubs in the attic. But the poor thing had no talent. She was kept close by her mother, who seemed to have been some sort of a termagant, and I understand her father was a tyrant, who could not bear the idea of any man ever touching his pure, his chaste daughter. He had no idea of what would happen when he hired a refugee from the Spanish Civil War, a handsome young man, to work in the vineyards. The boy must have been in his twenties and the girl about thirty, then. They had an affair, and the father found out. . . ."

"Was she pregnant?"

"I don't know. She does say those things. . . . M. Adhémar admits he heard rumors at the time, but no one was ever certain. In any case, she was sent away, to live with relatives in Brittany and didn't return until well after her father had died."

"Would it be too melodramatic to imagine she had lost her mind when she returned?"

"It certainly would be, and yet that's probably what happened. No one saw much of her after she came back. Her mother told everyone that 'health' problems kept her close to home. M. Adhémar remembers seeing her in church a few times from a distance, but nobody could approach her. When her mother passed away, he was appointed manager of the estate, and he found her the way you saw her today, with glimpses of memory, but absolutely no idea of time."

"And nobody ever heard of the handsome Spaniard?"

"On the contrary! If he went away at all, he didn't go very far. . . . In any case, he soon bought a small vineyard, then a larger one and became, in time, an important wine grower of the area. You've probably seen his label, the best restaurants serve his *Côtes-de-Provence*."

"And he married and forgot her, is that it?"

"He did marry, but he has been a widower for a long time now, and no, he did not forget her. He visits M. Adhémar now and then to inquire about the lady and bring gifts for M. Adhémar to deliver: a lace shawl, such as she used to wear when they were young, tortoise-shell combs, gloves, posies of artificial flowers. . . . All the things he remembers her liking."

"Did they see each other again?"

"He *did* try to visit her once, after her mother had died. It turned out a disaster. Although she didn't seem to recognize him, she went into a fit of terror, sobbing that her father would kill the man and that her mother would die if she knew. She was trembling uncontrollably, so that a doctor had to be called to sedate her. As you can imagine, the visit wasn't repeated."

"I take it that's not him living upstairs."

"*Nobody* lives upstairs! She's the only occupant of that *hôtel particulier*, which, by the way, is worth a great deal, or will be, after necessary renovations are done. The lady's heirs, distant cousins, will probably take care of those after her death."

I cannot take my mind off the handsome young Spaniard, who is not so young anymore:

"He must be an old man, too, by now?"

"Yes, he is, probably 80 or so. But still handsome, standing erect, with a mane of white hair. I know him by sight, he is *quite* a personality around town, mayor of his village. I even think he was a deputy to the National Assembly in Paris at one time. . . . Come to think of it, isn't it a shame her parents made it all turn out that way? He'd have made an excellent match for her. Except, of course, for that age difference. Nothing could ever change *that*." Liz shakes her head sadly. "*Nothing*. It is a stigma to be an older woman, you know."

Frankly, I do *not* know. I suppose I should, since I am several years older than my husband, but I have never felt inferior or the need to apologize for the age difference. However, I reside in the States, in California yet, where one lives and lets live, and I send grateful thoughts to that much maligned American culture where personal happiness takes precedence over prejudice. Liz, meanwhile, is blowing her nose on a Kleenex, pretending to be absorbed in the budget sheets spread out on her desk.

I pull up a chair next to hers.

"Tell me something, Liz. Am I guessing wrong, or are you thinking of Stan?"

She looks up, tears welling in her blue eyes:

"How did you guess? He has been so discreet! Do you think anybody else has noticed, too?"

"No, it's just me, and only because you and I are such good friends and I care about you. I learned enough about your home life and how unhappy it is to understand *anything*. Tell me more if you feel like it."

"There isn't much to tell, except that I have never been so happy and felt so tortured at the same time as I am now. Never thought myself capable of such intensity of feeling after years so . . . so emotionally barren. . . . You see, my husband considers that his role is to be a provider for the family, *period*. He is rarely home, barely speaks when he is, except to complain and criticize. We have no life, sexual or otherwise, as he shows no interest in me, only to ridicule me whenever he can. For years, there was only this void. . . . Affairs? He makes no secret of having affairs! 'My business, not yours,' he'll say. 'What I do doesn't concern *you*.'"

"And you had resigned yourself to that! Why? On account of the children? But they're grown now!"

"Yes, I was resigned, but then I took this job and it brightened my life! Meeting all these great kids, organizing activities, contact with the university people and with America, all that is exciting and right up the line of what I like to do. I never thought. . . . But Stan came along, and he says he is in love with me. . . ." She adds defensively: "And he isn't all *that* young! Thirty-four to my forty-three." And, I comment silently, a handsome forty-three. She is like a full-blown rose and normally exudes irrepressible energy and optimism.

She continues, holding the Kleenex under her nose:

"We liked each other right away, from that first day in Paris. He told me how lonely he's been since his wife died and how he's sought that job in West Africa to try and find new horizons. It's a coincidence I've lived there myself and loved it when my husband's job took him there some years ago. . . . Now, Stan wants me to leave with him, get a divorce so we can get married as soon as possible, and. . . ." She covers her eyes.

I lean over and put my arm around her shoulders.

Stan often waits for her after our office closes, and I have watched them walk together: both tall, she blonde, and he looking older than his years, with an already receding hairline. Hard to tell about any age difference, and anyway, who cares? Not him, certainly. But for her, it's a different matter where age isn't everything. It would mean abandoning home, children, husband. The children are grown, well on their way to complete independence, but still. . . . One is a mother for life, *n'est-ce pas?* Doesn't motherhood mean end of life as a *woman?* Burdened by her education and all the *préjugés* of a town where she's spent a good part of her existence, the decision to throw it all away, taking a chance on love and a new man—a foreigner! A younger guy!—would be superhuman. Hasn't she any shame? the gossips would cry.

Strangely enough I found that France, with all its free ways where love is concerned, flirtation a form of socializing and men feeling they have no excuse not to sleep with their wives' friends, France can be as straightlaced as any small American town. But not quite in the same way: Blame here accrues to the *woman* who errs, while her male partner—and one certainly does *not* err alone—will be admiringly described as a *chaud lapin.* I remember the term used in reference to cadaverous-looking President Mitterand when it was revealed in the press that his mistress *and* an illegitimate daughter both lived near the Élysée Palace, and again, when the two ladies surrounded the very legitimate Madame Mitterand in his funeral cortege. . . . The French register delight when their president, who, after all, *represents* his constituents, does them honor as a male. So, they totally failed to understand the Clinton-Lewinsky brouhaha, and the more they learned about it, the greater their sympathy grew for that virile American president, who could prove himself in the eyes of the world—thus honoring his constituency—such a *chaud lapin.* They even almost forgave him for doubling import taxes on foie-gras and Roquefort.

"Stan says he wants to make a new life with me, that he delights in me, in my presence, my laughter. . . . He tells me that I am beautiful," she adds, almost shyly, drying her eyes and smiling through the last tears. "I've never heard anything like this before . . . and I believe him. He is solid, sincere, he opens a window on love and happiness for me. . . ." She pauses, shakes her head:

"Only, you see, it can never be. I told him, over and over again, but he will not give up. So it's all very hard. I know, without a doubt, where my duty lies: right here, with the man I married for better or worse, even if it turned out a lot worser than I bargained for."

Worser? By now we are both laughing, a bitter laugh. She is accepting her fate as a woman and I understand. Would I do the same under equal circumstances? Probably. . . . But wait:

"Stan says I have until the end of the Program, in June, to make up my mind and that he'll never stop trying to talk me into leaving with him."

I tighten my arm around her shoulders, but remain silent.

"And I must confess I love hearing his arguments. We sit on a bench, in a secluded corner of the Parc Jourdan and talk for hours. *He* talks mostly, telling me what life would be like for the two of us, and how he would love to see me first thing in the morning, smiling at him. All this is so new to me it feels like . . . like champagne for the soul. It lulls me, it intoxicates me, but then I shake myself awake: no, I have to. . . ."

A knock on the door interrupts the flood of confessions. Liz throws the wet Kleenex into her wastebasket and summons a smile for the student who walks in. I look up, too, supposedly from the budget spreadsheets. It is Mona.

Mona hasn't been around much, and neither has Larry. They came from the same campus, looking like a couple, always together and not much involved in group activities. She is a slender girl, with sensitive, lovely features, only right now her eyes are reddened with tears and reflect tragedy.

"Madame Lenard, could I speak to you privately?"

"Of course. Come into my office."

As I close the door, Mona bursts into tears, her entire body convulsed with sobs. It takes a long time before she can calm down and tell me:

"It's Larry."

"What happened to Larry?"

"He left me and moved in with some French students. That's what he said, but I think it's a girl. . . ."

As if speaking the words aloud renewed the horror of the facts, she buries her face in her hands again, trying to stifle the sobs.

"For some time now, he's been telling me he needed space, we should both see other people. But I don't want anybody else, just him. . . . I never loved anyone before and never will . . . I told him!"

Sure Mona, you told him over and over again that he *had* to be with you, and he felt you were cutting off his air; you had him cornered into a room that you locked on the two of you. And he was . . . what? Scared? Bored? Curious to see what else was around the corner? Only, I am not going to tell you any of that because it would make it all worse. You didn't come to me for reasoning, scolding or advice to the lovelorn. You just needed to cry this out.

So, I sit next to her on the little bench along the wall, take her hand in mine and tell her softly, "I am so, so sorry, Mona, so sorry. . . ." After a moment, she puts her arm on my shoulder, and hesitantly, shyly, kisses my cheek. I hug her tight in return.

"I wish my mom was here," she whispers.

The Mediterranean coast is rocky, and when storms rise, waves do not come to die gently upon sandy shores. Instead, they hurl themselves against cliffs and crags where they explode in thunder, throwing great spumes of foam into the air. Loves that flourish in Provence are not safe, either, from coming to break upon these . . . these rougher shores.

Experience Romance
Seeking Smoother Shores

The Mediterranean shores may be rocky. Still, they will reveal smooth beaches and sensuous adventures for you.

Explore the Secret Charms of Marseille
Sure, it is a bad girl of a city, home to the French Connection drug traffic, a rowdy, bustling port! So forget about the town and explore Marseille-by-the-sea.

A Mysterious Message
The centrally located Vieux Port, the original 5th-century B.C. Greek harbor, is now a marina and mooring for the tour boats to the islands that dot the coast.

Board one to the Château d'If. The Château d'If is actually a small, fortified island where the Man in the Iron Mask was imprisoned. Forget for the moment controversies on the subject, and allow yourself to shudder as you visit his stark cell. Peer through the window from which he managed to hurl a pewter plate on which he had scratched a message.

The fisherman who found the plate brought it to the governor of the fortress, who asked: "Can you read?" "No, sir, I cannot," replied the fisherman. "Well, my good man, this has just saved your life," declared the governor.

Back on land, still pondering the ominous message, you might, nevertheless, have recovered enough to think of a bite to eat.

An Oyster Feast for Lunch

The catch of the day has arrived, and in front of the little cafés that line the Vieux Port, vendors are shucking oysters to serve on a bed of fresh seaweed. Not only oysters, but *violets*, urchins, mussels, a bounty of *coquillages*, shellfish, fragrant from the sea. A glass of flinty Bandol or Cassis white is the perfect complement, to savor as you gaze upon the swaying masts of yachts at anchor.

Sun on the Uninhibited Prado Beach

The Marseillais like to keep secret the fact their city possesses one of the great beaches of the Mediterranean. The *Plage du Prado*, a little beyond the Vieux Port is vast, not too crowded, and sandy, unlike the gravelly ones of the Riviera.

Swim there, and sun with or without a top, as you prefer. No need to be shy, as you'll see plenty of local beauties in the process of acquiring a seamless tan and quite uninhibited about it.

A Breathtaking Drive Along the Corniche

From the beach, continue along the drive, the *Corniche*, which will rise to offer you stunning views of the coast, the sea and the flock of islands lying offshore. Drive on to where the road ends, at a quaint little harbor, home to a dozen fishing boats. Then, turn around and experience a different aspect, as you are now against the light. Are you getting a bit of an appetite?

What Is Your Idea of a Romantic Dinner Tonight in Marseille?
Are you thinking classic Marseille *à la Pagnol* or elegant cuisine with a view?

Chez Fonfon (140, Vallon des Auffes; Tel: 04-91-52-14-38; Fax: 04-91-59-27-32) is just the place if you feel like stepping right into a Pagnol movie and the best for a classic bouillabaisse. Although right in Marseille, it seems remote, sitting in the Vallon des Auffes, a tiny harbor on an inlet, straddled by the pylons supporting the Corniche road.

Le Petit Nice (on Anse de Maldormé, exit the Corniche at #160; Tel: 04-91-59-25-92; Fax: 94-91-59-28-08; www. petitnice-passedat.com; e-mail: hotel@petitnice-passedat). Most elegant and spectacular place in Marseille, on top of a small peninsula jutting into the sea, a location to die for. The cuisine rates two Michelin stars, a rarefied company. The selection of Cassis wines is unequalled.

Should you not feel like driving tonight, or cannot bear to abandon that view, the rooms are wonderful, with the song of the sea at your feet.

Simple and Sensuous
A Mediterranean Dinner *à deux*

A superb, easy dinner, full of Mediterranean flavors.

Melon au Xérès
Homard grillé
Pilaf de riz au curry
Tarte aux pêches

Melon with Sherry or Sweet Wine
   2 small cantaloupes
   2 small glasses of sherry or other sweet wine
   4 strawberries and a sprig of mint

Cut off top of melon (in a wavy line, or else a sawtooth pattern). With a spoon, scoop out seeds. Pour sherry into melon, adding two sliced strawberries. Replace top of melon. Place in freezer for 10 minutes to chill. At serving time, decorate top with a strawberry and a sprig of mint on a toothpick.

Broiled Lobster Tails
   2 lobster tails
   Salt, white pepper, butter

With cleaver, split lobster tails lengthwise. Season with salt, pepper, generous pat of butter. Broil until top is lightly browned, finish in oven until cooked through, but no longer.

Curried Rice Pilaf
    1 box prepared rice pilaf
    1 tablespoon curry
    2 tablespoons raisins

Cook pilaf following instructions on box. When cooked, stir in raisins and curry and serve after 5 minutes.

Peach Tart
    1 ready-to-bake pie crust, frozen
    3 or 4 ripe peaches, or 1 16-ounce can peaches, drained
    2 eggs
    ½ cup sugar, plus 3 tablespoons
    ½ pint sour cream

Prick bottom of crust so it doesn't bubble and bake at 350°F until very lightly browned. Arrange peach halves (peeled if fresh) on crust.

In a small bowl, beat eggs with ½ cup sugar and sour cream. Pour over peaches. Bake at 350°F until set.

Take out of oven. Sprinkle with 3 tablespoons sugar and slide under broiler until sugar bubbles and browns.

To Drink
A flinty, Bandol white would be great. But a *white* Châteauneuf-du-Pape? Now, that would be super.

Do you have seashells? Glass fish?
Something that evokes the Mediterranean regions
that you can arrange creatively as a centerpiece?

Aphrodisiacs
for the Soul

"The Mas Tourteron is serving *ortolans* tonight! Odile called to let me know because they weren't able to get that many and prefer to reserve them for clients who can really appreciate them," says Bill, excitedly, on the phone.

Our level of ignorance is so dismal that we have to be told just what kind of a treat that is. Even my dictionary doesn't help, as it simply offers "ortolans" as a translation for *ortolans*. But Bill, as usual, is full of information.

Ortolans are birds, songbirds, tiny ones and they are caught—cruelly, to be sure—by spreading glue onto the branches of bushes where they alight to rest in the course of their yearly migration. Their flesh is incredibly fragrant and tasty on account of certain berries they feed on this time of year. Once plentiful, they've become a rarity today, so rare in fact that one could not possibly miss such a seldom-available delicacy. Very few lucky gourmets, specifies Bill, will *ever* be offered a chance to *déguster* a dish of roasted ortolans. And *déguster* is one of those French words that elude translation, only because the relationship to food is entirely different in France. "To sample," "to savor," "to taste," "to enjoy" would all be needed to give even a faint idea of the intensity of a true *dégustation*.

Informed of the event, Wayne's first reaction is one of sorrow for the little birds, treacherously trapped as they trustingly settle for the night—sorrow that escalates into horror when I unwisely describe to him, as euphemistically as possible, the kind of death they met, helpless on those sticky twigs. "Outside of being cruel, don't the French realize that their greed thins out the number of reproductive birds, leading therefore to almost certain extinction of the species? Already, you tell me, those birds are getting rare. . . ." After a pause: "*You* go with Bill, if you must, but count me out. I'll stay here and cook myself some pasta."

He wants pasta every time he thinks of the inevitable death that preceded his chicken, veal or beef dinner. Hard to feel sorry for spaghetti, even when I suggest they were harvested in some Italian field, ruthlessly mown down in the bloom of their vigorous youth.

Now, he's revved up: "I might even fax the Sierra Club. I'll bet they'd have a thing or two to say on the subject! Educate the French a little."

Now, the French are notoriously hard to educate, I've already found. They feel strongly that they *already* know everything that's *worth* knowing and do not take well to suggestions from foreigners that they should modify their culture in slavish imitation of others.

"You want to stay? That's fine with me. I hope you realize that, according to Bill, ortolans are so rare, you're lucky to be offered a chance to taste them once in a lifetime. Furthermore, listen, you cannot help these poor little birds *now*; they're *already* dead! If you do not eat them, somebody else will, and you'll never, *ever* know what you missed. I'm sure you'll regret it if you stay home tonight. As for the Sierra Club, I fear the French would laugh at any injunction coming from them."

I can see him weakening, and he weakens to such a point that he is, in fact, the first one in the car tonight. Anyway, ortolans or not, he loves the Mas Tourteron, a discovery of Bill, where we eat as often as we can afford it, so that, during the drive, he only grumbles occasionally about the thoughtlessness and cruelty of man.

The Mas is a small stone farmhouse, isolated in the country not far from Gordes, in the direction of a village called Les Imberts. Not long ago, it was taken over and restored by a youngish couple, he the chef, she in charge of the dining room. A romantic story is even attached to them: Odile used to be married to the prosperous owner of a large hotel restaurant in Avignon when she fell in love with Gérard, the young chef hired by her husband. She left everything for him—French divorce laws hardly favor the woman—and together they started this new restaurant on a shoestring.

After we leave the main road, a dirt track leads to the Mas. We park at the edge of a field, walk across the small courtyard planted with herbs and lavender, knock on the door, for it is locked, and Odile opens it a crack to ascertain we indeed have reservations before she welcomes us in.

Only five tables occupy the room, and at practically each visit, we notice that something new has been added: antique embroidered tablecloths one day, better silver settings, or translucent porcelain demitasses another, purchased, no doubt, from the many dealers in nearby L'Isle-sur-la-Sorgue. We always rejoice at these signs of increased prosperity.

No tourists frequent the Mas Tourteron. How would they ever discover it? Only locals, and of the upper ranks, for the Mas isn't cheap. So, there are surprised glances, often followed by friendly smiles, when diners hear us speak English. I learned right away, in Provence, that if there is hostility—and I personally haven't encountered any—it is our government's actions the French dislike, but have nothing at all against us as individuals. And since, as I often tell my French friends, we are not, ourselves, necessarily crazy about what goes on in Washington, there is more to agree about than disagree.

The menu is succinct, but refined, and offers only a few appetizers, entrees and desserts. (Don't forget, when reading a French menu, that *entrée* means "appetizer," the "entrance" into a meal, while the main dish is the *plat principal*.) All, however, are exquisite. I am partial to the *parfait de foies de volailles*, smooth as satin and flavored with Armagnac, which loses a lot when called as "chicken liver pâté."

(Names of French dishes often do not survive translation.) Once, Wayne enjoyed so much the orange and madeira sauce of his *magret de canard*, sliced duck breast, that I had to stop him just in time, as he was going to pick up his plate to lick it. Frustrated, he decided to appeal to a higher authority, stood up, walked over to the next table, occupied by a group that we'd been told included the mayor of Gordes, introduced himself and asked, in his own personal version of the French language, whether they'd be offended if he were to lick his plate.

The mayor beamed, stood up, shook Wayne's hand and assured him that, in fact, he'd been wishing to lick his *own* plate, but was deterred by the presence of those elegant Americans, pointed to by his wife. So the two men shook hands again, licked their plates in unison and, afterwards, both groups joined for coffee and cognac. I took advantage of the situation to explain we were in France with a group of American students, eager for cultural exchange, and this resulted in several invitations for the kids.

Americans who feel that the French are difficult to approach should see how Wayne goes about it, totally unconcerned about his—shall we say—imperfect command of French, intent only in establishing friendly contact.

Tonight, all other tables are occupied as we enter—no stragglers on ortolans night! Odile is serving the Mas house apéritif of champagne with pear brandy *and* pear liqueur all around, with little plates of hot *feuilletés* and green faience jars of almond stuffed olives. After a pause, she brings out *amuse-gueule*, palate teasers. Today, five tiny porcelain cups on a saucer offer: a spoonful of peppery melon soup with muscat wine, one garlicky escargot, one smoked oyster, a dollop of *poutargue*, the Provençal caviar made with mullet eggs and a taste of smoked salmon pâté. These are *not* part of the ordered menu; rather, they come as the chef's fun gift, a warm-up for the meal itself. The appetizers that come next are quickly disposed of, nobody paying much attention because a heavenly aroma wafts in from the kitchen: the ortolans are being prepared and anticipation hovers in the air.

I am not positive about the recipe for cooking ortolans because I figure that my chances of ever having to prepare such a dish are of the same order as winning the lottery jackpot. I think the birds—the size of a walnut—are roasted whole, innards and all, then flambéed in cognac or Armagnac, and served resting on a slim toasted *croûton* that will soak up the exquisite juices. As Odile brings out the first plates, four birds to a serving, a quiver of excitement sweeps the room.

The ortolans resemble perfect, miniature chickens, sized for some doll dinner party, with tiny folded wings, plump little thighs and feet held together with a gold string tied in a bow. Unless you are a Philistine, you do not just *eat* ortolans. As you would with a rare vintage, you exercise your senses: you look, smell, poke delicately with your fork, and, as you verbalize your sensations, untie the golden bow with cautious fingertips. Then, so none of that scrumptious fragrance be lost, you place a large white napkin over your head, extending to cover the plate. You read me right: *A napkin over your head,* and the sight of a roomful of distinguished people sitting there, with napkin-covered heads, the flap held daintily with two fingers of the left hand, is something to behold.

Since such napkins, heavily starched and crisply folded, have been placed next to our plates, we unfold them and drape them over our heads, too, with enough hanging in front to trap the exquisite fumes. Silence reigns. You do not converse while *dégusting* ortolans. It would be like jabbering away during the most sacred moment of the Mass, when they ring the little bell to announce that you must bow your head, because, at this very instant, the wafer is being morphed into the body of Christ. Even if you harbor some doubt that this is *really* happening, or simply believe none of it, you know enough to keep quiet. Same thing here. Surrender to the sacredness of the experience, and religiously crunch away at the tiny bones and the bit of flesh. One mouthful to a bird. It is good manners to exhale a sigh of orgasmic release after each one. So, to your silent picture of napkin-draped diners, please dub in now, for sound effects, the ethereal counterpoint of those ecstatic sighs.

All right. I know you have a question at this point, and I am aware that you wonder, "But how do ortolans *taste*?" This puts me in a difficult position. They taste *good*, no doubt about it. "But do they taste *that* good?"

Look: Are you seeking a lyrical, sacrosanct experience with your food, or do you just want to *eat*? If the latter, you probably need not bother with the ortolans' four little mouthfuls, and you can skip making a fool of yourself with that napkin. But if, on the other hand, you are hoping for a feast of all six senses—the mind included, *and not the least*, enhanced by rituals—ortolans are part of what you'd go to Provence for.

At a table near the door, a group that includes a monsignor in black cassock and biretta, violet silk cummerbund laced with a heavy gold chain and crucifix, has finished eating. Only the monsignor, napkin still draped over his head, is relishing the last fumes, bending over his empty plate. Wayne, impressed, follows his example. . . . I am tempted to tease him by reminding him of the awful way those innocent songbirds met their end, but I refrain. No need for me to be cruel, too.

Am I witnessing a conversion? Wayne, born in Los Angeles and American through and through—part of his charm, as far as I am concerned—is embracing, under my very eyes, a new faith: food as a source of ritualistic, elaborate ceremonies, food as an object of worship. Has he, God forbid, joined the ranks of the French?

But this was only a momentary lapse: He looks up and says, "Wasn't I reading something about the new European codes that would protect species like ortolans? When that happens, these poor little creatures will be safe. . . ." He smiles at the thought: "They can gorge on berries and afterward sing their little heads off, perched on those bushes. Then, whenever they feel like it, they can merrily fly away and live to sing some more." The image of a flock of ortolans winging their way into the blue rather than ending up in a roasting pan dissipates any lingering remorse. The Sierra Club could again recognize him as one of their own.

Now, Odile walks from table to table and whispers a few
words. Conversations, which had resumed, stop as she
speaks and visages become thoughtful. . . . Finally she
approaches us, "For dessert, tonight, we have Father Antoine's raspberries." The words are pronounced with such
reverence that we understand: There are raspberries and
then, there are Father Antoine's. We become thoughtful,
too, even though we have no idea of the identity of Father
Antoine, as we realize that these must be the ortolans of
berries. So, we abandon thoughts of Gérard's *moëlleux au
chocolat*, his triumph. (*Moëlleux* is another word that suffers
no translation: It is soft, yielding, giving, something you
sink ecstatically into. A goosedown bed is *moëlleux*. "Try
me, I am *moëlleux*," a plump young man whispered to the
girl he wished to entice.) No *moëlleux* tonight. We order, no
we ask for, no we petition for raspberries.

These arrive in footed crystal cups, placed on large
Limoges plates over a lace doily. No sugar, no cream, no
liqueur is offered. Just the dozen or so smallish, intensely
red berries. When I taste the first one, after breathing to
intoxication its aroma that rises like the soul of raspberry
itself, I understand: The fruit bursts with such an intense
flavor, it can only compare in sensation to a small electric
discharge on the palate. It is the spirit of the fruit explod-
ing on your tongue, and I see Wayne closing his eyes in
meditative introspection.

"Eat them slowly, one by one, and take only sips of
water. No wine, it would drown the flavor," advises Odile,
who tours the room again. The same silence accompanies
the raspberries as the ortolans, broken only when some

loutish type comments loudly that a little raspberry brandy over them would kick things up nicely. Indignant looks from several tables silence him, and his companions pointedly move *their* chairs away from his just a bit.

We will not leave tonight before we know how to find Father Antoine. We could not bear never to experience those berries again.

For one thing, he is difficult to find. A few days later, in late afternoon, as prescribed by Gérard, we attempt to follow the directions: After the abbey of Sénanque, take a narrow lane that branches off the road and climbs through scrub and pine forest, along the side of a mountain. When you get to where the car can no longer pass, leave it there and continue on foot, turn right where two paths cross, then left at a big rock, then right again when you glimpse the river way down, up and down, and then up again, remembering the sun is *west* and you want to go *north*. After several wrong turns lead us to impossible cliffs, we are suddenly there: a narrow plateau, sitting close under the top of the mountain, bordered by a precipitous fall down to an encased valley below.

Before us stands a stone shepherd's hut with no windows, only a door. Adjacent to it is the small *jas* that shares the wall with it, a semi-circular shed where the flock would take shelter. A handsome Alsatian dog looks out, then ambles over to greet us and silently wags his tail when I give him my hand to sniff. Father Antoine appears, stooping in the low doorway.

He is a Cistercian monk, wearing his order's coarse white

woolen robe tied at the waist with a knotted cord from which hangs a rosary, its beads made of olive pits, barefoot in rough sandals of wood and leather, obviously home-made. A tall, strikingly handsome man, ascetically lean, with a deep tan, silver hair surrounds the ritually shaved crown. He smiles, calls back the dog, waves his welcome. Did we disturb him from some important occupation?

"Not at all. I just completed my afternoon office of prayers. I was sort of expecting you, as Gérard told me you might come. Would you like to step into my chapel?"

Wayne and I, intimidated, follow him into the former sheepfold. No windows. No doors: the sheep transited through the shepherd's hut, and sheep do not need light. Only a small, handkerchief-sized window has been man-aged in the wall, near the top, and fitted with a foot-square stained-glass window in yellows and orange.

"I see the sun rise through it during my second morning devotions. It was a gift from a stained-glass artist who lives down in the valley." We know. We have passed the studio many times.

"And this, my altar, was a grindstone left from an old olive oil mill not too far from here. The Gordes Boy Scouts spent several weekends helping me roll it up here, so I can celebrate mass in proper fashion and render God grace for his bounties."

I am entranced by the tall monk and by the life he must be leading, so devoid of all comforts that it is hard to con-ceive of it. No electricity, of course, or running water. (And is there, even, any water at all?) No furniture, not even the semblance of a bed. Only two tree stumps, one to use as a table, I guess, and the other to sit on. So I question him relentlessly.

"I was a lawyer living and working in Lyon before I joined the monastery. The contemplative life always appealed to me, though. . . . Finally, one day, I realized the vanity of all my activities when my only concern on this earth should be to prepare for the salvation of my eternal soul, in addition to praying for others. So I was blessed when the monastery accepted me. . . . I remained several years there, in our mother house of Cîteaux in Burgundy. But then one day, our prior called me in. 'My son,' he said, 'you are *too* happy here. For one does not enter into the service of God to find personal happiness, but mortification of the flesh and the spirit. So, I order you to leave, go into the wilderness, alone, and make a life by the sweat of your brow, remaining faithful always to the rule of Saint Bernard, our founder.' He directed me to this area because of the proximity to Sénanque, where no monks are in residence now, and only one comes on Sunday to say Mass for a handful of faithful. Whenever I am needed to assist or replace him, I descend to the abbey. The rest of the time I celebrate Holy Mass here on this stone altar, watching the sun rise in the east, as our Lord rose from the dead himself."

I have visited Sénanque and read about the life of the monks who, for centuries, resided there. So I know a bit about the ascetic rules dictated by Saint Bernard for his Cistercian Order. Minimal food, never more than three hours of sleep at one time on a bare floor wrapped only in the coarse monachal robe, barefoot in sandals winter as well as summer, the hours marked by the prescribed prayer services.

And then I wonder: how could Father Antoine be expected to be self-sufficient on that barren plateau, sun-baked now, but snowbound or mistral-swept in winter? I visualize him, when the icy wind howls over the mountain tops and down in the deep gorges, getting up in the freezing dark, alone, to kneel on the stone floor of the small chapel, reciting the predawn offices. How much harder to do in solitude than when surrounded by others to follow or to lead!

"And you adhere to the rule of Saint Bernard, here, all by yourself?"

"I try, madame, I try to do my best. But it requires sainthood to follow it to perfection, and I am but a sinner. Good will isn't always enough to vanquish temptation, so all I can do is pray for God's help and His forgiveness."

Wayne is awestruck, seeking ways he could help Father Antoine, so he asks about the raspberries. The monk smiles, a radiant smile:

"Come, I'll show you how blessed I really am."

A little farther on the high plateau, overlooked only by the mountain peak, we discover his field: Maybe two hundred raspberry plants, thorny little vines, in neat rows, with a shallow well dug in the dirt at the foot of each. They look surprisingly green and leafy in that sere landscape, now pitilessly roasting under the sun. That is when Father Antoine proudly shows his secret.

The edge of the plateau falls precipitously from a cliff, down into a narrow gorge. At the bottom runs a brook, probably a torrent in winter, but not much more than a trickle now.

"God sees to us, doesn't He?" he beams.

He has painstakingly carved footsteps into that almost vertical wall, which makes me dizzy just looking at it, and planted sticks, anchored in the rocky soil, to grab, instead of a banister, so that he can climb down and then back up. . . .

"After I finished that, I prayed for some way to bring water to my plants. In an answer from God, the Boy Scout troop came a few days later and left me an old pail. I patched it up and my problem was solved! All I have to do is descend to the brook and climb back up again with a pailful. I do that as many times as possible; still, it isn't enough for the berries to grow very large, but I'm told they are all the tastier and sweeter. . . . All that sunshine and cold mountain nights are good for them, too."

"Do people come to buy them?"

"There is never a big crop! Only the man from Mas Tourteron comes now and then and takes whatever is ripe at the moment. He leaves me bread and cheese in exchange, or else he pays me, so I can buy the few things I need: matches, wicks, a little oil for a lamp."

"You eat some of those raspberries, don't you?" asks Wayne, hopefully.

"Oh, no, that would be contrary to the rule. As I told you, bread and cheese and a few vegetables I grow over there are all that is allowed."

"Do you have any to sell us?"

Unmindful of the thorny boughs that protect the berries, Father Antoine gathers about a cupful of the red,

red berries that, warmed by the late afternoon sun, waft an aroma that distills all the magical powers of the earth. . . .

When we return to the shepherd cabin, I discover bundles of wicker leaning against the wall, and a few baskets, some half completed.

"Another gift from God. There are willows on the bank of that brook, growing a little farther down-current. So, I harvest their young shoots in the spring when they will remain pliable, and I am trying to learn how to weave them into baskets. So far, the results are not very good, they all seem to come out lopsided. . . ."

Yes, they are lopsided, clumsy and infinitely touching. I buy the four completed ones and insist on paying a little more than the few francs Father Antoine hesitantly names.

"Thank you, madame. You will enable me to be charitable in your name," he tells me.

During these months, Father Antoine's raspberries become Wayne's spiritual food. Raised without any religion at all, totally ignorant of any Catholic, Protestant or Jewish dogma, he has grown up unaware of what *belief*—or even *disbelief*—in God means, and always regarded the many churches and temples of Los Angeles as social clubs, not all that different from others, except that people seemed to sing there, rather than play golf.

But now, there are moments when he feels a void and seeks something beyond the world he captures in the lenses of his cameras. He has tried to practice Eastern meditation, but there again, at least as it is taught here, it demands no more than an emptying of the mind in a quest for inner peace. So, as often as he reasonably can, he will now seek Father Antoine and try to help him with his chores, both in silence, until the monk must perform the next devotions of his liturgical day.

Then, Wayne will stand against the wall of the little chapel, motionless and respectful, trying hard not to understand but to share a little in the overwhelming love that has brought Father Antoine to lead a hermit's life on this isolated mountain.

When, the following winter, we are back in California, I often think of Father Antoine. After being told on the phone that the mistral has been sweeping Provence with ice-cold fury, I wake up that night thinking of him. I didn't even see a fireplace in that stone hut. . . . How can he endure such cold?

So, the next day, I find an Army/Navy surplus store and buy a complete set of what the salesman calls "watch gear": a peacoat, rubber boots lined with fleece, muffler, thick gloves, a woolen cap to pull over the brow, and mail the package to the Gordes post office with a note asking them to deliver it to Father Antoine. And I smile inwardly, for I can again enjoy my warm bed, knowing that soon Father Antoine will be more comfortable.

But I am wrong.

A few weeks later, a letter arrives, and I realize what a project this must have been: purchasing paper, envelope and pen, then trekking to Gordes again for stamps and mailing. But he did it. And he writes:

Madame, my sister in Christ,

I received your generous gift and thank you for your thoughtfulness. It has brought me the greatest possible joy, that of being able to help a poor man I know who is ill, all alone, and lacking warm winter clothes. So, let us render grace to God who has allowed this charity. My prayers include you and your husband, as I ask for His divine protection upon both of you.

Your brother in Christ,
Father Antoine

Experience Romance
Foods to Love By

The High Flavors of Provence and Nostradamus's Elixir of Love
Provence, with its sere, high plateaus and fertile valleys all drenched in sunshine, is a land of low fat, but high-flavored foods: Look for lamb, delicate goat cheeses and truffles, not to mention wines. You'll even find there Nostradamus's Elixir of Love.

Feast on Thyme-Scented Lamb in Sisteron
A new freeway, A51, along the Durance Valley, brings you to picturesque Sisteron. This is the Route Napoléon, followed by the emperor when, escaping from exile on the island of Elba, he landed near Fréjus, marched on Paris

and regained his throne . . . for only a hundred days, ending with Waterloo.

Sisteron sits in a narrow spectacular gorge, dominated on one side by a gigantic rock, constantly being scaled by ant-sized climbers. The lofty fortress, opposite, is proud to have surrendered without a shot to the returning emperor.

But to me, Sisteron's real claim to fame is its lamb, *l'agneau de Sisteron*. Flocks graze on nearby slopes, munching on rosemary and the various kinds of thyme that grow there in abundance. It is served rosy, tender and fragrant, as in all of Provence, but you'll find its flavor unequalled in the Sisteron restaurants like the *Grand Hôtel du Cours* (Allée Verdun; Tel: 04-92-61-04-51; Fax: 04-92-61-41-73; www.sisteron.com/html/hcours.html; e-mail: hoteldu cours@wanadoo.fr) or the *Touring Napoléon* (22, Ave. de la Libération; Tel: 04-92-61-00-06; Fax: 04-92-61-01-19).

Graze on Goat Cheeses

Fresh, they're mild and creamy; a little older, they become firmer, *demi-sec*; finally, allowed to dry, they are *sec*.

When presented with the cheese tray, which, in Provence, is likely to be a selection of goat cheeses, ask the waiter for a sliver of each kind: *crèmeux*, *demi-sec* and *sec*, to *déguster* in just that order, as you finish the last drops of your bottle of Côtes-du-Rhône.

There are many sorts of goat cheese. In the Luberon, my favorite is *banon*, named after the village that produces it. It is entirely worth a trip to Banon, ancient and perched in the mountains above Apt. Have your camera handy as you pass Simiane-la-Rotonde, high above the lavender fields.

Buy a dozen of the pungent little cheeses that come wrapped in dry chestnut leaves.

A Rare Food for Lovers, with Potent Properties
Truffles are gathered in fall and winter. Our friends Christian and Marie-Françoise, who came to visit us in California for Christmas, tried to bring us a large one, found in
the forest near their village. They'd sealed it in plastic,
wrapped in layers of tin foil and buried among sweaters.
But at the Miami Airport, where they were rerouted
because of weather, a dog of the Beagle Brigade detected
the pervasive aroma. The truffle was confiscated and incin-
erated on the spot by horrified inspectors. This confirmed
in whoever heard the story, back in Provence, the convic-
tion that America lags far behind in *gastronomie*.

Truffles have always been considered a potent aphrodisiac. Madame de Pompadour, the ethereal mistress of
Louis XV, is said to have subsisted on a diet of truffles,
oysters and celery in an attempt to match the king's ardor.

Nostradamus's Love Potion
In Salon, the home town of Nostradamus, you'll learn that
predicting the future was only a sideline for the good doctor. He was also the author of a treatise, *Cosmetics and the
Health of the Senses* (1552), and at his former home in Salon
you can purchase products made from his original recipes.
One is a *sachet de modestie* to "calm the ardor of the senses,"
but I didn't see anybody buying that. Instead, great interest
was shown in the "Philter of Medea: Amourous Beverage
for the Perfect Love." It comes in four little packets of

herbs to be mixed and brewed like tea, and smells deliciously of lavender, thyme and other fragrant herbs I could
not identify. Not having used it yet, I cannot report on its
effect, but I suggest you conduct your own research and let
me know your conclusions.

(Maison de Nostradamus, 13, Rue Nostradamus, 13300
Salon-de-Provence; Tel: 04-90-56-64-31.)

The Wines of Provence
You'll see vineyards everywhere. Their grapes give wines
that, light-hearted and full of sunshine, will cool your
throat and warm your soul.

Wines of recognized quality, produced in certain limited areas—and laws are strict—rate the Controlled Origin
Appellation label, AOC. There are several AOC wines in
Provence. For instance: Côtes-du-Rhône, with Châteauneuf-du-Pape as its crown jewel, and, for rosé lovers, Tavel,
a pink Châteauneuf.

Côtes-de-Provence lies east of the Rhône, with Château
Palette as one of its best known. Côtes-du-Luberon, grown
in the foothills and on the slopes of the famous little
mountain range, is proud, among others, of its Château La
Verrerie.

Many villages boast their own cooperative winery, *Cave
Cooperative Vinicole*, where participating growers truck their
grapes. Wine made in the fall is for sale year round. Locals
bring their own jugs, but wine is also bottled, with attractive labels. Light and fruity, these wines are best young and
they beautifully enhance local foods.

AOC Hay?

AOC is not limited to wines. A few other products, whose place of origin is paramount to their quality, rate the AOC label: *Échiré* butter, for instance, Roquefort cheese or green lentils from Le Puy.

Provence has the distinction of producing the only AOC hay anywhere. In the plain of the Crau, near Arles, hay grown under tightly controlled conditions and containing percentages of prescribed grasses is AOC. Most of it is exported, I am told, to be served to prized race horses belonging to Middle Eastern oil princes, but I don't know on what kind of dinnerware.

Simple and Sensuous
An Anniversary Dinner *à deux*

Do you celebrate the day you met? Your wedding day? Some other important landmark in your lives? Here is a delicious and easy dinner to help you mark the occasion.

Salade au miel
Saumon fumé
Pommes de terre au caviar
Crêpes Suzette

Salad with Honey Dressing
I cup diced apple
I cup sliced celery
I can mandarin orange sections, drained
½ cup walnuts
Salt and pepper to taste

In serving bowl mix apples, celery, mandarin oranges and walnuts. Season lightly with salt and pepper.

At serving time, toss with salad dressing.

Dressing: Use the basic vinaigrette recipe (p. 47), adding honey to taste.

Smoked Salmon with Salmon Caviar Potatoes
8 to 12 small rose potatoes
Sour cream
I jar red salmon-egg caviar
½ pound smoked salmon

Potatoes should be smaller than an egg. Peel, leaving little strips of pink skin. Cut a small slice off bottom so potato can stand and cut out a little hollow at the top. Boil in salted water until just done. Drain and keep warm.

At serving time: Place a dollop of sour cream in each and top with a scant teaspoon of caviar. Lay slices of salmon on serving dish, arrange potatoes around and garnish with parsley.

Sauce for the Salmon
Juice of I lemon
¼ cup olive oil

1 tablespoon capers
Cracked pepper

Mix all ingredients in a small bowl. Pass sauce to spoon over salmon.

Crêpes Suzette

(If you prefer, you may buy the crêpes ready-made. In that case, just add the butter-orange sauce and flambé.)

Batter for Crêpes

1 pint milk
2 eggs
½ cup cake flour
Salt

Suzette Sauce

½ stick butter
1 tablespoon frozen orange-juice concentrate
¼ cup sugar
3 tablespoons Grand Marnier or other orange liqueur
(Cointreau, Triple Sec)

To flambé: ½ cup Grand Marnier

Make the batter by mixing milk, eggs, flour and a pinch of salt in a medium bowl. Batter should have syrup consistency. Add milk if too thick.

With a wad of paper towel rubbed in butter, grease non-stick pan. When hot, using soup ladle, pour just enough batter to cover bottom of pan, as you swirl pan around. Cook for a minute or two, flip over and cook other side until lightly browned. Stack crêpes.

Make sauce by melting butter in small pan with orange concentrate. Add and dissolve sugar. Add liqueur. Do not allow to cook.

Spread sauce over crêpes. Fold in fours and arrange, fan-wise, on a plate. Sprinkle generously with sugar.

To flambé (as in original recipe): In very small pan, warm liqueur but do not allow to stand or boil. Light with long match. Pour flaming over crêpes. Shake plate to keep flames burning.

To Drink
A cool Riesling would enhance this light dinner.

> Find some memento, meaningful to both of you,
> to place on the table with a few flowers.

Love Is Always in Season

"*N*ah," Madison is saying as I push open the dining room door. "I don't take the bus, I hitch-hike."

"You hitchhike to where?" I ask. She turns in my direction, "To Marseille, of course." I blanch.

It is noon, and half a dozen kids are sitting around the table, talking and waiting. They know I'll be closing my office for lunch, so they find some reason to need to speak to me just about this time. Because everybody is hungry, we first check the refrigerator and usually find tomatoes, olives, eggs, potatoes and frozen green beans. We boil the potatoes and beans in the same water as the eggs, keeping the beans in their plastic bag. Cans of tuna are stacked in the cupboard. Enough to make some approximation of a *salade niçoise*, which the kids call a *comme-ci, comme-çoise*. Somebody is delegated to the bakery for an armful of baguettes. All else failing, there is always Jeannot's pizza truck parked at the end of the drive, a choice spot for business with starving kids coming and going at all hours. Only, walking back up the drive to the Villa balancing a pile of pizzas is a challenge because Jeannot doesn't know about cardboard boxes.

Now, the idea of hitchhiking, and into Marseille yet, is enough to send shivers down my spine.

"I was tired of the *dojo* here," says Madison, between mouthfuls. "Making no real progress. So, now I go down to the one in Marseille."

"When do you go?"

"Evenings, three times a week. See, they're all black belts there, the *sensei* is a former European champion! As I was saying, buses would take forever. It's much faster to hitchhike, *faire de l'autostop*," she winks, sticking up her thumb. The kids laugh.

At night? And into that big port city where danger is rife? Madison is 19, an adult (I know, I know). Still, there is reason to worry.

"Now, Madison, you shouldn't take risks of that sort. Those men who pick you up might. . . ."

"Man, I'd worry more about any dude who'd get fresh with her, like," interrupts Kevin, all curly head now, with Dana at his side, practically not scowling anymore.

"I for one know what she *can* do," interjects Maria. "I was going home with her after the movies the other night. Two punks came after us! 'You girls want to have some fun?' and they grabbed us from behind. 'I *love* to have fun,' said Madison, and she threw one over her shoulder. He landed—splat—flat into the gutter and the other took off, fast like. Enough fun for him."

Laughter is general, but I am still not reassured. How would her parents feel about all this?

"My parents?" asks Madison incredulous. "My *parents*? Say, may I use your phone? Thank you. California time, they're asleep, but they won't mind."

She dials. "Hi, Mom, sorry to wake you, but you need to speak to the Director here. She worries about me. Would you please tell her whether or not I should hitchhike into Marseille?"

And she passes the phone to me.

Well, Madison's mother—a martial arts instructor herself in the gym she and her husband operate, she tells me—thinks the best protection her daughter can have is her ability to self-defend, and confidence in that ability. "We've always let her do what she feels she can handle, and go where she can take care of herself. But," she adds, "I am grateful for your concern. Madison writes that all the kids like you."

Well, I like them too. It is just that nobody would guess Madison has steel muscles and quicker-than-a-cobra reflexes! With that slender build and her braid of pale gold, whoever tries to take advantage of her is in for a surprise. . . .

Now, the conversation veers to the events of the night before, as the two principals, Rosalind and Amanda, walk in, apparently fully recovered, eager to inform anyone who hasn't heard of what happened to them.

"We were walking home last night, a little past eleven, when that guy on a moped passes us, turns around, leans the bike against a tree, and starts pacing backward in front of us. He's saying things I can't understand," begins Rosalind. "I looked. . . ."

Rebecca interrupts: "The mistral was blowing, dust got into her eyes, she'd taken off her contacts. So, she couldn't see a *thing*."

"It was dark, too," protests Rosalind. "Anyway, he's walking backward in front of us, and suddenly he opens his raincoat, points his finger down and. . . ."

Howls of laughter: "And he flashes you? Man, crazy, like!"

"She couldn't figure out *what* he was showing," gasps Amanda. "Blind as a *bat*! So, she leans down, real close, peering at the guy's. . . ."

They're strangling with laughter; Rosalind squeals in high decibels.

"That is called *une bitte*, isn't it?" asks Michiko, leafing through her notebook. "Does it take one or two t's?"

"Either spelling is acceptable, I checked," replies Keiko.

"When I finally could see what it was," continues Rosalind between fits of laughter, "I got so nervous I couldn't stop giggling. Rebecca, too. All we could do was hold onto each other and laugh like crazy. . . ."

"That made him real angry," continues Amanda. "He is

so mad, he turns around, lifts the *back* of his coat: 'Perverts,' he yells, 'that's what you are! Perverts! So look at *this* if that's what you *want* to see!'"

They're falling off their chairs. "So, you got mooned, too, like! Man, oh man, they got mooned!"

Only, last night, when the girls frantically ran up to the Villa and rang the doorbell, *I* wasn't laughing. A flasher! And what else is the man capable of: Abuse? Kidnapping? Rape? Murder? Back home, we are used to considering the worst scenario, and I feel responsible for the protection of these *kids* (regardless of what my handbook might call them) from whatever deviates roam the darkened streets.

So, taking the two young ladies with me, I drove to the police station. There we were greeted as old friends by none other than the potbellied chief who danced with me the night of our memorable party. Other *flics* were playing cards, a bottle of wine on the table. A little calmer now, the girls recounted their adventure.

The chief listened. Then:

"And it happened near the casino, right? A little after eleven? I thought so. A thin guy, with longish hair and a mustache? That's him. We know him well. He works as a croupier at the casino and leaves work every night about that time. So you mean he's at it *again*?"

Apparently, he *is*. So, this is a *repeat* offender we are dealing with?

"Oh, yes, he's done the same thing *many* times before, ever since starting work at the casino."

Aix, with its mineral water baths is a spa, and therefore,

under French law, entitled to a gambling casino. So, our croupier is a *well-known* flasher, and apparently a respected one, I comment ironically.

The chief is conciliatory.

"I'll grant you," he says, "that he *shouldn't* be going around flashing young ladies. We've *told* him many times, so he *knows* it. We've spoken pretty rough to him, even issued a warning that he'd get into trouble if he kept that up. *Alors,* he promises to behave and he does. But after a while, though, there he goes again!" The chief shakes his head. "Can't help it, I guess, he just likes to *show off.* . . . It's a shame, not a bad guy, got a wife and kids. . . ."

"Couldn't you lock him up for a while, as a lesson?"

"Oh, madame," the chief is aghast, "that would serve no good purpose. Who would feed his family? And the embarrassment, for those innocent people! Have you thought of it?"

Now, I wonder, with all these considerations, is there *something* the police can do?

It seems there is. Listen:

"I'll tell you what, *mesdemoiselles,*" says the chief, addressing the young ladies. "Just stay *away* from that street by the casino, especially around eleven at night when his shift lets out. Tell your friends to do the same thing. This way you won't run across him and there should be no more trouble. . . ." After a pause, he adds: "But, should you meet him by accident, please, don't *laugh.* He's sensitive that way, no point in hurting his feelings."

Back in the car, both the girls and I are impressed with the simplicity of the solution. One only had to *think* of it.

"In California," comments Rosalind, "that dude would be in jail, hurt feelings and all, learning how to commit worse crimes, home lost, wife and kids on welfare. . . ."

"And *we'd* be undergoing mandated psychological treatment for trauma recovery," giggles Amanda. She adds, turning to Rosalind: "Next time, keep your contacts *on*, just so you don't make a fool of yourself again, peering down close like you did, laughing like a loon. Remember: No hurting the guy's feelings."

After all the noontime excitement, the afternoon seems quiet and passes quickly. For once, I want to leave the office on time for I am invited out to dinner, and I'd like to get my hair done and dress up a bit.

Several weeks ago, Wayne, taking pictures near Pertuis, cut his finger on the sharp edge of some equipment. When he couldn't staunch the bleeding, he walked into a doctor's office there. The young doctor bandaged his hand, commented with admiration on the cameras strung around Wayne's neck, who in turn remarked on the sports car parked outside the office. They talked about America, where Dr. Christian had been several times, one memorable summer in particular, driving at breakneck speed all over the Southwest, missing not a single National Park or canyon, and only a *few* Indian reservations. They enjoyed themselves so that they decided we should all have dinner soon, and thus we met his pretty, fey wife, Marie-Françoise.

One thing led to another, and soon they brought *their* friends, Bernard and Jacqueline, also their neighbors in a beautiful, historic village near Pertuis.

This is how, this morning, Bernard called to invite us for dinner and was sorry to hear Wayne would be away for a while.

"Come by yourself, then. We have a basket of *cèpes*, wild mushrooms, the best, and the first of the season. This time of year, they grow only way up high near the top of the Luberon mountains. Under dry leaves, yet, which makes them all the harder to find. Too bad Wayne can't be here."

These two couples represent the *new* Provence. All four are professionals, born in this region, proud of it and they speak with its lilting accent. Their homes are Provençal in spirit, with wooden *volets* painted in the warm hues of the ocher quarries, terra-cotta floors, and oriented to avoid the harsh afternoon sun. But instead of the small windows that, in old homes, kept out the elements, but also the light, their French doors open wide onto terraces. Their sound systems are state-of-the-art, the stacks of CDs mostly American. Bernard's communication room, which he needs for his work, would impress any computer freak. Swimming pools sparkle in their yards, and Bernard's even boasts a small palm tree on an island. "People make fun of me, with that palm tree. 'Won't live out the winter,' they say. But I just wrap it in straw, and it's doing fine."

Both couples travel each year to exotic destinations, the Seychelles Islands a favorite. Bernard and Jacqueline, some years ago, even went and got married, on a lark, in Las

Vegas and proudly show their legal documents, delivered by the French Consulate in Los Angeles.

Yet, in that bright blue and ocher–tiled kitchen that opens wide onto the dining room—even with the avant-garde English group *The Cure* playing in the background—you know you are in Provence, and this could be nowhere else. For one thing, a hint of forest scent floats in the air: The mushrooms are in the oven.

With the ritual apéritif of orange wine—a specialty of Jacqueline's mother—olives are served: two kinds, the green, unripe kind, and the black, ripe, wrinkled ones. "I pick some in October, when they've just plumped up, and the rest at Christmastime, after the frost," says Jacqueline. "All from the tree here, in front. The crop from the other six in the back, we take to the mill in Cucuron and we get our oil supply for the year."

I have once tasted an olive from a tree and found it both sour and bitter. "How do you prepare olives like these?"

"It's very easy: Place them—either the green or the black ones, it makes no difference—in a large *tian*. Cover them with coarse salt you change about once a week, as it absorbs the bitter water from the fruit. After a month, take the olives out, rinse them, dry them, and put them in jars with enough oil to cover. They'll keep for months that way, getting more mellow all the time."

The first course of scrambled eggs, laced with thinly sliced truffles, comes as a luxurious surprise: "But aren't truffles terribly rare and expensive?"

"They certainly are, but not here," smiles Marie-Fran-çoise. "They grow right in the foothills of the Luberon.

Christian's mother has a knack for finding them. She brought us a whole salad-wire basketful the other day."

I visualize an elderly woman, kerchief-covered head, leading a . . . pig, isn't it? to some secret grove, muttering, perhaps, some truffle-finding incantations.

Wrong again: Christian's mother is no crone.

"Weekends—she's a professor at the university, you might meet her there—she puts on boots and there she goes! All it takes is a stick, a walking stick if you like. She looks for oak trees with no grass underneath, only lots of dry leaves. Stirs the leaves with her stick. At some point, a small blue fly may rise and hover above the spot. She pushes the leaves away, digs into the ground just a bit—she uses an old dinner fork for that—and, with any luck the truffle is there. You see, that fly lays her eggs just above it."

"Some truffles are the size of a peanut," adds Christian. "Many like a walnut, but this time, two or three were as big as an egg." The flavor—or is it aroma?—of a truffle beggars definition: musk, earth and something ineffably potent and mysterious . . . haunting even.

A hush around the table greets the heavy, lid-covered *tian* that Jacqueline brings in next.

"Now, if you don't like this, or if it makes you sick, blame it on Christian," jokes Bernard. "He brought it, the gift of one of his patients. So we don't know whether it was a reward or a revenge."

It has to be a reward because the *civet de sanglier*, stew of wild boar meat in red wine, is sumptuous, the meat highly flavored but not gamy, fork tender in a sauce . . . rich is the first word that comes to mind.

"Boars are plentiful in the forests of the Luberon," Christian tells me. "So, after the hunting season opens, that patient of mine, whose wife is a fabulous cook, brings me *civet* like this on occasion." He adds: "And don't worry, Bernard: He's the type that would shoot, rather than poison."

And now, even before the mushrooms are served, I understand the invitation wasn't *just* for the *cèpes*. Generously, they wanted to share with me, with us, the bounties of the season and of their land. The atmosphere around this table is like the food, like their homes, like the spirit of Provence: warm and imbued with *joie de vivre*, the reflection of fulfilled, happy lives, lived exactly as these people want their lives to be. What they are offering me tonight is a great deal more than a dinner invitation, I know.

Full attention is now turned to the mushrooms, glasses exchanged for fresh ones in honor of the *white* Châteauneuf-du-Pape Bernard is uncorking. They are prepared *à la provençale*, I am told: stems finely chopped with *jambon*, garlic and parsley, sautéed and used as stuffing for the caps. The whole baked—in a *tian*, of course—with a good dash of olive oil. My mind is running out of adjectives, after all these complex and extraordinary flavors. Yet the first forkful followed by a sip of the equally savory wine summons the last of my vocabulary: heavenly.

"I hadn't seen mushrooms like these yet, this season," remarks Marie-Françoise. "Where did you get them?"

Bernard relishes the question.

"The gendarmes found them."

"The *gendarmes*? Where?"

"Near the top of the Luberon. The *Grand* Luberon."

"What were they doing up there? They patrol the Luberon now? Regularly?"

"Not regularly! This was special. A missing person case! Very serious. You know the Peyronnet's grandfather, the *papy*, we say here," he explains for my benefit. Christian nods: He knows the family well. Several members have been his patients. "He disappeared yesterday. They all were frantic, as you can imagine! The family had gone to the Pertuis market, leaving him in the care of a great-granddaughter. Anyway, he is 94, can walk only a little with his cane and doesn't see much, either. So, the girl left him sitting outside in the shade and went over to her girlfriend's next door. When she returned, the armchair was empty and no sign of the *papy*. She looked everywhere, shouted out for him, nothing. *Alors*, her dad called the gendarmes when he returned."

"So they took their SUV and climbed *to the top* of the Luberon, looking for him?" asks Marie-Françoise in wide-eyed, feigned wonder.

"They looked *everywhere*," replies Bernard, just as straight-faced. "That's how *thorough* they are."

"And a good thing they did," adds Jacqueline. "They saw no sign of the *papy*, but there were all these mushrooms. . . ."

"And since they happened to have pails and baskets in their van, why, they were able to pick them and bring them back," continues Bernard. "So, when they stopped me on the road to ask if I'd seen the *papy*, I chanced to see those baskets of *cèpes*, and they spotted my cases of Châteauneuf. They suggested a swap, and here we are. How do you like them, Yvone? Not bad, are they?"

Not bad indeed. Every bite releases the soul of the forest in autumn. . . . But what about the *papy*?

"That's the problem, you see. No, they didn't find him on top of the Luberon."

"Surprise," exclaims Marie-Françoise, still wide-eyed. "I'd have thought he'd thrown away his cane and climbed up there to hide under the leaves!"

"They asked around," continues Bernard, imperturbable. "Knocked on every door, questioned everybody they could find. Finally, at a loss, they went to sit at the Bar des Sports. Best place to continue their investigation because that's where everybody will stop sooner or later . . . but nobody had seen the *papy*."

Christian cannot stand it much longer: A little muscle twitches at the corner of his mouth. They all know the story's end, of course. This is only a show they're putting on for my benefit—and I enjoy it as much, if not more, than they do. Christian interrupts:

"It's tough work for gendarmes, sitting there, because *everybody* wants to buy them a drink, but hey! they're on duty: One drink, two, okay, but the rest, they *have* to refuse."

So, it seems they were about to quit for the day when that kid wheels up on his bicycle: The Raynaud boy, tall for his age, those Raynauds from the big farm near here.

"Are you looking for the *papy* Peyronnet? Some kid told me he's missing. He's not missing at all! He's sitting out in our backyard with our *mamy*, both fast asleep."

Well, further investigation reveals that the *papy*, unsupervised, has walked—yes, walked, he was that determined—all the way to the Raynauds' house, almost a quarter mile away. Nobody thought him capable of that feat.

Now, the Raynauds have that *mamy*—she used to be an Auberti girl—and it seems the *papy* had been talking about her. "Says he used to dance with her at the fairs when they were young. I think he mentioned something about her being promised to him, sort of, but she jilted him to marry one of the Raynaud brothers, who own all that land," says his daughter-in-law. "If *only* we'd known he wanted to see her! But he never let on. Just mumbling and rambling about her. . . ."

At the Raynauds' house, the *mamy* is being coquettish.

"*Peuchère*, you could have knocked me over with a feather when I saw that boy. Still handsome, no doubt, but just the same troublemaker he always was, I bet. A couple of drinks and he'd get into fights at every fair! Mostly about me, it was, couldn't stand it if I danced with anyone else. . . ."

And:

"Marry him? I'd never have married him! No good he was, and from that family. . . . I remember his mother: She wore a hat with *feathers* to go to market. Never knitted a man a single pair of socks so long as she lived. Both he and his father wore store-bought socks, never any good ones."

When asked if it would be all right if the *papy* came to visit her now and then, she refuses indignantly: "No, sir, I wouldn't have *anything* to do with that hot-tempered young man." Then she relents:

"Oh, let him come, if he wants to so bad! He might sit with me awhile. Won't hurt him to see how decent folks live. We could talk of those times, and believe me, I'd give him a piece of my mind."

A little later:

"Could stay and eat with us. I bet they don't look after him properly in that house. My father never thought much of the Peyronnets."

A little later in the day, she asks, "When did you say that boy was coming?"

And she sits waiting in her armchair. She has started some new knitting: the first of a pair of socks in mixed blue and gray yarn.

Experience Romance
Provence's Gift of Nature and Gift of Art

The gift of nature is lavender, the gift of art is the fabled Moustiers faience. Let them both enchant you on this lovely summer day on the high plateaus of Provence.

Intoxicated by the Lavender Fields of Valensole
In July, lavender blooms everywhere in Provence (or else, it is its close cousin, *lavandin*). But to experience the true glory of the largest fields, with the richest, most flower-laden, deeply scented lavender, drive to Valensole (north on A51, exit at Manosque, east, direction Valensole), and do not forget your camera.

Drive through the little town, stopping only for pictures of the unique fountain in the square. It is half-covered with calcite accretions, plants and flowers, spectacular and quaint, so your camera will not be the only one there.

Past the town, you climb to open country. Continue until you see the lavender fields stretching into infinity. Do not fear to drive down little dirt roads, and you'll be surrounded by those fields, as by a lavender-scented tide. In this rocky, reddish soil, unwatered, drenched in sunshine, the lavender bushes droop under the weight of their spikes, heavy with intensely fragrant and violet-blue flowerets.

You'll see photographers—professionals and others. Join them, images are crowding around you: a long shot, with mountains in the distance; close-ups, with bees in each floweret; your love, in the midst of those painted rows.

Stop at the lavender grower's farmhouse turned into a boutique, and stock up on lavender cologne, lavender essence, lavender oil, soap and sachets.

A lavender kiss. A Provençal lover uses lavender cologne as an aftershave and invites his lady to kiss his cheek and nuzzle his neck in the ritual of *étrenner la barbe*, to get the first of a fresh shave. I see no reason the custom should be confined to Provence, so long as you bring back a provision of lavender cologne. *Definitely* something to try at home, unless you fear the effects the scent of lavender, combined with that of the man you love, might have on your more sober judgment.

Under the Sign of the Star: Moustiers-Sainte-Marie
A 20-mile drive along a picturesque little road brings you to Moustiers, one of those "Most Beautiful Village" award winners.

The first thing you'll see is a long chain, strung between two mountain peaks, punctuated by a star at its center. Tradition has it that a crusader fighting in the Holy Land made a vow to present such a chain to the Virgin Mary should he return home safely. He did and the chain was duly installed. Taken down during the Revolution, restored later, it endures today. It is said to be forged of solid silver.

The Moustiers Faience
You'll see the faience displayed everywhere in the village. It is beautiful, with a distinctive white glaze, thin enough to let the pink clay show through. Its traditional decoration shows the "potato flower" in blues and greens with a bit of yellow.

There are majestic tureens to use as centerpieces, platters, dishes, vases, candelabra. I bought a pair of double-armed candelabra that a village electrician fitted for me as lamps. Moustiers pieces are not cheap, but are entirely worth the price, as they will be cherished for generations.

If you do not want to bother transporting a tureen, you might gift your lover with some small Moustiers object for his or her desk, like a pencil cup or a paper-clip dish.

And Is There Ever a Romantic Place for You!
La Bastide de Moustiers (below the village, take D952 and then Chemin de Quinson; Tel: 04-92-70-47-47; Fax: 04-

92-70-47-48; www.bastide-moustiers.com; e-mail: contact @bastide-moustiers.com). Chef Alain Ducasse, of Paris three-star fame and also chef at Monaco's fabled Louis XV restaurant in the Hôtel de Paris, bought and restored this *bastide* for his personal use. Then, he couldn't resist turning it into a charming, welcoming inn.

Settle on the terrace, under the trees, with the valley at your feet. *Apéritif maison* is champagne with almond liqueur. There are only two menus to choose from, but both are three-star quality, with reasonable prices. You'll love the Bastide.

There are rooms, too, all different, in a style I'd call country elegance.

Moustiers is at the entrance to the Gorges du Verdon, which offer a world-class, spectacular drive along the gorges of the river, called *La Corniche Sublime*. So, if you are seeking more of the magic of Provence, check your map, and *bon voyage*.

Simple and Sensuous
A Figure-Conscious Dinner *à deux*

If you feel like a particularly light dinner tonight, you'll enjoy this simple menu, as you discover the "poor man's asparagus" and a novel, reduced calorie take on the classic pizza.

Poireaux vinaigrette
Portobello pizza
Grains de raisin à la crème

Leeks Vinaigrette
Some humble vegetables, like leeks, cabbage and turnips, are being rediscovered by French cuisine and given a new twist. You'll find these leeks on the menu of some excellent restaurants in France.

    4 leeks (6 if small)
    Salt
    Vinaigrette (p. 47)
    1 hardboiled egg (optional)

Split and wash leeks to remove any sand. Discard dark green part. Cut crosswise into 5 inch sections. Hold together with a rubber band and cook in boiling salted water 8 to 10 minutes. Cut off rubber band. Arrange in oblong dish. Garnish, if you like, with sieved hardboiled egg. Serve with vinaigrette on the side.

Portobello Pizza

2 large Portobello mushrooms
Olive oil
1 small yellow onion, chopped
2 cloves garlic, chopped
Salt and pepper to taste
½ cup tomato or spaghetti sauce
½ package shredded mozzarella
Hot sauce (optional)

Wipe mushrooms but do not wash. Remove stems if any. The mushrooms are probably too thick to broil properly, so with a sharp knife, cut slice off the top and reserve. Brush mushrooms with olive oil and broil for about 5 minutes. Turn over and grill other side. Season. Meanwhile, chop stems (if any) with the slice you cut off the top. Sauté in a little olive oil with onion and garlic. Season with salt and pepper and a little hot sauce, if you like.

Divide and spread onion-mushroom mixture on underpart of caps. Top with sauce and a generous heaping of mozzarella. Slide under the broiler until cheese is bubbly and browned.

To accompany this pizza: If you are not watching calories too closely, spaghetti cooked al dente, seasoned with butter and cracked pepper would be great.

Otherwise, a box of frozen, chopped spinach, cooked according to directions on the package and seasoned with a little olive oil and garlic would be nice and very low cal.

Grapes with Cream
Grapes are *raisin* in French and raisins are *raisins secs*. What we are having are fresh grapes. This is a traditional way to eat grapes in Provence as they ripen on the climbing vine that frames the kitchen door.

2 cups white seedless grapes
½ cup light sour cream or crème fraiche
Brandy
Brown sugar

Wash and dry grapes. Pull off stems. In a bowl, mix grapes with cream and a little brandy. Serve in glass bowls, sprinkled with brown sugar.

(If grapes are not very sweet, you might want to add a little sugar when mixing with cream.)

To Drink
If you are not too fanatical about dieting, a Chianti Classico or a red Côtes-du-Rhône would complement the pizza nicely.

> Perhaps you'll arrange grapes and other fruit
> around the base of your pillar candle.

Making Love at
the Royal Convent

"*Y*ou don't know about the Royal Convent in Saint-Maximin? Very romantic! I am told local couples—not necessarily married, you understand—will drive out there for dinner, even spend the night. That last part may only be a rumor, though," adds Professor Bugatti cautiously, watching us. (You never know, Americans can be such *Puritans!*) He looks more seductive than ever tonight in his black velvet blazer, sporting a new red suede vest.

We are not shocked. As a matter of fact, spending the night in a *convent*, and a *royal* one yet, boggles the mind, admits Wayne, who would like to know more, but Bugatti is now absorbed in the menu.

When we asked him for dinner at Les Deux Garçons, on the Cours Mirabeau, he accepted, apologizing that he couldn't make it before 10:00 P.M. Would that be all right? We know he has telescoped all his classes for the month into a single week, during which—if we are to believe the kids—he must also fit his carefree bachelor living, before returning to his family in Paris. No need to convince us that his schedule is *full.*

The late hour suited us perfectly, since today we drove all the way to Monaco to *visit* with the students who'd left yesterday for their long-awaited weekend on the Riviera, accompanied by Liz and a lady professor.

"Why aren't you coming with us?" they asked. "It's more fun when you're there!" I am flattered, but Wayne and I have other plans.

"My husband has been away, he just came back. I'd like a little time with him, and I need a *rest.*"

"A *rest*? From *what*?" They have no idea that this seven-day-a-week, early-morning-to-late-night job might be a bit of a drain.

"Rest from *you*! Great as you all are, I get enough of you, sometimes!"

They are piqued, "We get fed up with *you,* too, like when you nag about studying," replies Steve, as Keiko and Michiko shake their heads vigorously, appalled by such undue familiarity.

"Hey, man, check that out! They want to be like *lovers!*" The idea of Wayne and me as such convulses them.

"Come just for a *day,* then," they insist. Their desire for my company intoxicates me so that I agree, in spite of Wayne's grumbling, yes, we'll look in on them the next day and see how the Riviera agrees with them.

That is why Wayne and I drove out all the way to Monaco.

The students have spent the night in a formerly luxurious villa, a bit rundown now, built in a location to die for, right into the cliffs of exclusive Cap d'Ail. It was willed, some years ago, to a student organization by a philanthropic American lady, who specified that U.S. students be given priority. So, Liz needed only make reservations, and the entire place was ours, with its pool cut out of the rock and private little beach below, *salade niçoise* and pizza for dinner, the night and breakfast and all next day if we want it.

When I arrive, Constance is waiting for me.

"Are we really going to the beach today?"

"That's the plan. A private beach club in Monaco invites you all as guests. Madame Liz has arranged it."

"Could the plans be changed?"

"Only if it's the wish of the majority. Why? Would they prefer to do something else?"

"Oh, no! They all want to go! Is it true *nudity* is allowed on beaches here? Like *down to the waist*?"

"It is allowed, but not compulsory, you understand. Only whoever, men and women, wants to can go barechested—or bare-breasted, as the case may be."

"But this is *immoral!* Indecent! Can it be prevented?"

"I don't see how. They have their own codes here, and don't care about ours, so it's up to us to adjust. Does it bother you *that* much?"

"Bother me? It just simply shocks me! I find this *obscene,* intolerable. . . . Do I *have* to go?"

"Of course not. You can do what you want: Stay here, sun, swim, read. The little beach is private and ours for the day."

"I don't want to be left here, all alone."

"Then, come along with the others! While they're at the beach, you can visit Monte-Carlo, see boutiques, the exotic gardens. . . . Hey! they have that aquarium. . . ." I don't mention the casino.

She pouts, "I don't feel like wandering around all day in a strange city with tourists ogling me."

"Would you see a movie?" Remembering Jean-Luc, who left and has been replaced by an older man, "Keep the driver company, if you like."

But my suggestions only annoy her: "I discussed all that with Madame Liz, but she told me the same things. Where does that leave me?"

A desperate measure, and I don't care if Wayne kills me, "My husband and I will be going to lunch somewhere, would you like to join us?" To my relief, she shrugs off the invitation. "It's not my idea of a day on the Riviera to. . . ." Say no more, Constance, I am relieved. We are looking forward to lunch at La Chèvre d'Or, in nearby Èze, and definitely would prefer to be alone.

So, she'll stick with the group, none too happy about it.

We follow the bus to the beach club, where the kids start ecstatically to photograph everything in sight. They're sure the woman sunning over there is Princess Caroline—or is it Stéphanie? As they settle down on the sand, I notice among the girls one- and two-piece suits, bikinis, but no bare breasts.

"Let's go," urges Wayne. "They wouldn't take off those bras in front of us."

Lunch at La Chèvre d'Or is an enchantment, served under vast umbrellas on the top terrace of that eagle's nest crowning a rocky promontory, looking straight down at the Mediterranean's expanse of cobalt and milky turquoise, the Cap Ferrat marina in the distance with toy yachts and sailboats plying the bay.

Back at the beach at four, we find the kids ready, dressed again, showing off their new tans, leaning on the balustrade. They surround us, giggling, pointing down.

Constance is there, lying on the beach. Am I seeing right? The bottom part of her two-piece suit has been rolled down as far south as decency permits, while the top has been altogether removed. A group of Japanese tourists stands a short distance away, taking pictures with *telephoto* lenses, magnifying her already generous curves. Liz looks at me questioningly.

I shrug: What is there to say?

Only, Constance remains deaf to our calls, and I have to stumble down onto the sand to remind her we're leaving now. I don't mention our earlier conversation and neither does she, acting perfectly normal, not embarrassed in the least, only a little disgruntled because we're going, now that the sun's just right. But the others are eager to get on the way: Driving back, they're going to stop in Cannes where the film festival is in full swing, and they can't wait to check out the scene there.

Now, on the Deux Garçons terrace, our kirs have arrived. Professor Bugatti comments on the Constance episode I have just recounted: "You can see why men will *never* be able to understand women. Men think *logically,* while women's thoughts and actions follow no recognizable system. Only intuition, or else instinct, guides them. Or could it simply be whims? That is why they can be puzzling, trying, even infuriating to us men, but so *endearing,* nonetheless. Don't you agree?" he asks. Wayne only nods noncommittally, not wanting to look too savvy in front of me.

"I did notice that young lady in my Petrarch seminar," adds Bugatti. "Well endowed . . . intellectually, of course. Great potential, I suspect."

Yes, *of course,* intellectually. Only now, Wayne wants to hear more about that Royal Convent where couples go to make love, if he heard right. "Do they take just *anybody* in that convent? Like *us*? Did you say in Saint-Maximin?"

Driving along the autoroute to the Riviera, you cannot miss Saint-Maximin. We passed it twice today, going to Monaco and returning. A small, self-contained town snuggled at the foot of a mountainous range, it is dwarfed by a huge church, a basilica, read the signs, way out of proportion with the city. We never stopped, but did wonder why so much church for so little else.

Professor Bugatti is vague, wouldn't want us to think he's been there. Yes, they'll take us, if we have a reservation, that is. As a matter of fact, he just might happen to have the number here in his notebook.

So now, Wayne cannot wait to get to a phone. Yes, reservations are available for next weekend. Do we prefer a regular or a deluxe room? Deluxe rooms in a convent? Hey, check that out, as the kids would say.

Such luxury is still a week away. Next morning, a large group, much larger than the usual *comme-çoise* contingent, is waiting for me at noon. Man, oh man, do they have a story for me!

"In Cannes, like, there was this crowd on the promenade, the Croisette, it's called, right in front of some building, all white, big stairs with a red carpet, baskets of flowers on each side of the door. They were showing some movie there, like. Man, there were photogs, TV trucks, minicam crews with mikes. . . . So we pushed to the front to see."

"Limos were stopping, people dressed to kill were getting out, walking up those stairs. The papparazzi were going crazy, man, flashes all over. . . . Guess what Faustino did?"

I have no idea. "Took pictures, too?"

"No, no! Man, he's wearing white jeans and a blazer—you know him, always looks dressed up. So, he grabs Carola. She's got on that long beach skirt and a halter, and man! Like, with that tan, and her hair, she looks like a movie star! So, they just make like they're getting out of one of those limos. Bulbs are flashing; 'Who's that?' some photog shouts. 'It's that new American porn star,' another yells back. So, like, the crowd applauds, cheers, the photogs, they're falling all over each other, they shove a mike into her face. . . ."

And I had to miss that! "What did she do then?"

"She just walked up those stairs like a queen, holding on to Faustino's arm, stopping every few steps to turn around, wave, blow kisses. Feeding frenzy, like, man, with all those cameras!"

"At the top of the stairs, Faustino gets down on one knee, kisses her hand, and the crowd is yelling, applauding, we're all whistling! Man, you could go blind with those flashes!"

And that's not all:

"They were on the news last night with all those dressed-up dudes. And this morning! Get a load of that front page."

Sure enough, *Le Provençal* newspaper features a front-page color photo of blonde Carola, handsome Faustino kissing her hand: "Rising American Stars at the Cannes Film Festival."

"Some guy told Carola he was a press agent, wanted to take her to a party on a *yacht* with Arab princes," contributes Jennifer. "Only she wouldn't go. That's dumb. I'd have gone."

"Previous engagement," winks Carola, busy cutting photos out of the newspapers. "I didn't want to miss the bus."

"I want to go back tomorrow, walk up those stairs and get it on video to send my mother," demands Dana. "You're going nowhere, and you're climbing no stairs," retorts Kevin, suddenly sounding like an alpha male. "You're staying right here with *me*." Dana beams; as Kevin himself would say, looks like she's found her groove.

With such events and their fallout, the week passes quickly, so that we are now in Saint-Maximin on a very hot afternoon, looking for that mysterious convent. Signs, plenty of them, direct to *Basilique* and *Couvent royal* in different directions, but when we try to follow them, we lose sight of that enormous church, engage in a labyrinth of narrow, one-way streets and the signs disappear. Driving in apparently widening circles, we end up in the outskirts, where a lady, fanning herself on her doorstep, kindly puts us on the way.

"Just down that street. Turn left at the end, you'll see the basilica."

"But it's the *convent* we're looking for."

"Walk into the basilica, that's where you'll find it."

Next, we are stepping into an immense nave, bigger even, it seems, than Notre-Dame, reveling in the sudden coolness. Finally, we learn why such a gigantic monument: This, reads a plaque on a pillar, is where a crypt holds the body of Saint Mary Magdalen, the woman who, according to the Gospels, poured perfume on Jesus' feet, accompanied him through his preaching mission, stood at the foot of the cross and met him on Resurrection morning, the sister of Martha and Lazarus who was brought back from the dead. In other words, someone from the upper echelons of Bible aristocracy.

We wander, join a group following a guided tour, catch a few words: "This basilica was founded in 1295, in honor of the relics of Mary Magdalen found resting here, by Charles of Anjou, King of Naples and Count of Provence. At the same time, he founded the adjoining convent."

Adjoining! Now, we've found it. Just exit through the lateral portals *directly* into the cloisters, a covered walk under Gothic arches, open to a central garden alive with oleanders and myriads of roses, the ironwork of a well ethereal in a veil of star blossoms.

But tables are set under those arches, elegant in pastel cloths, flowers, silver and crystal. More tables, more crystal gleams in the vastness of another Gothic room. Nice for a convent, no wonder couples—not necessarily married—seek out the place! More romantic, one could not find. Following the cloisters, we step into a *bar* (A *bar?* In a *convent?*) with club chairs and bottle-covered walls, then a salon and, finally, the reception, which opens onto a small recessed square we'd never have found on our own! There, a large brass plaque on the outside wall announces: *Hostellerie du Couvent Royal,* and the mystery is solved: Some time ago, the convent was turned into a hotel.

"Trust the French to think of it," comments Wayne.

When we are led to our deluxe room, we find that, in its own way, it is just that.

"Rooms have been created from the cells formerly occupied by monks. For rooms like this one, a partition was knocked down to double the size."

Even so, it is not large. The walls are whitewashed, the floor bare, terra-cotta tiles polished to a low luster. But the armchair, the drapes and the bed coverlet, all in the same orange and white printed fabric, spill pools of sunshine, further brightened by the late afternoon rays that pour through the small window, open onto the jumble of roofs, flying buttresses and spires of the basilica. The bathroom is so stark and gleaming, I hesitate to sully it with our toilet kits.

Wayne has already set his camera on a tripod and whistles softly as he sights through the lens, returns to turn down the bed covers, and, pulling a sunflower from a vase on the bureau, lays it invitingly across the *traversin*.

"The stock agency always needs shots of hotel rooms. Bet they won't have too many taken in a convent, a royal one, yet."

Later, we find our table reserved in the delicious coolness of the cloister arches, where candlelight casts wavering shadows. We especially enjoy the *tian* of lamb flavored with fennel and thyme, and tell the young chef when he comes on his post-dinner rounds. That's when we notice a distinguished older couple, at the next table, smiling at us. We are soon in conversation with them and discover they'd been curious about us but, hearing only English, were hesitant to try out their half-forgotten school English, until they heard us complimenting the chef in French.

M. Rivière, it turns out, is a fountainhead of information. A retired architect, the author of several books on the region, local history is his hobby. He finds it hard to believe we know *nothing* beyond the fact we've just learned: Mary Magdalen is entombed here.

"Yes, a sarcophagus was found, containing bones which, legend affirms, are those of the saint. . . . Much later, science had progressed enough to determine they *are* those of a small woman of Mediterranean type, in her 50s, with long, dark hair, of which a few strands still adhere. Are these the remains of the woman who wiped perfume off Jesus' feet with her tresses? The church believes they are, and while not proven, it's a possibility."

"But what would Mary Magdalen have been doing *here*? She lived in what is Israel today, didn't she?" I ask.

"Yes, Judea then. But after the execution of Jesus by the Romans as a rebel to their rule, his family and followers were forced into exile. Provençal tradition affirms that Mary Magdalen, her sister Martha, their brother Lazarus and a few others, like Maximin, Mary Jacobe and Mary Salome, were pushed into a bark without oars, rudder or sails and set adrift onto the sea."

"Don't forget their servant Sara," interjects his wife.

"Oh, yes, Sara, their black servant from Yemen, was left ashore, despairing and begging to join them. So, Martha, I think it was, threw her cloak over the water and Sara walked, dry-footed, into the boat. You don't see that sort of thing nowadays."

"They ran aground here in Provence," adds Madame Rivière, "on a beach called, since then, the Saintes-Maries-de-la-Mer, the Holy Marys from the Sea. From there, they scattered: Maximin came here and eventually became head of a budding Christian community. Martha went on to Tarascon on the Rhône, where she tamed the *Tarasque*, their local monster. As for Magdalen, tradition has it that she preached Jesus' word in Marseille, in particular, in front of the Temple of Artemis, to be exact. As for Sara, there's no record of her activities, only that she died and was—still is—buried in the church of Les Saintes-Maries-de-la-Mer near the shore where they landed. She became the patron saint of gypsies, who gather there each year in a festival honoring her."

So that's it, that gypsy festival the students have been asking me about! Now, I know a little more.

Dinner is over, and at my insistence, the Rivières move over to our table for coffee because I don't want the conversation to end yet.

"We've been coming here each year since the *hostellerie* opened," confides Monsieur Rivière, "to celebrate our wedding anniversary. Perfect place to kindle or rekindle romance, under the auspices of a woman who loved so passionately and so devotedly, don't you think?" He must be right: many of the tables earlier occupied by attractive couples—and, I thought, when I first came in, not *necessarily* married—are now empty, although it is not late. He continues: "The next day, we climb up the Sainte-Baume, in reverence to the saint. The Sainte-Baume? That's the mountain right in back of the town."

"What do you find there?" I want to know.

"There is the grotto where Mary Magdalen supposedly spent the last 30 years of her life in contemplation and remembrance. Then, a little higher, you come up to a chapel and a small bookstore, where I sometimes discover monographs of interest."

"Is the climb difficult?"

"Not at all. More like a walk, a bit steep at times, but cool under the canopy of trees. And a lovely fountain, with icy water, gurgles halfway up. Takes about an hour."

"Can we join you?"

Madame Rivière nods her pleased agreement, and thus it is decided that we'll walk up the Sainte-Baume in their company.

Monsieur Rivière leans over, lowers his voice confidentially, "She was the wife of Jesus, you know."

What? "But we've always been told that Jesus lived and died a single man!"

"That's the version fostered by the Church, during the first centuries, when monastic tradition was developing. Celibacy was encouraged then because the fruits of labor of single persons—nuns and monks—accrued to the Church; so, Jesus had to be presented as a role model. But don't forget: He was Jewish, a rabbi, as his disciples always called him and, according to the laws and customs of his time, would *have* to be married."

For me, raised in Catholic schools, this is . . . blasphemy, I fear. I try to recall the teachings of the good nuns. . . . And how does Wayne, who's been seeking spirituality in the company of Father Antoine, feel about this?

Wayne is looking at his watch. Trying to catch my eye, he discreetly indicates the doorway to the stairs. Then, he elaborately stifles a yawn under his hand. "It's getting late don't you think? We shouldn't keep you up on this important day."

So, we excuse ourselves. Madame Rivière, whose blue-tinted white hair gleams under the candlelight, smiles as we say our goodnights—did I see her wink at me? Holding on to my hand, Wayne pulls me up the winding stairs, whistling:

> *Pour un flirt avec toi*
> *Je donnerais n'importe quoi. . . .*

Hardly a fitting tune for a convent, royal or otherwise, but who's complaining?

Next morning finds us climbing up the Sainte-Baume—
I've found out that *baume* is the Provençal word for "cave."
The sun, already hot, cannot penetrate the cool of the
night still trapped under the heavy foliage of arching
branches. Our pace is brisk, I feel, until a troop of Boy
Scouts passes us, running up and down, chasing each other,
led—or rather followed—by a portly master who puffs
and strains to keep up with them.

"You see," Monsieur Rivière is picking up where he left
off last night, "I believe there is a great deal more to the
Mary Magdalen story than the Church will admit. As I
mentioned, she had to be Jesus' wife—remember how
familiar they were, according to the Gospel writers? How
she accompanied him everywhere, how he kissed her pub-
licly? That wouldn't have been possible in the climate of
the time, unless they were man and wife. And what about
the Wedding Feast at Cana, where Jesus changed water into
wine? We're not told whose wedding it was, but suppose it
was his own? Why, otherwise, would he have felt responsible, at his mother's urging, for seeing to the refreshments?
Which he did, changing all that water into wine—600
liters of it, to be exact. Must have been *some* affair! But
then, they were not ordinary people: more like royalty,
descended from King David."

Any thoughts of protest vanish as the fountain appears,
under a bush covered with clusters of tiny white flowers.
My hands turn numb as I dip them into the little basin,
where clear water trickles. Wayne rinses out one of his lens
caps and offers it as a drinking cup, but cupped hands

work very well, bathing most of your face at the same time in that icy water that smells of moss and iron filings.

Back on the trail, Monsieur Rivière continues:

"Then, after Jesus was arrested, convicted as a rebel— remember, the Romans accused him of wanting to be King of the Jews, that's what the inscription on the cross says— she accompanied him to his execution and saw to his sepulture. . . . A wifely duty."

I am sure the nuns of my school years would have me stop my ears to such iconoclastic talk. . . . Their teachings, however, are long ago and far away. . . . And there's more, as I listen, spellbound:

"What's to say that, when forced to leave Judea, she did-n't bring with her . . . their children? At least, their child?"

"What would have become of that child, then, as he grew up?"

"In Roman-occupied Provence, his life would have been far from safe, so he had to be hidden, his identity kept secret. Only initiates would know of him, of his blood-line. . . . I have always felt the Holy Grail legends of the Middle Ages were a way of transmitting that secret with-out revealing it openly."

"I don't understand. Wasn't the Grail some sort of a ves-sel that had held the blood of Christ?"

"Exactly. The *blood* of Christ! The words in French are *Saint Graal*. But pronounce it *sang* (blood) *réal* (or royal), properly linking the *g*. See? *Sangreal*, or *Saint Graal*."

"You make it sound almost credible, and in any case, fascinating. . . ."

"Thank you. So, it wasn't a matter of a little coagulated blood at the bottom of a dish. No. The *Saint Graal*, or Holy Grail, referred to living blood, a bloodline, a descendance, a family with royal origins dating back to King David."

"And what do you think happened to that line?"

"Much has been written on the subject, but the mystery remains. Did they marry into the first dynasty, the Visigoths, that reigned over Southern France? Would the concept that French kings ruled by divine right originate there? Some think the fleur-de-lis of French royalty harks back to the lily of Judea, emblem of David. But then, there is so much we do not know. . . ."

"Henri," interrupts his wife, who, in a light blue T-shirt and shorts with matching espadrilles is stepping lightly over rocks that stud the path, "Henri, the subject never bores you but it might be a different matter for our friends! Forgive him, please, if he rides his hobbyhorse roughshod over anybody's beliefs! I hope you're not offended."

Not offended at all, just wondering, and pleased with what I see as an exercise in opening the mind. I do remember the nature of that mysterious Grail is never specified in the legends. As Monsieur Rivière says, so much we do not know!

"Ah, now, this is the *baume*, where Mary spent all those years, or so we're told." The small cave, just a hollow in the mountainside with a rock overhang is dark and damp, water steadily dripping onto a long, flat stone in the back. "Her bed, you see." Moss and ferns grow out of cracks. I almost shudder.

"Hope she wasn't arthritis-prone," comments Wayne.

"Whatever the truth about her," ventures Madame Rivière, "I find hers a beautiful love story. Forget about sainthood and all the trappings that must have been added much later. But what we have is a woman who loved completely and forever. I visualize her as beautiful, with long hair and green eyes—like many Mediterranean people have—falling in love with that strange young man, who was consumed with a mission, espousing his cause, following him all the way to the hill of his execution, watching him expire from a distance. . . . And later, here, in this strange country, trying to perpetuate his memory, speaking in his name. . . . And when all was done, retiring from the world to remember . . . nothing but *remember* until the end came. Let's think of her neither as a saint nor a sinner, but as a woman who knew how to *love*."

Our silence is punctuated only by the drip, drip of a rivulet over that flat stone—her bed.

Only a short distance remains, a flight of stairs hewn out of the rock, and here is the chapel, and the little bookstore crowded with books, religious magazines, souvenirs, rosaries and small statues of the saint carrying her perfume jar. The Boy Scouts are jostling for attention at the candy counter.

Alone, on a shelf level with my eye, a single, large book is propped against the wall. It's cover shows a color photograph of the little grotto we've just seen. The title follows me as I move across the room:

NO GREATER LOVE

Madame Rivière was right.

On Monday, I try to tell the students about our trip to Saint-Maximin, stressing its educational aspects rather than its romantic ones. But they make a show of indifference, pointedly ignoring even my offer of lunch. They ask no questions and simply shrug off mine. Who cares what *you* did? their attitude plainly says. They only want to know when *our* (meaning *their*) next outing will be. Puzzled at first, I finally understand. They are jealous! I went somewhere and had a good time without them, so they don't want to hear about it. *That* will show me. They even seem to suspect that I might prefer Wayne's company to theirs, and don't like the idea.

"Watch out," cautions Wayne. "Next thing you know, they'll be calling you *Mom*."

I certainly wouldn't try to take their real mom's place. However, it would please me greatly to think I've found a little place of affection in those kids' hearts.

They, I know, have just that spot in mine.

Experience Romance
Passion and Paradise

The Guide "Esprit de France" Lists Places Like the Royal Convent
If you enjoy hotels and restaurants installed in historic buildings that range from medieval fortresses to sumptuous castles, and from abbeys to fortified farmhouses, check the guide *Esprit de France* (Esprit de France, 93, Rue de Lille, 75007 Paris; Tel: 01-47-05-48-40; Fax: 01-47-05-41-18;

e-mail: esprit.france@wanadoo.com; www.esprit-de-france.com).

There are several other guides representing different associations, like *Relais et Châteaux*, for instance. If you seek quiet and secluded hotels, the guide *Relais du Silence* is for you.

Hostellerie du Couvent Royal (Tel: 04-94-86-55-66; Fax: 04-99-59-82-82).

A Pilgrimage to Love

Climb the Sainte-Baume. It is a lovely excursion. Browse through the little shop for souvenirs of the saint.

Give more than a passing thought to that woman who was made a saint because she loved passionately, and wonder whether *you*, too, are, on that score, a candidate for sainthood.

Let the Tarasque Scare You in Tarascon

If you are interested in Mary Magdalen's story and/or in the most beautiful Provençal fabrics, you'll enjoy a trip to Tarascon.

This is Saint Martha's territory. She was Mary Magdalen's sister, and they came to Provence together with Maximin and a few others, expelled by the Romans after Jesus' execution.

While Martha was evangelizing the area, a *tarasque* monster would periodically creep out of the Rhône to devour a few residents. This prompted survivors to call upon that holy woman. With a sign of the cross, she tamed the beast, and, untying her sash, she used it as a leash to lead it away.

She is buried in the church, and you'll see there a spiky, wooden *tarasque* the faithful take out each year in a procession that re-enacts the event.

Tarascon Is Home to the Soleïado Fabrics Sold by Pierre Deux
The Demery family, there, discovered some old print blocks in their attic, and the rest is history. Their Soleïado (*sunny*, in Provençal) patterns and colors are unequalled. Visit the shop: There are great buys in discontinued patterns and remnants.

Take the Photo of Your Life at the Pont-du-Gard
This is the perfectly preserved, great aqueduct built by the Romans to bring water to the city of Nîmes. Time your arrival for late afternoon: You'll avoid the madhouse of tour buses, crowds, fast food and souvenir stands, and the place will be yours alone.

Then watch, camera in hand, as the shadows of sunset paint the old stones blue, while brilliant gold illuminates the arches.

For a Most Romantic Dinner
There is a nice hotel-restaurant, very close to the Pont-du-Gard. *Colombier* (Tel: 04-66-37-05-28; Fax: 04-66-37-35-75; www.le-colombier.com; e-mail: info@le-colombier.com) is fine, and if you stay there, you can look at the Pont in the moonlight. Nothing wrong with that.

But read on for a surprise.

Le Vieux Castillon (Tel: 04-66-37-61-61; Fax: 04-66-37-28-17). Just 4 kilometers away, in Castillon-du-Gard, a hilltop medieval village, complete to cobblestone paving, you'll find this enchanting restaurant-hotel. The cuisine is Michelin-starred. The décor will delight you and you'll want to whisper words of love across the table.

If you do not feel that anything better awaits you elsewhere, why not stay overnight? You won't be disappointed when you discover how comfortable your bed is under that canopy.

Simple and Sensuous
A Springtime Dinner *à deux*

Spring is in the air, and this easy dinner makes use of the season's products: spring lamb, asparagus, strawberries. You'll love all the delicate flavors.

Asperges vinaigrette
Agneau grillé aux flageolets
Fraises Romanoff

Asparagus Vinaigrette
    1 bunch plump, green or white asparagus
    Salt
    Vinaigrette (p. 47)

Peel the stems of the asparagus. This is important because the skin is stringy and imparts a bitter flavor. Cook vertically in pot of salted water, covered. If too long, shorten them a bit, or else, instead of a lid, wrap top of pot in foil. Only steam should reach the delicate tips. Cook until tender but do not overcook. Drain. Serve on oblong dish.

(To eat asparagus: In France, you tilt your plate by placing a bit of bread under it. This creates a well for the vinaigrette. Pick up asparagus and dip in vinaigrette.)

Grilled Lamb and Flageolet Beans

 2 slices of leg of lamb
 1 16-ounce can green flageolet beans (or white beans)
 1 whole head of garlic, roasted
 Salt, pepper, minced parsley
 2 tablespoons butter

In a very hot pan, sear lamb on both sides, and, lowering heat, continue cooking until done to your taste. Remove from pan and keep warm.

The Beans: The ideal complement to grilled lamb are the pale green "chevrier" or flageolet beans, available in many markets. If not available, white beans will do.

Drain and rinse beans. Heat in same pan, add butter and flavor with roasted garlic.

How to Roast Garlic: Take an entire head of fresh garlic. With a sharp knife, cut it across in two. Wrap in foil. Bake in toaster oven 10 minutes (longer in a conventional oven) or until soft. Unwrap and squeeze. Roasted garlic will come out in a purée consistency. Use this to flavor the beans and the meat, and even spread a little on your bread.

Optional: You might slice a vine tomato in two and grill the two halves, cut side down after you remove the meat. Flatten a bit with a spatula. It takes only a minute or two. Season well, garnish with chopped parsley.

On Your Plate
Season lamb with salt, pepper and garlic. Serve with beans (and tomato half if desired). Garnish with parsley.

Strawberries Romanoff
   I pint strawberries, washed and hulled
   ½ cup strawberry liqueur (or other fruit liqueur or
      red wine)
   ½ pint strawberry ice cream
   Whipped cream

Slice strawberries and marinate for 10 minutes in liqueur. If using wine, add sugar to sweeten to taste.

Serve strawberries in dessert dishes with a scoop of strawberry ice cream in center, liqueur poured over the top. Decorate with whipped cream if you like.

To Drink
Wouldn't you say a red Bordeaux? Or perhaps a California Merlot?

A bowl of your decorated Easter eggs
would make a great centerpiece.

Love Makes
the Sun Rise

*I*s my authority waning in these last few weeks of
the Program? The students—mostly the men—
are not *asking* to be taken to the gypsy festival in Les
Saintes-Maries-de-la-Mer, they are *demanding* it. Is it because, abandoning the suits I felt this job required, I am
now appearing in narrow jeans? "Hey, cool!" exclaimed the
girls, and the guys went, "Right on, Madame L!" Or is it
because I catch myself sounding like them, as when one of
the guys reported forgetting the date of an exam: "Like
zero smarts, man!" I exclaimed, instead of, "Now, that was
thoughtless of you, wasn't it?"

"We did go to the festival once," cautions Liz, "on my
first year with the Program. But I always advised the Resident Directors against it afterwards. Massive, unruly

crowds, rampant thievery, better tell the kids to forget about it."

So, I try to cajole the group: "Not much to do or to see there, you'd get lost in the crowds. . . . Wouldn't you prefer to return to Avignon? I know, you've been there; only this time, you could visit the Palace of the Popes, see the bird-hunting fresco in John XXII's room? No? Then how about Nîmes? There's a famous Roman temple there, the Maison Carrée, that you should see. . . ."

But someone—I don't know who—has told them one must *not* miss the gypsy festival and promised them delights there that nobody will tell me about. Whatever it is they expect to find at that festival rules out any old fresco or the Maison Carrée.

And that is why we are today on our way to Les Saintes-Maries, having crossed the Rhône at Arles, where it divides into the *Grand* and the *Petit* Rhônes, arms that embrace the triangular delta. The part of the Camargue we cross is a flat expanse of rice fields, spreading their short, bright green stubble and rather anemic-looking vineyards—I know these produce the Listel des Sables, a wine called *gris* because it is a pale, almost gray rosé. I found the taste, dry and flinty with a hint of salt, strangely enticing. The *manades* we pass are farms that breed bulls for fights in the nearby arenas of Arles and Nîmes, and also for other venues all over the southwest of France. The black bulls are there in numbers, rather small, but armed with fearsome horns, grazing in pastures distant from the road.

The driver, who is from Camargue, tells us these bulls are wild, totally unused to human presence.

"Aren't they, like, taken in at night? Into a stable, like?"

No, they never leave those fields where they eat, live and sleep. That is why, one day, when the gates of their dark holding pens swing open to the arena, as the bull is propelled into blinding sunlight and the roars of the crowds, he'll show no fear, but instead charge the red moving cape. . . .

Some of the students have seen those bullfights on TV, when the bull, half paralyzed by the banderillas stuck into his spine, sinks to his knees almost to the ground, still trying to attack the maddening red cape. They are horrified by that senseless torture of an innocent animal and root for the bull, hoping to see the toreador gored instead. The girls are almost in tears: They'd like to get out, walk over to those bulls, pet them, kiss their noses, perhaps bring one home. . . . The guys take a tougher line: "You could, like, sneak up to those paddocks, slip the bolts open and let the bulls out! Give them a chance, man!"

But you cannot fight destiny, and these bulls are destined to die in the arena. "They know it, too," comments the driver.

Even before we reach the urban sprawl that girds the ancient city of Les Saintes-Maries, we come upon empty land turned today into gigantic parking lots, and looking for a spot, drive through acres of parked buses. Many are touring *autocars* like our own, which brought tourists like us. Others, ranging all the way from luxurious motor coaches to rusting heaps, bear plates from Poland, Ukraine, Hungary, Romania, Czechoslovakia. "Chartered by gypsies," comments the driver.

We are passed by a young couple, all in black leather, who roar away on a Harley-Davidson with Italian plates. "See that sign on the back fender? It's in Romany, their language. It means they're gypsies," says the driver. In turn, we pass a horse-drawn caravan all painted in bright colors, tasseled curtains at the windows, the same sign on the back. On the woman sitting next to the driver gleams a mass of gold chains and bracelets. We are passed again, this time by a Rolls-Royce with British plates, the same sign on the fender.

Now is the time to take out the plastic bag I brought, together with a box of baggies. Let's try to express tactfully what I must tell them: "You'll be exposed today to a culture different from your own that may not place the same emphasis on personal property as we do." What I mean is, "Like, man, watch out or you'll be robbed blind." But the delicacy of language does not fool them. I've touched the nerve of political correctness.

Boos interrupt me. Part of the group is indignant: "You mean, like they're going to *steal* from us? Man, it is *racist* to stereotype any ethnic group!" Others join in: "Right on! No racist talk." A few, though, are beginning to slip off rings and watches and reach for their wallets. I don't give up:

"All right. You are not *forced* to do anything you don't want to do. Those of you who wish to may place their things in a baggie, which will go into this big bag, to be locked in the cargo hold." The driver adds: "I'll stay with the bus if I want to find tires and even wheels on it when you return." Several baggies with green U.S. passports, watches, rings, folders of travelers' checks are dropped into the bag. Still not reassured, I insist, "It's not because you'll stash your stuff where you can keep an *eye* on it that you're being racist." I know how unsafe back jeans pockets can be, and several times we've found wallets and their contents behind chair cushions or on the floor of the Villa.

The driver, who missed the exchange in English, tries to warn: "Gypsies will take anything they can grab, except silver jewelry. Silver is bad luck for them, unless it is a watch or money. Gold rings, chains and the like are not safe with them. Passports they like—easily sold at a good price." He tells us how a young Arab man, bearer of such a purchased passport issued in the name of Sue Ellen Anderson from Bridgeport, Connecticut, was detained upon arrival in New York. Sue Ellen's picture had been replaced with his own, mustache and all, so he couldn't understand why there should be anything suspicious about his ownership of the document.

Before they scatter: "We'll meet again at the bus at four. Meanwhile, should you need me, I'll try to stay as close to the church as possible. Look for me there." I am the lone chaperone today, for Liz has begged off, arguing important errands, and come to think of it, Stan is not here either.

Much has been said and written about the mysterious, haunting charm of Camargue, its immense sky, the decoupage of land and lagoons, where flights of flamingoes rise like pink clouds. I saw all that in the course of a solitary drive this past winter, when, taking a whole day off by myself, I pushed way through the delta to the Salins, a sort of end of-the-world place where evaporating flats draw a giant checkerboard in colors ranging from azure to magenta, as salinity and mineral contents rise. I watched, at twilight, while the sun set and a full moon rose, *sauniers* gathering the *fleur de sel*, those rare crystals that form on the surface of the water. I even climbed one of the sparkling mountains of salt. . . . Afterwards, driving home in the dark, I kept touching my lips to my arm, recapturing the salty tang, and later, I brushed salt dust out of my hair.

But today, we'll see none of that. Only crowds, crowds, appalling crowds, all converging on the fortified church where, today, the relics of Saint Sara are going to be raised from the crypt where they lie and carried on men's backs to the sea.

The gypsies are here en masse. If there is any organization, I fail to detect it. They push and crowd, all men, for the women take no active part in this phase of the ceremony—we'll find out later what *their* role is. Right now, they stand on the sidelines, a baby on their hip, an infant suckling a breast, children hanging from skirts, intently watching the surging mass of tourists who push to see . . . what?

A vociferous group carrying the saint's catafalque and her effigy loaded with jewelry and dressed in robes piled on top of one another is walking out of the church, following a priest in gold vestments and choir boys swinging censers as an incantation rises in some language that must be Romany. With a mob following, encircling, hundreds of hands reaching up to touch the relics, the bearers attempt to make their way to the beach nearby. But some constantly try to push them out of the way and take their place, or at least help to carry, as others bend down to slip under, for extra blessings, I suppose, as the load lurches and angry shouts arise.

Finally, the coffin-like box and the overdressed, bundled-up statue, swaying more dangerously all the time, have reached the water. The men step into the surging surf, with waves rising above their waists, still surrounded by hundreds of shouting, praying, chanting gypsies. Many kneel, water up to their chins, are trampled, disappear to emerge spluttering. Meanwhile the priest has also stepped into the water, but remaining close to the edge, holds up a crucifix and recites prayers as acolytes swing their censers.

I watch this mad show from the comparative safety of a little ledge against the church wall protecting my back from pushes and shoves. That's when Amanda comes running, all her little braids flying:

"My ring, my ring! My grandmother gave it to me when I graduated from high school! It's gone! That woman took it! I want it back, call the police, please, oh please, get me back my ring! . . ."

The police? In this mob? "First, try to calm down, Amanda, and tell me what happened."

"I was watching them walk into the water, and this woman comes up to me. *'Love makes the sun rise, sister,'* she says. 'Cross my palm with silver and I'll tell you your fortune.' So, I give her a coin, and she's holding my hand, pressing it to look at the lines. Suddenly, I feel she's slipping my ring off, and at the same time, somebody is tugging away at my backpack. I turn around, but I don't see anybody, and now the woman is gone, too, with my ring. Please, oh please, get it back for me."

Not much hope. . . . Still, I ask, "Would you recognize the woman?"

"I'm not sure. . . . Dark, with a head scarf, a shawl and a long skirt, I think."

Well, that describes about 10,000 women here today. Looking everywhere, I manage to spot a lone policeman who stands, watching the turmoil with a distant gaze. He shakes his head:

"Now, what do you expect me to do? Arrest every woman with a shawl and a long skirt?" Amanda is crying, "It was gold, with an aquamarine, my birthstone, a real one. . . ." Now, she hugs her backpack to her chest.

The saint's relics are being returned to the church, amid the same insane mob scene. This apparently marks the end of official ceremonies and leaves the thousands of tourists milling around, with nothing much to do except spill into the streets where the gypsy women are prowling. Lunch will be hard to get, as the small restaurants are already crowded and refusing customers. Yet, Amanda and I are lucky because we find a small table at the terrace of a café, where we can, at least, escape the jostling.

We are sinking gratefully onto the hard, plastic seats when Rosalind runs by, looking for me. I call out to her.

"Oh, I'm glad I found you! Come quick, quick, it's terrible! Something happened to Rob, he can't move, he is paralyzed."

I dash out, followed by Amanda still hugging her backpack to her chest.

A short distance away, I see a group: Steve, Keith and Rob, who's looking very pale leaning against a wall, all lopsided, his right shoulder and arm hanging down.

"What happened to you, Rob?"

"I'm paralyzed. See? I can't move this arm. But the pain is better now."

I take his hand, try to lift it. It falls back limply. Now, I am panicked: Could someone so young be the victim of a stroke? I guess anything is possible. He can speak, he is conscious, even standing up, more or less. But I'm not sure: What exactly are the symptoms of a stroke?

"When did that happen?"

"When that girl put a curse on me."

Ah, so it is a *curse*, rather than a stroke! I breathe a small sigh of relief. Perhaps not easier to treat, but I won't go looking for paramedics yet.

"Why did she put a curse on you?"

"I was just walking down the street, like, with a couple of other guys. She comes up to me and says, '*Love makes the sun rise, brother.*' So we all laugh because we expected something like that and I answer: 'It sure does, sister!'"

"That chick was a knockout, man," interjects Keith. "Twenty maybe, long black hair, didn't even *look* like a gypsy."

This from an expert, I think wryly. "Go on. Then what?"

"So, she takes my hand, and I don't mind that, I'm thinking like 'Hey! Right on, man!' Then, she wants some money to tell my fortune, so, just to play along, I give her a ten-franc coin. But she says no, it's a hundred she wants. Man, that's like 20 bucks, way too much, I tell her, and I pull my hand away. . . ."

"So?"

"So, she fixes me with those dark eyes, points to my shoulder muttering something, makes a sign with her fingers: 'There. You are cursed! You won't be able to move your arm again *ever*.' And I feel a pain shooting like hot iron all the way down my arm and into my fingers. So I screamed and found what she said was true: I was paralyzed."

"That's when she got my camera," puts in Keith, "when I rushed to see what was the matter with Rob. Must have cut off the strap."

"My passport, too," adds Steve sheepishly. "From my back pocket. I know, I know, no need to scold me."

Jennifer has joined the group: "What did you think she meant with *Love makes the sun rise*? She was in love with you? Man, they *all* say that when they want money! Two of these women came on to me like that . . . only, I'd left my things with the bus."

I am not scolding anybody. Those kids are punished enough. Only, now who will help restore the use of that arm, hanging loose and limp, dragging Rob's shoulder down? I don't see anyone, so, *I'll* give it a try.

"Rob," I say as sternly as I am capable, "there's *nothing* wrong with your arm. You can move it if you try. Come on, don't be a *wuss!*" (I told you that I'm beginning to sound like them.)

He makes a weak effort, but the arm remains useless: "Nothing doing. It's like, paralyzed for *life*, she said."

Will it do any good to explain that this is hypnosis by suggestion? Hypnosis does not affect the body, only the mind, by supplanting your own will with someone else's . . . but only if *you* let it happen. "Don't tell me you'd let that girl take over your own will, man!"

"I can't move it."

"You can if you *want* to."

Rob looks at me, shakes his head sadly. "But you see," he says at last, "I'm not sure that I *want* to."

The other kids laugh at that, but the arm is still paralyzed when we return ahead of schedule to the bus, and find many already sitting with the driver or converging. They've had enough. Let's go.

But Madison is not here, and as we wait for her, we tally the losses: In addition to the gold ring, two watches are missing, with neither owner having any idea of how that could have happened; one passport—Steve's—and three cameras including Keith's, their straps probably neatly sliced away.

Nothing can be done, unfortunately, about the missing objects. Except for the passport, and Steve cheers up when I inform him that I'll just take him into Marseille where the U.S. Consulate will replace the missing document.

At the Consulate, the employee shows exasperation. "This is the sixth this weekend! Tell me, were you at the Gypsy Festival, too, by any chance?

When Madison comes running, something is different about her, and it takes me a moment to realize that her long blonde braid is now much shorter and unraveling.

"I'm standing in a crowd watching gypsies do a dance with tambourines and a white goat tethered in the middle. I feel a tug on my hair, turn around. Two guys are there, one with scissors, the other holding the end of my hair in his hand. They were trying to cut off lots more; it's only because I turned around so quick that they didn't get it all." So, she threw them one after the other in two quick moves, and recovered the piece of braid, which she holds like a trophy: Ten inches of white blonde strands that looks like angel hair from some Christmas tree . . . angry, but pleased that she got even. As the bus pulls out, she shakes her remaining hair loose; it still hangs shoulder length. No longer skinned away from her temples, it now frames her face.

"Hey, look!" somebody exclaims. "Madison *is* beautiful!"

The plastic bag has been recovered, the baggies redistributed. Rebecca is disconsolate about her ring. Keith, whose camera was insured (if you knew Keith, you'd know it would be) is figuring out the claim procedure. The other two are casual about their losses. As for the watches, one was valuable: "I think my dad carries insurance on it." The other one wasn't worth much, declares the owner.

There is still something I need to know.

"Now, please, tell me: Why did you want so badly to go to that festival? What did you expect to find there?"

"It was the guys, we just went along," say the girls.

The guys look sheepish. "Can't we just forget it, like?" But I am stubborn.

"Did somebody tell you that you should go?"

They all look in Rob's direction. Finally he bursts out:

"That guy from Algeria, who said he didn't like Americans. Then, he turned real nice and told me he had a tip:

'Go to that festival, 'cause, man, sex is yours for the taking there all over the streets. Just wait 'til a girl comes to you and says *Love makes the sun rise*, man that means, like, she's *ready*,'" confesses Rob. Then, suddenly enraged:

"Just let me find that bastard again! Man, I swear, I'll kill him for sure!" yells Rob shaking his fist.

His *right* fist.

And now, this is the last day of our program. To ward off wistful thoughts that this group will never be together again, we are closing the year with a party on the terrace, just as we opened it. The students are all here, the same, yet different in ways we cannot fathom, and some have already set out on unexpected pathways.

Is this Pomme, the girl whose French lessons so entranced Phil on the first evening in Paris? Bangs down to her eyes, but demure in a white dress, she stands with him and his parents—I can barely distinguish Phil from his father, so striking is the resemblance. Pomme shows off her ring, the engagement part of a sweetheart set that belonged to Phil's grandmother, and I explain to her how it will lock together with the wedding band. "The *wedding* band?" she says, wide-eyed. "I haven't even thought much about *that* yet." She snuggles close to Phil, "Chéri, tell me it is all *pour de vrai*, for real?"

Those last weeks were heady. The students—why do I find it harder to call them *kids* now?—are high with plans for the summer. Several have bought cars, three or four pooling budgets to acquire a Renault or a Citroën on its last legs, hoping it will last long enough for a spin they're going to take before heading home. They sailed through exams, much more confident this time, no tears, nobody rushing into my office to complain about unfair questions or wail they'd surely flunked. . . . I see them less than earlier in the year, the *comme-ci, comme-çoise* lunch set has dwindled, as many have made a life for themselves, found friends and traced their paths in the city. Faustino dropped by to inform me mysteriously that he might soon have some stunning news to share.

We are notified that the General Director, on an inspection tour of the European facilities, will stop in Aix on his way from the Program in Florence to the one in Madrid. I already like, but have learned to admire and respect, the General, as I still privately call him, finding him the perfect administrator, always available and supportive, willing to trust the good sense of his appointees rather than sabotage their initiative.

When I suggested a welcoming committee, so many hands shot up that we had to draw lots to select six volunteers. Those turned out to be seven because Keiko and Michiko had written both their names on a single slip. By way of apology, they immediately proposed preparing a welcome sign. The "sign" came as a cloth-wrapped bundle they could barely carry, which unfurled into a 20-foot banner with "Welcome to the General Director" calligraphied in almost Japanese strokes amid minutely painted flourishes.

When the railroad station police, alerted by what looked to them like a student demonstration, converged, the "committee" explained: *"Non, non, nous ne protestons pas! Au contraire. Nous sommes contents de voir ce monsieur!"* So, the *flics* stayed to help hold up the long banner, and this is how Liz, seven students, two *flics* and I greeted the General with grinning faces above the banner.

Parents are in for a surprise when they see the changes the year has wrought in their children, and even more when they discover the changes run deeper than their altered appearance.

Kevin, pictured on his application document with a shoulder-length mane and who arrived with a clean-shaven head, has matured into a well-barbered, young executive type. And Dana! Dana, the snarling veteran of counseling, who overdosed on sedatives, charcoaled her eyes into dark holes, Dana seems to have found whatever she needed in Kevin's company. He clearly cares for her, will tolerate no eccentricities, and she revels in this newfound authority that she must have craved.

As more guests arrive, it looks like another engagement yet! Carola, in a black sheath dress, hair blonder and straighter than ever, is helped out of a Mercedes by a young man I recognize as Fabrice, the son of the Villelaure mayor. All year, I heard of the other girls' envy whenever they caught sight of that Mercedes waiting to pick up Carola for another weekend at the wine estate. "Wow! That place looks more like a castle, and with those vineyards all around . . .," gasped Rosalind, invited there once by Carola. Now, the ring, a large solitaire, gives them even more reason to turn green. Jennifer cattily remarks, "The *first* marriage is always the most romantic, don't you think, Carola?" I learn that the happy fiancée will not be returning to the university and the wedding is planned for

August. "Such a lovely girl!" beams her future mother-in-law. "We'll have beautiful grandchildren!" Her husband adds: "Quite competent, too. She insisted on working in our office and showed us how to reorganize our files."

Keith, the loner, is still overweight, but not so lone anymore. He has brought his friend, a sturdy Danish girl, who, he proudly announces, will visit him next month in San Diego.

Liz is here, of course, active and efficient as ever, but dark circles ring her eyes. I draw her aside.

"Stan left last night. Until the last minute, he was still trying to convince me that I should go with him, 'Don't even bother to *pack*,' he said, 'and there's no need to say *anything* to anybody. Plenty of time later to explain. See? I bought you a ticket, so just get on the plane with me and tomorrow we'll be in Gabon. You'll see, when you're far away, you'll worry less about what you left behind. Your children? They'd be the first to agree that you deserve happiness at last. Your husband? He'll find someone else to cook and do his laundry, or else he'll learn how to do it himself. You are abandoning nothing but ashes here, come with me, I swear that I'll love you forever!' It all made it the harder to say no, and he insisted I repeat it, no, no, he wanted me to be sure. . . . And then he left without turning around. . . ."

Laughter, conversations surround us, but cannot penetrate the desolate little circle that engulfs us.

Until Faustino comes up—has he grown even taller this year?—practically floating above the ground in his excitement: "I have been appointed as assistant to the organist in the cathedral! They'll even *pay* me, although I can't quite believe that yet!" The General congratulates him and learns the appointment is for the summer. Faustino will return home to finish his degree, and he has been promised a permanent position upon graduation.

One has to admire the way the General converses in French with our guests, and I have heard that he is equally fluent in Italian, German, Spanish and even gets along well in Chinese. And now, he is laughing as Rob recounts his early suppository episode and the recent gypsy festival misadventure. Good sport that he is, Rob sees it all as a good joke on himself.

A moment later, Liz and I find ourselves leaning together against the balustrade. "So, you're not going to see Stan again?" She hesitates. "His job does not start until two months from now. . . . The plane ticket he bought me is in my purse. . . . You see, he hasn't given up yet. I found a note folded in with the ticket saying that he wants to come back a month from now—it's not such a long trip from Gabon to Marseille, Air Afrique has a direct flight."

"Perhaps you'll find you miss him too much to stay apart?"

She dabs at her eyes: "I do know that I will miss him. What I do not know yet is how much courage I can summon. . . . Will I find enough within myself to say no to him once again?" A call interrupts us, as one of our girls runs up: "Madame Liz! My Irish friends here invite me to visit them. What's the best way to get to Dublin?" So, Liz smiles and begins talking about student-priced flights and how to go about getting information.

All year, the students have besieged Liz and me with never-ending questions about everything: "What is the schedule of trains to Paris and how much does a ticket cost? Find me an inexpensive hotel in London and how do I get there in the first place? How do I get my laundry done on a Sunday, when the laundromat is closed? How can I borrow money from the Program until my check arrives? How do I find this book I need? What is the least expensive ski resort in the Alps? How do I lose the pounds I gained because I cannot pass a pastry shop? How do I say in French, 'I like you, but I don't love you?'" I thought even Liz would be stumped when one girl came one day, almost in tears: "I realize that since I came here, I have done nothing to help humanity; I want to read to the blind." The difficulty was compounded by the fact the young lady didn't at the time know enough French to read aloud intelligibly in that language. Unbelievable as it may seem, Liz found a visually impaired elderly *English* lady living in Aix who'd welcome inspirational readings from the *Reader's Digest*. "Great!" enthused our student, who showed up *once* and never again. "I met this guy, see, and . . .," and humanity was left to fend for itself, taking second place, once more, to love. . . .

Now, no escaping it, there will be speeches.

The *recteur* congratulates the students on their achievements and encourages them to refer to principles of French wisdom in their future endeavors. . . . The mayor of Villelaure, whom I have asked to speak as representing the families who hosted our students during the year, declares: "Your country could have no better *ambassadors*. . . ." Did I hear *ambassadors*? Perhaps *they* have, but *I* haven't forgotten those statements of purpose, and that expressed wish to come to France as "ambassadors of culture." Starting from that beginning-of-the-year party, where they saved me, until today, it does look like they've met their goal.

The General thanks all the families who have entertained our young people. Several have even invited them to stay on for the summer in their *résidence secondaire*, that vacation home that so many French people seem to own.

When my turn comes to speak, I disregard the paper I prepared last night. What is there to say? They have run me ragged, worried me, exasperated me at times, taken up every moment, including most of my evenings and weekends, even resented it when I got away *once* with my husband. I had no life of my own this year, instead, I shared in all of theirs. But I don't trust my voice because it is choking with emotion: Is this *really* the end? It all went so fast. . . . Couldn't we start the year over again? I'd know how to look after you a lot better this time. . . . Better conclude before I break down.

"You made me very proud with those questions you kept asking, which showed you trusted me to know *everything*. But I was never as flattered as the day I heard, "Madame L., will it stop raining in ten minutes?"

I am still speaking when I see a hand go up: "Yes?"

"Remember, on that first day in Paris, when we asked you what the French do with those *traversins* on their beds? You said that if we didn't find out on our own, you'd tell us on the last day. Well, I don't know about the others, but *I* still haven't found out. So now, you tell me."

Everybody is waiting. The General looks at me questioningly; perhaps he, too, wonders what the French do with those *traversins?*

"I am glad you reminded me. What do the French do with those *traversins? Why,* they *sleep* on them, of course."

Do I hear good-natured boos mixed in with the applause?

Experience Romance
Blood Runs Hot in Camargue

Camargue is the triangular delta of the Rhône, its wider branch running into the sea at Port Saint-Louis. The city of Arles stands at the apex of the triangle.

Visit Van Gogh in Arles
Seduced by the works of Japanese artist Hiroshige, van Gogh dreamed of a voyage to Japan. Instead, he came to Arles, where he found the light so pure and brilliant that he became obsessed with capturing it on his canvasses.

Visit the *Van Gogh Foundation* in an ancient chapel, where works of famous painters, conceived as their homage to van Gogh, are displayed. In *Espace van Gogh*, a cloister garden, once painted by van Gogh, has been lovingly restored.

Lunch with Vincent at Café van Gogh
Remember the *Night Café* and the *Yellow Café?* These are van Gogh's view of the same establishment, still located on the

lively Place du Forum. It has been restored to its exact appearance in the artist's time, painted in the same ocher yellow color. Food is brasserie-type and very good. Sit on the terrace, fantasizing that Vincent is joining you for lunch, and share in a moment of Arles' vibrant life.

Stirring Up the Flocks of Flamingoes

You must drive deep into Camargue, leaving the heavily traveled tourist roads in favor of narrow, sometimes dirt lanes, in the *eastern* part of the delta. There, you'll find the elusive charm of that flat land of lagoons and beaches, where flocks of pink flamingoes rise "like dust shaken out of a carpet," says Lawrence Durell, revealing the flash of magenta of their underwings.

Camargue is famous for its horses, but these are not the dejected ones you'd pass, tethered in rows to await tourist riders. Instead, you'll see the celebrated white ones, prancing in reed-bound pastures, and the fierce little bulls bred for the arenas.

Emulate Lucien Clergue's "Born of the Waves" Photos

The beaches of Camargue are vast, made of pure, dazzling sand. They'll intoxicate you with light and sun *and* they are practically deserted. Sunbathe in *any* kind of attire.

Born of the Waves (Née de la Vague), an album of nudes, photographed on those beaches, established Lucien Clergue's fame. None show the face of the model, retaining thus the mystery of anonymity, but all associate the sensuousness of the female form with the caress of the sea.

So, *monsieur*, why not whip out your camera, coax your

companion into a little modeling and see if you cannot do Lucien one better?

Is Fleur de Sel Really an Aphrodisiac?

At Salins-de-Giraud, the great saltworks, buy little autographed boxes of *fleur de sel*. Gathered on the *surface* of the evaporating flats, it is pure, untreated and retains the soul of the sea. Some element in it, which defies chemical analysis, is supposed, the locals will tell you, to arouse one of men's and women's better instincts, which is to make love tenderly, passionately and soon.

Straight from the Sea: Food in Camargue

Removed from the tourist circuit, mostly known to initiates, *Le Mazet du Vaccarès*, also known as *Chez Hélène et Néné* (in Méjanes; Tel: 04-90-97-10-10; Fax: 04-90-97-12-32) offers no printed menu. Eat what has been prepared today and you won't be sorry.

On a recent visit there, in the company of our friends the Clergues, we were served: First, as an hors d'oeuvre, a large bowl of *tellines*, the small white Camargue clams, steamed in white wine. Next came an aïoli composed of a vast platter of boiled vegetables and a pot of steamed *bulots*, the big, spiny sea snails you pull out with a pin, accompanied by a generous bowl of *aïoli* (garlic mayonnaise). Another vast platter followed, this time of assorted fried fish. We begged off the cheese tray, and proceeded directly to a dessert of light-as-air fruit tarts.

Simple and Sensuous
An It's-Too-Hot-to-Cook Dinner *à deux*

This has been a scorching day. As soon as you arrive home, you want to slip into something comfortable and you might splash on some lavender cologne for extra freshness. If you prepare this flavorful dinner, you won't have to face any more heat tonight.

Gazpacho provençal
Salade de poulet au curry
Brésil Brésil

Iced Raw Vegetable Soup
    1 cup chicken broth
    1 bouillon cube
    4 vine tomatoes cut into quarters
    1 large cucumber, peeled, not seeded, cut into chunks
    ½ sweet (or red) onion, peeled
    ½ sweet red pepper, seeded, cut into chunks
    3 tablespoons olive oil
    3 tablespoons balsamic vinegar
    Salt and pepper
    Tabasco
    3 tablespoons sour cream (plus 2 teaspoons
        for garnish)

In blender, put chicken broth and bouillon cube. Add tomatoes and purée. Then, add cucumber, onion, red pepper. Purée all until smooth.

Add olive oil, balsamic vinegar. Season to taste with salt and pepper, add a few drops of Tabasco. Blend. You can pulse to blend in the sour cream, or just swirl it in serving bowls.

Garnish with a dollop of sour cream. If you have plenty of time before serving, gazpacho will cool nicely in the fridge. If not, place it in freezer to speed up icing.

Curried Chicken Salad
> 2 cups diced meat from a fully cooked, cold barbecued chicken
> 1 red apple, cored and diced, not peeled
> 2 stalks celery, chopped
> ½ cup cashews
> Vinaigrette (p. 47) with 1 teaspoon curry

In serving bowl, mix chicken, apple, celery and nuts. Toss with curried dressing.

Optional: You can decorate with hard-cooked egg slices and tomato wedges, if you like.

Brazil Brazil (Coffee Ice Cream with Coffee Liqueur)
> Coffee ice cream
> Coffee liqueur (like Kahlua or Tia Maria)
> A few coffee beans

In sorbet dishes, place a scoop of coffee ice cream (or coffee with nut brittle). Pour a generous topping of coffee liqueur. To add extra coffee flavor, press a few coffee beans into the ice cream. (I have seen it served with crystallized violets pressed into the ice cream. Lovely color effect!)

To Drink
Is it still too hot for wine? If you have an open bottle of white in your fridge, you might think of a wine cooler made with Perrier.

A glass bowl filled with ice cubes mixed with flowers
and flower petals is sometimes used in Provence
as a centerpiece on very hot days.